MW00379412

Computation of Fractions

Math Intervention for Elementary and Middle Grades Students

Bradley S. Witzel

Winthrop University

Paul J. Riccomini

Clemson University

PEARSON

Upper Saddle River, New Jersey
Columbus, Ohio

Library of Congress Cataloging-in-Publication Data

Witzel, Bradley S.
  Computations of fractions : math intervention for elementary and middle grades
students / Bradley S. Witzel, Paul J. Riccomini.—1st ed.
      p. cm.
  Includes bibliographical references.

  ISBN-13: 978-0-205-56738-6
  ISBN-10: 0-205-56738–X

  1. Fractions—Study and teaching (Elementary) 2. Fractions–Study and
teaching (Middle shcool) 3. Mathematics—Study and teaching (Elementary)
4. Mathematics—Study and teaching (Middle school) 5. Children with
disabilities—Education. 6. Learning disabled children—Education. I. Riccomini,
Paul J. II. Title.
  QA137.W58 2008
  372.7—dc22

Executive Editior and Publisher:	Virginia Lanigan
Editorial Assistant:	Matthew Buchholz
Senior Marketing Manager:	Krista Clark
Production Editor:	Gregory Erb
Editorial Production Service:	Progressive Publishing Alternatives
Composition Buyer:	Linda Cox
Manufacturing Buyer:	Megan Cochran
Interior Design:	Carol Somberg
Cover Designer:	Linda Knowles

This book was set in Sabon by Progressive Information Technologies. It was printed
and bound by Bind-Rite Graphics. The cover was printed by Phoenix Color
Corporation/Hagerstown.

For Professional Development resources visit www.allynbaconmerrill.com

Copyright © 2009 Pearson Education, Inc., Upper Saddle River, NJ 07458.
All rights reserved. Printed in the United States of America. This publication is pro-
tected by Copyright and permission should be obtained from the publisher prior to
any prohibited reproduction, storage in a retrieval system, or transmission in any form
or by any means, electronic, mechanical, photocopying, recording, or likewise. For information regarding permission(s), write to: Rights and Permissions Department, 501
Boylston Street, Suite 900, Boston, MA 02116, or fax your request to 617-671-2290.

Pearson® is a registered trademark of Pearson plc
Merrill® is a registered trademark of Pearson Education, Inc.

Pearson Education Ltd.   Pearson Education Australia Pty. Limited
Pearson Education Singapore Pte. Ltd.   Pearson Education North Asia Ltd.
Pearson Education Canada, Ltd.   Pearson Educación de Mexico, S.A. de C.V.
Pearson Education—Japan   Pearson Education Malaysia Pte. Ltd.

10 9 8 7 6 5 4 3 2 1

Merrill
is an imprint of

www.pearsonhighered.com   ISBN 13: 978-0-205-56738-6
                                 ISBN 10: 0-205-56738-X

Table of Contents

Introduction

This manual contains the information you will need to implement the *Computation of Fractions Math Intervention* for elementary and middle grades students who have yet to fully master computation of fractions. In the first section, we explain the three basic stages in the concrete to representational to abstract (CRA) instructional sequence and why CRA should be used. Next, we provide a brief overview of the National Council of Teachers of Mathematics (NCTM) Process Standards and how the sequence developed for this intervention is aligned with the sixth to eighth grade standards. Although this intervention is designed for students in grades six to eight, it is applicable to students of any age who have not completely learned fractions. The next section includes a list and description of all manipulatives necessary for the implementation of this intervention. In the final section, we provide an overview of the lesson scripts to be used as guides during teacher-directed lessons. All teacher-directed lessons are presented in the form of scripts. These scripts were designed as guides to help you to use this intervention. We strongly encourage you to become familiar with scripts prior to presenting lessons to your students. Please note, this intervention is intended for students who have already received instruction in the area of fractions and have struggled; therefore, a well-prepared teacher is essential to maximize the effectiveness of this intervention. Students should already be aware that fractions represent a precise point on a number line, a form of division, a part of a whole, and part of a set.

WHY FRACTIONS?

Students entering algebra often struggle with precursor mathematics skills such as fractions. Within algebra, students must accurately compute fractions when solving and graphing equations, interpreting decimals, working with ratios, and using ratios and proportions. Even though this program will help explain the concept to students, the lessons within the program focus on computation.

OVERVIEW

Proficiency in mathematics depends on a continuous development and blending of intricate combinations of various critical component skills. Gaps in any of these component skills will cause students to struggle in many aspects of their mathematics education. This is especially true for students with math disabilities (MD). The challenges that students with MD encounter during their mathematics instruction are substantial and well documented. Difficulties experienced in mathematics begin early and continue throughout their education, and are magnified as students progress toward secondary-level mathematics courses (Maccini, Mulcahy, & Wilson, 2007). The deficits in mathematics for students with MD are documented in the areas of basic facts, computation procedures, fractions, and solving word problems. Since many of these deficit areas are prerequisite skills for algebra, it is easy to see why these students will struggle with algebraic concepts.

Recently, the struggles of students with MD have received a great deal of attention from educators and researchers with renewed emphasis on providing evidence-based instruction. Efforts to move students toward mathematical proficiency have taken many different forms. One especially developed and effective instructional approach is the concrete to representational to abstract (CRA) instructional sequence. The CRA sequence of instruction includes teaching students through three levels of learning, from concrete objects to matching pictorial representations and then finally to abstract numerals.

The CRA instructional sequence systematically and explicitly instructs students through three levels of learning: (1) concrete, (2) representational, and (3) abstract. The purposeful transition through each of the three stages encourages students to learn the concepts as well as the procedures and computations that are so important in mathematics. The CRA instructional sequence is a three-level learning process in which students solve mathematics problems through the physical manipulation of concrete materials, followed by learning through pictorial representations of the concrete manipulations, and ending with solving mathematics through abstract notation (Witzel, 2005). Other terms that have been used to describe this sequence of instruction have been the concrete to semiconcrete to abstract sequence of instruction and graduated instruction (Gagnon & Maccini, 2007).

Teaching students through the three learning stages in the CRA instructional sequence has been shown to be beneficial to secondary students with mathematics difficulties (Butler, Miller, Crehan, Babbitt, & Pierce, 2003; Hutchinson, 1993; Jordan, Miller, & Mercer, 1999; Maccini & Hughes, 2000; Witzel, Mercer, & Miller, 2003). Success using this sequence of instruction has been beneficial—from small-group settings to whole-class instruction—for students with and without learning difficulties (Witzel, 2005). While other CRA approaches may exist, this one has a history of powerful effects. In the CRA stepwise approach implemented within this instructional series, students with learning disabilities performed at two to three times the success rates of their traditionally taught peers (Witzel, Mercer, & Miller). Moreover, students with a history of performing at or above grade level scored significantly higher than their traditionally taught peers when instructed on using this approach (Witzel).

There are many reasons why the CRA instructional sequence has been so successful. First, multimodal interactions with concrete materials and pictorial representations increase the likelihood that students will remember stepwise procedural options in mathematics problem solving. Students are more likely to memorize, encode, and retrieve information when information is presented in a multisensory format: visually, auditorily, tactilely, and kinesthetically. Using the concrete objects and linked pictorial representations described in this program, students will gain access to difficult abstract instructional ideas. What's more, even when students are presented with abstract questions in mathematics, they may turn to previous levels of learning (pictorial or concrete) to solve the problem. Thus, the student can solve difficult abstract problems without thinking fluently at the abstract level.

Computation of Fractions Math Intervention for Elementary and Middle Grades Students is designed to help improve mathematics instruction for students who traditionally struggle with learning fractions at both the conceptual and procedural levels. This intervention is designed to more thoroughly teach fractions by systematically presenting instruction to help students process important fraction concepts from the concrete level through the abstract level. Although many have advocated for the use of the CRA instructional sequence, very few programs are available for teachers. The Computation of Fractions Intervention was developed to help guide teachers' instructional planning for students with MD in seven essential areas involving fractions: (1) division with fractional answers/mixed numbers, (2) multiplication of fractions, (3) division of fractions, (4) finding equivalent fractions, (5) reducing and comparing fractions, (6) adding and subtracting fractions with like denominators, and (7) adding and subtracting fractions with unlike denominators.

NCTM Process Standards

The development of this program is meant to supplement a mathematics program designed around your state's standards. However, the organization of this program is much different from most textbooks. Unlike the typical spotty introductions and occasional lessons that are strung across several grades, we wanted this program to take students from being taught the concept of a fraction to being able to solve fractional computations. Much of the development of this program revolved around the NCTM process standards. Refer to Table 1 for a summary of the process standards outlined by NCTM.

TABLE 1

NCTM Process Standards Summary Table

Process Standards	Description
Problem solving:	• Solving problems using mathematics—analyze problems. • Apply and adapt strategies. • Monitor and reflect on problem solving. • Word problems in the instructional program series are arranged to increase difficulty with organization as well as to continue developing the current concept of the lesson. Students should be taught to continue using the strategies from previous lessons.
Representation:	• Create and use representations to communicate mathematical ideas. • Translate representations to solve problems. • "Students need a variety of representations." • The representations cannot be ends to themselves. • Representations should be used as tools.
Connections:	• Connecting mathematics ideas within fractions. • Show how solving fractions connects to solving basic computations and how the two are interconnected. • The generalization activities and cumulative reviews help connect the skills within fractions and mathematics. • Consistent mathematical language across subskills helps build connections.
Reasoning and Proof:	• Developing mathematical shortcuts based on justified reasoning. • Students evaluate problem-solving approaches. • Students learn the logic to mathematics.
Communication:	• Designed for two-way interactions on the concepts and skills, starting with the teacher as an expert and then scaffolding student learning from one skill to the next. • Analyze and evaluate problem-solving approaches. • Learn and use mathematical language built within the scripts and outlined lessons.

Source: National Council of Teachers of Mathematics (2000). *Principles and standards for school mathematics.* Reston, VA: Author.

The Sequence and Standards

The NCTM advocates that all students in grades three to five should learn about fractions through varying visual models or representations and should be able to demonstrate knowledge in equivalent forms to add and subtract frequently encountered fractions and decimals (NCTM, 2000). The necessity to understand and manipulate fractions greatly increases for students in grades six to eight. For example, the following list clearly demonstrates the need for students to develop a comprehensive understanding of fractions.

- Work flexibly with fractions, decimals, and percents to solve problems.
- Compare and order fractions, decimals, and percents efficiently and find their approximate locations on a number line.
- Understand the meaning and effects of arithmetic operations with fractions, decimals, and integers.
- Use the associative and commutative properties of addition and multiplication and the distributive property of multiplication over addition to simplify computations with integers, fractions, and decimals.
- Select appropriate methods and tools for computing with fractions and decimals from among mental computation, estimation, calculators or computers, and paper and pencil, depending on the situation, and apply the selected methods.
- Develop and analyze algorithms for computing with fractions, decimals, and integers, and develop fluency in their use.
- Develop and use strategies to estimate the results of rational number computations and judge the reasonableness of the results.
- Develop, analyze, and explain methods for solving problems involving proportions, such as scaling and finding equivalent ratios (NCTM, 2000).

The sequencing of this intervention works within the sixth- to eighth-grade standards as outlined by the NCTM (2000). When students struggle with fractions, typically there are difficulties with concepts, computational accuracy, and problem-solving procedures. The purpose of this intervention is to help build on students' early conceptual understanding of fractions and to help them develop better procedural understanding that leads to more correct answers in problem solving with fractions.

The sequence of this intervention was designed to work with elementary-based mathematics skills and to build to adding and subtracting fractions with unlike denominators. The use of this intervention does not need to end with the last subskill covered. Teachers can use this intervention to springboard to several other skills, such as division with larger numbers, computation with mixed numbers, and solving for ratios and percents. The sequence of fractional subskills within this intervention is described below.

DIVISION WITH FRACTIONAL ANSWERS/MIXED NUMBERS

Estimated at a fourth-grade level, solving fractions as mixed numbers involves understanding how fractions and division are similar. In addition, this subskill allows students to differentiate the use of numerators and denominators.

MULTIPLICATION OF FRACTIONS

It is important for students to understand multiplication and division of fractions before they find equivalent fractions. Numerators and denominators need to be multiplied separately but in the same pattern.

DIVISION OF FRACTIONS

Learning division of fractions is more than just memorizing to invert and multiply. The process of dividing fractions involves learning about the identity property. Within this subskill, students will learn to multiply the numerator and denominator simultaneously by different versions of one. Students will eventually learn the algorithm to multiply by the reciprocal of the second fraction, but, more importantly, they will learn why and how this happens.

FINDING EQUIVALENT FRACTIONS

Using the subskills of multiplication and division of fractions, students will learn to find equivalent fractions. This subskill, along with reducing and comparing fractions, helps students learn to manipulate equations in order to add or subtract fractions with unlike denominators.

REDUCING AND COMPARING FRACTIONS

As an extension of finding equivalent fractions, students learn to reduce fractions to their simplest forms and then to compare fractions based on their numerators and denominators. Reducing fractions to simplest form is also an essential subskill of fraction computation.

ADDING AND SUBTRACTING FRACTIONS WITH LIKE DENOMINATORS

The process of adding and subtracting fractions, whether with like or unlike denominators, should be consistent. By learning how to add and subtract fractions with like denominators using a consistent set of procedures, students practice how to add and subtract fractions with unlike denominators.

ADDING AND SUBTRACTING FRACTIONS WITH UNLIKE DENOMINATORS

Considered one of the most difficult middle school skills, this intervention ends with the subskill of adding and subtracting fractions with unlike denominators. It involves working with mixed numbers, finding equivalent fractions, and recognizing that only the numerators should be added or subtracted.

Description of Manipulatives

Inherent in the CRA approach are the hands-on interactions by teachers and students with the concrete objects or manipulatives. There is not a set of specific CRA manipulatives required; however, enough manipulatives for all students are required. The many benefits of a CRA instructional approach (i.e., improved math outcomes, deeper processing of math concepts) will only be realized when each student has had the opportunity to interact with the manipulatives in purposeful and engaging activities. Manipulatives take many different forms and are available for purchase through education supply companies as well as at your local Wal-Mart. Remember, implementation of a CRA instructional approach is not advised if materials are not made available to all teachers and students.

Students will need the following manipulative objects for the concrete lessons within this intervention. You can find templates for most of these manipulative objects in the Appendix of this manual. However, you will need to acquire popsicle sticks, a string for an equal sign, and condiment or bathroom cups for groups to make the following:

- 20 digit sticks
- 4 tens sticks
- 12 group cups
- 4 multiplication symbols
- 1 equal sign
- 8 minus signs
- 8 plus signs

 DIGITS

Digits are the most-often manipulated mathematical notations. It is important to use materials that are easily moved and that can be picked up with the least-deft fingers in class. Also, because so many digits must be used in solving the fractions, it is important to have ones that are easy to obtain and replace. We recommend short popsicle sticks because they are easy to pick up, readily available, and easy to see on a table top.

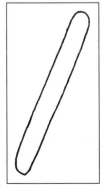

How to use: When students are learning through the concrete phase, you may refer to sticks as "sticks." However, teach them that the collection of sticks is considered a total number. For example, when looking at five sticks, refer to the set as "five sticks." When the students are being taught a representational lesson, refer to the set as five "tallies" or "tick marks." Always include the abstract verbal marker of five, however, because when students are being taught abstract lessons, you want to only say five.

TENS

While tens are not frequently used in the concrete stage of this instructional set, their place is important. You may find yourself helping students connect larger, abstractly written numbers to this concrete set of materials. Just as with base ten blocks, the ten should look significantly larger than the digits because as they physically represent a larger place value. We recommend using tongue depressors to match the small popsicle sticks.

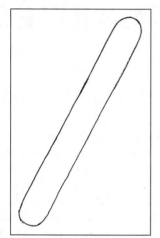

How to use: Use the ten sticks similarly to how you used the digit sticks. For example, for a representation of twenty, use two ten sticks during concrete lessons. During the representational level, use one ten for each darker straight line drawn.

 GROUP

Students with memory problems are often asked to memorize basic facts. There are many means for memorization when they are unable to do so. However, there are few attempts at explaining how we compute numbers and why the answers are what they are. For multiplication and division, using a physical representation for grouping is important. Using this representation allows for more explanation about what is occurring during the computation rather than requesting students to memorize basic facts that have not yet been mastered. For example, four times six and six times four are not the same computational problem. While their answers are the same, the purpose of each number is different. In the example, four times six means there are four groups of six objects each. Since multiplication involves totals, we look at the number of objects as the answer—twenty four in this case. Using the commutative property, these assignments can be reversed to achieve the same total number, but it is still important for students to learn that one number is acting on the other.

How to use: We suggest using paper condiment or bathroom cups to represent groups. They hold the small digit sticks well and are easy to obtain. When referring to groups at the concrete level, they may be referred to as "cups of" and eventually as "groups of." At the representational and abstract levels, the groups should be referred to as "groups of." For example, eight divided by two should be shown as eight objects split evenly into two groups. Since we are dividing or evenly distributing, we are interested in how many per group.

 DIVISOR LINE

The divisor line separates the numerator from the denominator. It simply means to divide such that if the numerator is seven and the denominator is fifteen, we can say seven divided by fifteen. We recommend using a colored paper strip to represent the divisor line.

How to use: Place the line between the numerator and the denominator and say "divided by" or "over" during the concrete, representational, and abstract lessons. After the computation is complete, the line should be removed. For example, in a concrete lesson, after dividing twelve sticks by four groups, there are three sticks in each group cup. Because the computation was just completed, the line should be removed, leaving only the four groups with three sticks each. A template for divisor lines can be found in the Appendix.

 ## EQUAL SIGN

Erroneously, young children conclude that equals means to solve when, in fact, it separates two equal parts of a mathematical statement. Using a vertically displayed  string is a quick way of separating two or more parts of an equation so that when a computation is added to one side of the equation it must be computed to the other side.

How to use: Place a string where there should be an equal sign in concrete lessons. For pictorial lessons, draw a curvy line below the equal sign. A five-inch cotton string works the best, as it lays flat and is easy to manipulate.

 ## POSITIVE OR PLUS SYMBOL

For computation, use the plus symbol interchangeably for addition or as a positive symbol. As a positive symbol, it means to the right on a number line. As an addition symbol, it means to combine or group.

 How to use: Place the symbol where the addition or positive symbol would be. Use the same language in each of the three stages of learning: concrete, representational, or abstract. A template for the plus symbol can be found in the Appendix.

 ## NEGATIVE OR MINUS SYMBOL

For computation, use the minus symbol interchangeably for subtraction or as a negative symbol. As a negative symbol, it means to the left on a number line. As a subtraction symbol, it means to remove or reduce.

 How to use: Place the symbol where the subtraction or negative symbol would be. Use the same language in each of the three stages of learning: concrete, representational, or abstract. A template for the minus symbol can be found in the Appendix.

 ## MULTIPLICATION SYMBOL

To help students recognize when multiplication is occurring, you may wish to use a multiplication symbol. Multiplication can be displayed through parentheses, a dot, 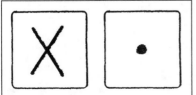 or a simple elementary ×.

How to use: You may place the symbol where a multiplication figure would be. Use the same language—"groups of"—in each of the three stages of learning: concrete, representational, or abstract. A template for the multiplication symbol can be found in the Appendix.

Organization of Materials

Using the materials described for this intervention requires an organizational system to be in place prior to beginning instruction. When setting up your organizational system, try to keep it simple and easy to use for both you and your students. Each student must have access to a complete set of materials. One cost-effective system we recommend is for each student to have a shoebox or a 1-quart, clear resealable bag containing all materials. The students can decorate their container of materials for easy identification. Although more expensive, you may consider using clear shoebox-size Rubbermaid containers because of their durability and ease of storage. We also recommend you have extra materials available to replace as necessary due to the wear and tear of day-to-day use.

The materials should be stored in the classroom for easy and quick access when needed; however, materials are not required for the representation and abstract lessons in this intervention. Students will not need to access their containers for every lesson. To reduce possible distractions caused by the materials, we recommend setting up a system to signal students when the lesson requires the materials. For example, the letter "C" can be placed in the corner of the board or beside the day's agenda to signal the lesson requires the use of their materials. Please keep in mind there is no single correct way to handle the materials; nonetheless, an organization system is important and can help minimize distractions and maximize instructional time.

Who Can Use this Intervention?

Computation of Fractions is written for both general and special education teachers. The effectiveness of this instructional sequence is supported by research in which certified teachers provided daily whole-class and/or small-group mathematics instruction based on the CRA instructional sequence within and outside the general education classroom. The CRA instructional sequence can be used to supplement the core mathematics curriculum of at-risk students as well as a targeted intervention for students with documented mathematics disabilities. The teaching activities outlined in this manual can complement instructional mathematics programs for students with disabilities as well as students who are struggling to learn fractions. It is important to note that the *CRA Mathematics Intervention Series* was designed to be fully implemented; results are not likely to be as strong as those obtained in the original research studies if only select parts of the CRA instructional sequence are used. In addition to the information and instructional guidelines provided in this manual, ongoing high-quality professional development for teachers is important in order to effectively deliver this program.

How to Use this Intervention

This intervention includes thirty carefully sequenced lessons with accompanying scripts and problems. All thirty lessons are teacher-directed lessons and are presented in the form of scripts. The lesson scripts were designed as guides to help you implement this intervention. In addition to the thirty lessons, this manual contains a pretest assessment, an initial advance organizer lesson, sets of cumulative review problems, a posttest assessment, and a teacher's answer key.

 PRETEST ASSESSMENT

The pretest assessment is used for placing students within the intervention sequence. In some cases, students may have some skills and should be placed further within the intervention. In other cases, the students may need to start with the first lesson. When placing the student, follow the best section that the student completed. For example, if a student scores three out of four in division with fractional answers and two out of two in multiplication of fractions, the student should go through Lessons 5 and 6, and if successful, the student should then move on to Lesson 10 and continue through the program.

Maximum scores (four out of four or two out of two) on any level subtest places the student at the next lesson. If the student scores two out of two on the last subtest, then the student need not complete any of the lessons in this intervention. However, in situations in which the student places high in one part and low in another, there are some areas of overlap that should be taught.

Subsection	Pretest score	Where student begins
Division with fractional answers	4 out of 4	Review the next section
	2 out of 4	Lesson 5
	0 out of 4	Lesson 1
Multiplication of fractions	2 out of 2	Review the next section
	1 out of 2	Lesson 10
	0 out of 2	Lesson 8
Division of fractions	2 out of 2	Review the next section
	1 out of 2	Lesson 13
	0 out of 2	Lesson 12

Sub-section	Pretest score	Where student begins
Finding equivalent fractions	2 out of 2	Review the next section
	1 out of 2	Lesson 17
	0 out of 2	Lesson 15
Reducing and comparing fractions	2 out of 2	Review the next section
	1 out of 2	Lesson 21
	0 out of 2	Lesson 19
Adding and subtracting fractions with like denominators	2 out of 2	Review the next section
	1 out of 2	Lesson 25
	0 out of 2	Lesson 23
Fractions with unlike denominators	2 out of 2	Focus on application
	1 out of 2	Lesson 29
	0 out of 2	Lesson 27

 ## INITIAL ADVANCE ORGANIZER LESSON

The advance organizer lesson is intended to introduce the purpose of using this intervention to your students. It also teaches students about the various materials they will be using and what each represents (i.e., a cup represents a group). This initial lesson should be taught prior to Lesson 1 and requires the students to have all materials. This lesson could be taught on a different day as Lesson 1 or on the same day, depending on the school schedule and learner characteristics.

 ## INSTRUCTIONAL LESSONS

Each of the thirty lessons in this manual follows the same format and presents information in a clear, systematic, and explicit approach. We strongly encourage you to become familiar with scripts prior to presenting lessons to your students; reading scripts during instructional episodes is discouraged. All thirty lessons contain four components: (1) model, (2) guided practice, (3) word problem, and (4) independent practice.

Model. Each lesson contains a section titled "Model" and includes two to four problems. The problems are designed to demonstrate the subskill for the lesson. The scripts were designed for students who struggle with fractions and need procedures presented in small, logical steps with multiple demonstrations. The scripts also contain clear and consistent language as well as mathematically correct terminology. Another aspect planned into the scripts is the importance of checking for student understanding through specific and purposeful questioning. If it appears that students are confused or are not following along during a lesson, it is recommended to repeat the demonstration problems as necessary.

Guided and Independent Practice. Each lesson contains a section for both guided and independent practice, with corresponding problems. This is one of the most important parts of the lesson. Students require well-structured and planned opportunities to practice newly introduced content. Adequate practice is essential and should include both guided and independent practice. Following the scripts in guided practice will allow you to work through several problems together with your students in order to ensure that they are ready for independent practice.

You may want to spend additional time on the guided practice problems before moving on to independent practice. Students who struggle with mathematics need more time in guided practice and a great deal of teacher support. It is beneficial to provide immediate corrections and feedback during the guided practice part of the lesson. It is impossible to develop scripts that can predict all possible scenarios; therefore, you may have to deviate from them. One final note, do not rush or skip guided and independent practice. Students need many opportunities to practice what they are learning. In the long-term, students will benefit by spending additional time on this part of the lesson. Rushing students forward will only increase the likelihood of overgeneralization and misconceptions.

 ## CUMULATIVE REVIEW SETS A–G

There are seven cumulative review sets in this intervention. Each set corresponds to one of the seven fraction subskills emphasized. For example, Cumulative Review Set A includes practice problems involving division with fractional answers. Beginning with the second subskill section, use the cumulative review sets to maintain fraction subskills. Use of cumulative reviews helps students to maintain earlier learned subskills and reduces the likelihood of overgeneralization of one set of procedures to another. Each cumulative review set includes problems from the most recent subskill covered as well as preceding skills within this intervention. In successive cumulative reviews there are more problems from recent lessons and word problems.

Peer-Tutoring Component. We recommend using a peer-tutoring format for the provided Cumulative Review Sets A–G instead of individual practice. The purpose of using a peer-tutoring format is to help students maintain newly learned skills and to encourage students not to forget what they have previously learned, and it provides each student with a partner to help promote better learning. Having a partner to discuss the concepts and procedures with will help students become more confident with each newly learned fraction concept or procedure. Peer tutoring is available in many different forms and can be a very effective instructional strategy if implemented properly.

A peer-tutoring format generally includes two or three students working together through a series of structured activities to practice important skills. Students often enjoy working together and are better able to provide each other extra support if needed. Peer tutoring also offers a way for teachers to differentiate instruction that is based on student instructional needs. Teachers must first teach students how to be supportive tutors. Explain to your students that a tutor doesn't just tell his or her partner the answer, but rather, helps his or her partner solve the mathematics problem by providing prompts and/or leading questions. Depending on the ability level of your students, teachers can provide students with various levels of prompts for the tutors to use. As a general rule, younger and more naïve students will need much more specificity in the tutor prompts. Prompts can be provided in a variety of forms. The ones provided with each cumulative review set are general in nature and are intended to be a starting point. Teachers can modify the prompts as they see fit, depending on the needs of their students.

Peer-tutoring sessions should run from twenty to thirty minutes or enough time for students to complete all problems included on the cumulative worksheets. Success or lack of progress should be recorded and monitored closely. If, in the best judgment of the teacher students are struggling (i.e., solving 20 percent incorrectly), the teacher should return to the lesson before the cumulative review sheet and reteach it. For example, if students are struggling with Cumulative Review Set A, the teacher should reteach Lesson 7 and provide students with additional opportunities in which to respond. It may be necessary to reteach several previous lessons. It is imperative for students to demonstrate proficiency with each new lesson, and rushing a student will likely result in later learning difficulties or gaps.

 ## POSTTEST ASSESSMENT

Once the intervention is completed, use the posttest assessment to determine the overall success of the students with fractions. A student successfully completed a subskill if he or she receives the maximum score for that section (four out of four or two out of two). If the student scores two out of two on the last subtest as well as on every other subtest, then he or she has successfully completed this intervention. However, if the student did not achieve mastery on a subtest, use the chart below to guide your reteaching process.

When placing the student, follow the best section the student completed. For example, if a student scores three out of four in division with fractional answers and two out of two in multiplication of fractions, the student should go through Lessons 5 and 6 and, if successful, the student should move on to Lesson 10 and continue through the program.

If you notice that the student included representational marks on his or her paper with the abstract notation, do not be alarmed. To determine what level the student is at, interview the student on his or her problem-solving approach. If he or she describes the marks in concrete terms, then the student may still be thinking at the concrete level. For example, if he or she describes two thirds as two sticks over three sticks, then he or she is thinking concretely. If, however, he or she describes the fraction two thirds as two over three, then he or she may be thinking in abstract terms. A student can still obtain correct answers and be at a level other than abstract. If so, help the student to develop fluency through more abstract and verbal practice.

 ## ANSWER KEY

The answer key located in the back of this manual contains answers for all problems used in the pretest and posttest assessments, the thirty instructional lessons, and the cumulative review sets. Answers are provided for the examples used in each lesson's model, guided practice, and independent practice problems. Because answers during the concrete and representational lessons will be displayed with manipulatives or drawings, a description is provided in terms of cups, sticks, and tally marks.

Subsection	Posttest score	Reteach from this lesson
Division with fractional answers	4 out of 4	Subskill mastered
	2 out of 4	Lesson 5
	0 out of 4	Lesson 1
Multiplication of fractions	2 out of 2	Subskill mastered
	1 out of 2	Lesson 10
	0 out of 2	Lesson 8
Division of fractions	2 out of 2	Subskill mastered
	1 out of 2	Lesson 13
	0 out of 2	Lesson 12
Finding equivalent fractions	2 out of 2	Subskill mastered
	1 out of 2	Lesson 17
	0 out of 2	Lesson 15
Reducing and comparing fractions	2 out of 2	Subskill mastered
	1 out of 2	Lesson 21
	0 out of 2	Lesson 19
Adding and subtracting fractions with like denominators	2 out of 2	Subskill mastered
	1 out of 2	Lesson 25
	0 out of 2	Lesson 23
Fractions with unlike denominators	2 out of 2	Subskill mastered
	1 out of 2	Lesson 29
	0 out of 2	Lesson 27

MATERIAL SAMPLES

Digit:

Ten:

Group:

Equal Sign:

Divisor Line:

Plus Sign:

Minus Sign:

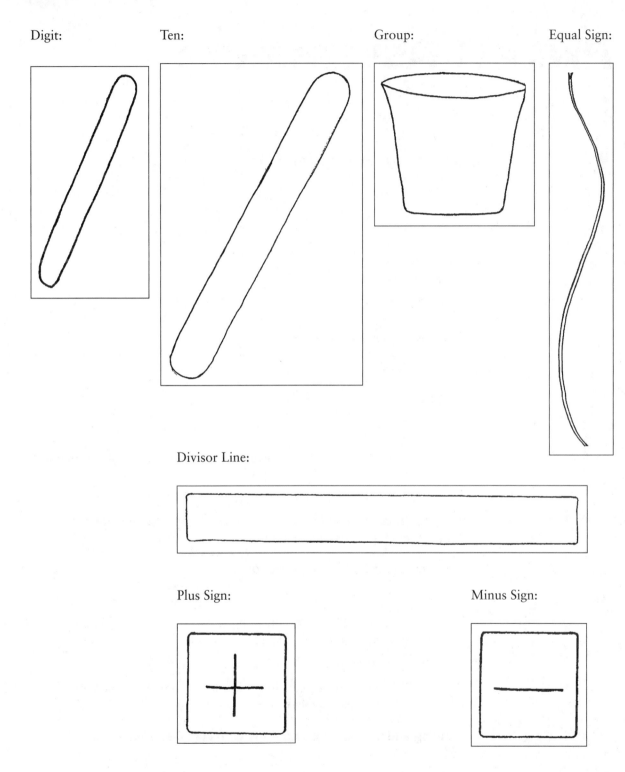

Pretest Assessment

Division with Fractional Answers

a) $\dfrac{8}{4}$

b) $\dfrac{5}{3}$

c) $\dfrac{14}{2}$

d) $\dfrac{11}{5}$

Multiplication of Fractions

e) $\left(\dfrac{2}{1}\right)\left(\dfrac{1}{3}\right)$

f) $\left(\dfrac{1}{3}\right)\left(\dfrac{3}{4}\right)$

Division of Fractions

g) $\left(\dfrac{3}{1}\right) \div \left(\dfrac{1}{4}\right)$

h) $\left(\dfrac{1}{2}\right) \div \left(\dfrac{1}{3}\right)$

Finding Equivalent Fractions

i) $\dfrac{1}{3} = \dfrac{2}{6} = \underline{\quad} = \underline{\quad}$

j) What was multiplied in the numerator and denominator to find the last equivalent fraction in part (i)?

k) $\dfrac{3}{4} = \dfrac{6}{8} = \underline{\quad} = \underline{\quad} = \underline{\quad}$

l) What was multiplied in the numerator and denominator to find the last equivalent fraction in part (k)?

Reducing and Comparing Fractions

m) $\dfrac{8}{12} = \underline{\quad}$

n) What was divided equally in the numerator and denominator to find the fraction in its simplest form in part (m)?

o) $\dfrac{3}{9} = \underline{\quad}$

p) What was divided equally in the numerator and denominator to find the fraction in its simplest form in part (o)?

Adding and Subtracting Fractions with Like Denominators

q) $\dfrac{1}{3} + \dfrac{1}{3} =$

r) $\dfrac{3}{4} - \dfrac{1}{4} =$

Adding and Subtracting Fractions with Unlike Denominators

s) $\dfrac{1}{3} + \dfrac{2}{9} =$

t) $\dfrac{3}{8} + \dfrac{1}{2} =$

Instructional Lessons

 ADVANCE ORGANIZER

Today we are going to start a new program for fractions. By the time we complete this series of work, you will be able to reduce fractions, find equivalent fractions, multiply and divide fractions, and add and subtract fractions. This new program should help all of you become masters of these skills. Before we start our first lesson, let's learn some of the items you are about to receive.

(Hand out each material immediately following its introduction.)

This is one stick.

(Hold up short stick.)

This represents the number one. If I hold up one stick, I am showing the number one. What am I showing when I hold up two one sticks? (Elicit response.)

(Hand out short sticks.)

Remember, our sticks are for mathematics use only. They are to be used for the problems we will go over together and are not to be used for pointing to items or touching others.

This is a cup.

(Hold up cup.)

The cup will be used to represent groups while multiplying and dividing fractions.

What does the cup represent? (Elicit response.)

This paper will be used as a divisor line between the numerators and denominators of the fractions.

This string will be used to represent an equal sign.

Where do we usually find an equal sign? (At the end of an addition, subtraction, multiplication, or division problem.)

We will also have addition, subtraction, multiplication, and division symbols that look just as they usually do.

Now that we have learned about all our materials, let's get ready for our first lesson on division with fractional answers. For this lesson you will need sticks, cups, and a divisor line.

LESSON 1

Division with Fractional Answers

1.C (sticks and cups method)

Describe/Model *(Answer is in sticks per cup.)*

Note: $\dfrac{8}{4}$ may also be represented as $8 \div 4$.

a) $\dfrac{8 \text{ sticks}}{4 \text{ cups}}$

b) $\dfrac{5 \text{ sticks}}{3 \text{ cups}}$

c) $\dfrac{3 \text{ sticks}}{4 \text{ cups}}$

d) $\dfrac{6 \text{ sticks}}{4 \text{ cups}}$

Guided Practice

e) $\dfrac{3 \text{ sticks}}{3 \text{ cups}}$

f) $\dfrac{9 \text{ sticks}}{2 \text{ cups}}$

Word Problem

g) A mother gave 10 dollars (sticks) to her 4 children (cups) to split up ($\div$) evenly. How many ($=$) dollars will go to each child? Show your answer using the objects provided.

What does the fraction in the answer mean?

Independent Practice

h) $\dfrac{4 \text{ sticks}}{3 \text{ cups}}$

i) $\dfrac{7 \text{ sticks}}{3 \text{ cups}}$

j) $\dfrac{6 \text{ sticks}}{3 \text{ cups}}$

k) $\dfrac{3 \text{ sticks}}{1 \text{ cup}}$

Teaching **LESSON 1**

Division with Fractional Answers

1.C (sticks and cups method)

Describe/Model *(Answer is in sticks per cup.)*

Note: $\dfrac{8}{4}$ may also be represented as $8 \div 4$.

(Problem A: 8 sticks/4 cups) **Eight-fourths, or eight sticks per four cups. How many sticks per one cup? Let's divide the eight sticks per the four cups.** Place one stick in the first cup below, the next stick in the next cup, and so on. In the end, you should have two sticks in each of the cups. **Are there even amounts of sticks in each cup? Good.** Remove the divisor line because it is no longer needed since the division is complete. **Now that we are done with the division, we don't need the symbol telling us to divide. What do we have left? How many in each cup? Yes, there are two sticks per each cup. Write 2 sticks/1 cup.**

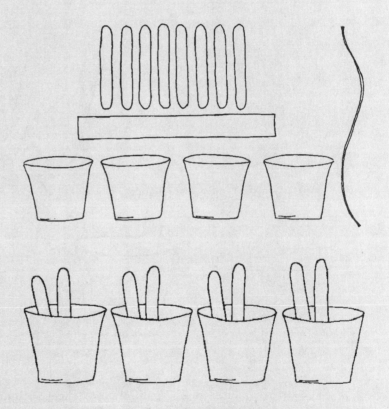

(Problem B: 5 sticks/3 cups) **There are five sticks per three cups. How many sticks per one cup? Let's divide the five sticks into the three cups.** Place one stick in the first cup below, the next stick in the next cup, and so on. In the end, you should have two sticks in two cups and one stick in the last cup. **Are there even amounts of sticks in each cup? No? Then let's back up one stick.** Remove the last stick placed into the second cup. **Are there even amounts of sticks in each cup now? No? Then let's back up one stick again. Are there even amounts of sticks in each cup now? Yes? Good.** Remove the divisor line because it is no longer needed since the division is complete. Now that we are done with the division, we don't need the symbol telling us to divide. **What do we have left? How many in each cup? Yes, there is one stick per each cup and two sticks that need to be divided into three cups. Write 1 stick/1 cup and 2 sticks/3 cups** $= 1\frac{2}{3}$.

(Problem C: 3 sticks/4 cups) **There are three sticks per four cups. How many sticks per one cup? Let's divide the three sticks per the four cups.** Place one stick in the first cup below, the next stick in the next cup, and so on. In the end, you should have three sticks in the three cups and no sticks in the last cup. **Are there even amounts of sticks in each cup? No? Then let's back up one stick. Remove the last stick placed in the second cup. Are there even amounts of sticks in each cup now? No? Then let's back up one stick again. Are there even amounts of sticks in each cup now? No? Then let's back up one stick again. Are there even amounts of sticks in each cup now? Yes? But they are all empty. The answer is going to be less than one.** Remove the divisor line because it is no longer needed since the division is complete. **Now that we are done with the division, we don't need the symbol telling us to divide. What do we have left? How many in each cup?** Yes, there are no sticks in the cups and three sticks that need to be divided into four cups. Write 0 sticks/1 cup and 3 sticks/4 cups = $\frac{3}{4}$.

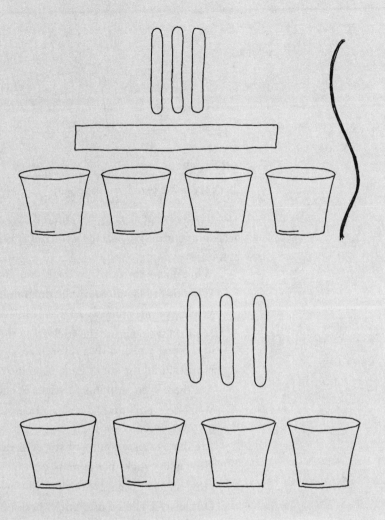

(Problem D: 4 sticks/4 cups) **There are four sticks per four cups. How many sticks per one cup?** Let's divide the four sticks per the four cups. Place one stick in the first cup below, the next stick in the next cup, and so on. In the end, there should be one stick in each of the four cups. Are there even amounts of sticks in each cup? Yes, very good. Now, we are finished with the division so we can remove the divisor line. **How many sticks are left in each cup? Yes, there is one stick in one cup.** Write 1 stick/1 cup.

Guided Practice

Let's try some problems together.

(Problem E: 9 sticks/2 cups) **How do we set this up? Let's complete it with the objects on your desks.** Ask the students a series of questions and have them repeat the questions.

> **What do we lay down in the numerator?** Nine sticks.
>
> **What do we lay down in the denominator?** Two cups.
>
> **What separates the two?** Divisor line.
>
> **How do we separate the sticks into the cups?** We should end up with four sticks in the first cup and five in the second.
>
> **Now that all the sticks have been moved into cups, what do we ask ourselves?**
>
> **Are there even amounts of sticks in each cup now?** No.
>
> **What do we remove?** The last stick put into the second cup. (Move back to numerator.)
>
> **Are there even amounts of sticks in each cup now?** Yes.
>
> **How many sticks per cup?** Four.
>
> **How many sticks were not put into a cup?** One.
>
> **Our answer will be four sticks per one cup and one stick per two cups, which is equal to $4\frac{1}{2}$.**

(Problem F: 3 sticks/3 cups) **How do we set this up? Let's complete it with the objects on your desks.** (Ask the students a series of questions and have them repeat the questions).

> **What do we lay down in the numerator?** Three sticks.
>
> **What do we lay down in the denominator?** Three cups.
>
> **What separates the two?** Divisor line.
>
> **How do we separate the sticks into the cups?** We should end up with one stick in each cup.
>
> **Now that all the sticks have been moved into cups, what do we ask ourselves?**
>
> **Are there even amounts of sticks in each cup?** Yes.
>
> **Are we finished dividing?** Yes. **Then, what can we remove?** Divisor line.
>
> **How many sticks per cup?** One stick.
>
> **We write our answer as 1 stick/1 cup; $\frac{1}{1}$; or 1.**

Word Problem

(Problem G) **Let's look at this scenario.** A mother gave 10 dollars (sticks) to her four children (cups) to split up ($\div$) evenly. How many ($=$) dollars will go to each child? We are going to show our answer using the objects provided.

> **Let's begin by setting this up.**
>
> **What are we trying to divide evenly?** Ten dollars.

Among whom or what? Four children.

So, let ten sticks represent ten dollars in the numerator and four cups represent four children in the denominator.

What separates the two? Divisor line.

Now let's split the "dollars" per the "children."

Start by giving one dollar to each child. Have all the dollars been given out? No.

Let's continue. Give all the children another dollar. (Two sticks per each cup.)

Have all the dollars been given out? No. Let's continue. (Two sticks in first two cups.)

Have all the dollars been given out? Yes.

Now, what can we ask ourselves?

Does each child have an even amount of dollars? No.

What should we do now? Remove the last two dollars from the first two cups and place them back in the numerator.

Now, do all the children have an even amount of dollars? Yes.

How many dollars per child? Two dollars/One child.

How many left over? Two dollars/four children.

So our answer is 2 dollars and 2 dollars/4 children or $2\frac{1}{4}$, which is equal to $2\frac{1}{2}$.

If we are dealing with change then we could evenly give each child two dollars and fifty cents.

Independent Practice

It's your turn to try some practice problems on your own. Use your sticks, cups, and divisor line to work out the problems. Be sure to draw a picture of your answer and the number answer on paper.

LESSON 2

Division with Fractional Answers

2.R (tallies and groups method)

Describe/Model *(Answer is in tallies per group.)*

a) $\dfrac{12 \text{ tallies}}{4 \text{ groups}}$

b) $\dfrac{8 \text{ tallies}}{3 \text{ groups}}$

c) $\dfrac{13 \text{ tallies}}{5 \text{ groups}}$

d) $\dfrac{15 \text{ tallies}}{2 \text{ groups}}$

Guided Practice

e) $\dfrac{5 \text{ tallies}}{5 \text{ groups}}$

f) $\dfrac{19 \text{ tallies}}{4 \text{ groups}}$

Word Problem

g) Three dogs (groups) are sharing dinner. The owner places eight scoops (tallies) of food into the one feeding dish. If each dog eats the same amount of food, how many scoops of food does each (÷) dog eat? Show your answer using the same picture format in this lesson.

What does the fraction in the answer mean?

Independent Practice

h) $\dfrac{9 \text{ tallies}}{3 \text{ groups}}$

i) $\dfrac{6 \text{ tallies}}{1 \text{ group}}$

j) $\dfrac{14 \text{ tallies}}{3 \text{ groups}}$

k) $\dfrac{18 \text{ tallies}}{5 \text{ groups}}$

Teaching **LESSON 2**

Division with Fractional Answers

2.R (tallies and groups method)

Describe/Model *(Answer is in tallies per group.)*

Today we are going to work some division problems much like the problems we worked yesterday. Yesterday we worked these problems using sticks and cups. Today we will be using tally marks to represent the sticks and groups (circles) to represent the cups.

(Problem A: 12 tallies/4 groups) **Twelve tallies per four groups. How many tallies per one group? Let's divide the twelve tallies per the four groups.** The problem should be set up with twelve tally marks in the numerator, a divisor line, and four groups (or circles) in the denominator. Place one tally in each of the four groups. Cross out four tallies from the numerator. Place one tally in each of the four groups again. Cross out four more tallies from the numerator. Repeat until tallies are evenly divided among the four groups. You should end with three tally marks per four groups. **Are there even amounts of tallies in each group? Good.** Write the tallies per group after the previous step without the divisor line because it is no longer needed since the division is complete. **Now that we are done with the division, we don't need the symbol telling us to divide. What do we have left? How many tallies in each group? Yes, there are three tallies per group.** Write 3 tallies/1 group.

(Problem B: 8 tallies/3 groups) **There are eight tallies per three groups. How many tallies per one group? Let's divide the eight tallies per the three groups.** Place one tally in each of the three groups until all tallies are distributed. In the end, you should have three tallies in the first two groups and two in the last group. **Are there even amounts of tallies in each group? No? Then let's back up. Remove the last tally put in the second group (move back to numerator). Are there even amounts of tallies in each group now? No? Then let's back up one tally again (move tally back to numerator). Are there even amounts of tallies in each group now? Yes? Good. What do we have left? How many in each group? Yes, there are two tallies per group and two tallies that need to be divided into three groups.** Write 2 tallies/1 group and 2 tallies/3 groups = $2\frac{2}{3}$.

(Problem C: 13 tallies/5 groups) **There are thirteen tallies per five groups. How many tallies per one group? Let's divide the thirteen tallies per the five groups.** Place one tally into each group until all tallies are distributed. You should end up with three tallies in the first three groups and two tallies in the last two groups. **Are there even amounts of tallies in each group? No? Then let's back up one tally.** Cross out the last tally from the third group (add it back to the numerator). **Are there even amounts of tallies in each group now? No? Then let's back up one tally again (cross it out of the group and add it back to the numerator). Are there even amounts of tallies in each group now? No? Then let's back up another tally. Are there an even amount of tallies in each group now? Yes. Now that we are finished, we do not need the divisor line. What do we have left? How many in each group? Yes, there are two tallies per group and three tallies that need to be divided into five groups.** Write 2 tallies/1 group and 3 tallies/5 groups or $2\frac{3}{5}$.

(Problem D: 15 tallies/2 groups) **There are fifteen tallies per two groups. How many tallies per one group? Let's divide the fifteen tallies into the two groups.** Place one tally in each group until all the tallies are distributed. You should end up with eight tallies in the first group and seven tallies in the second. **Are there even amounts of tallies in each group? No? What should we do now? Let's back up one tally. Cross out the last** tally placed in the first group (add it back to the numerator). Now, are there even amounts of tallies in each group? Yes? Very good. What do we have left? How many tallies in each group? Seven. How many tallies are left to be divided into two groups? One. Write 7 tallies/1 group and 1 tally/2 groups or $7\frac{1}{2}$.

Guided Practice

Let's try some problems together.

(Problem E: 5 tallies/5 groups) **How do we set this up? Let's complete it with paper, pencil, tally marks, and groups.**

> Ask the students a series of questions and have them repeat the questions.
>
> **What do we draw in the numerator?** Five tallies.
>
> **What do we draw in the denominator?** Five groups (or circles).
>
> **What separates the two?** Divisor line.
>
> **How do we separate the tallies into the groups?** One tally in each group.
>
> **Now that all the tallies have been moved into groups, what do we ask ourselves?**
>
> **Are there even amounts of tallies in each group?** Yes.
>
> **How many tallies per group?** One.
>
> **Our answer will be one tally per one group;** $\frac{1}{1} = 1$.

(Problem F: 19 tallies/4 groups) **How do we set this up? Let's complete it with paper, pencil, tally marks, and groups.**

> Ask the students a series of questions and have them repeat the questions.
>
> **What do we draw in the numerator?** Nineteen tallies.
>
> **What do we draw in the denominator?** Four groups (or circles).

What separates the two? Divisor line.

How do we separate the tallies into the groups? Five tallies in the first three groups and four in the last group.

Now that all the tallies have been moved into groups, what do we ask ourselves?

Are there even amounts of tallies in each group? No.

What should we do now? Back up a tally.

Are there even amounts of tallies in each group? No.

What should we do? Back up another tally.

Are there even amounts of tallies in each group? No.

What should we do? Back up another tally.

Are there even amounts of tallies in each group? Yes.

How many tallies per group? Four.

How many tallies in the numerator are to be divided into four groups? Three.

Our answer will be four tallies/one group and three tallies/four groups; $4\frac{3}{4}$.

Word Problem

(Problem G) Let's look at this scenario. Three dogs are sharing dinner. The owner places eight scoops (tallies) of food in the one feeding dish. If each dog eats the same amount of food, how many scoops of food does each ($\div$) eat? We will show our answer using pictures with tallies and groups.

Let's begin by setting this up.

What are we trying to divide evenly? Eight scoops of dog food.

Among whom or what? Three dogs.

So, let eight tallies represent eight scoops in the numerator and three groups represent three dogs in the denominator.

What separates the two? Divisor line.

Let's split the "scoops" per "dog."

Start by giving one scoop to each dog. Have all the scoops been given out? No.

Let's continue. Give all the dogs another scoop (two tallies per each group).

Have all the scoops been given out? No. **Let's continue** (two tallies in first two groups).

Have all the scoops been given out? Yes.

Now, what can we ask ourselves?

Does each dog have an even amount of scoops? No.

What should we do now? Remove the last two scoops from the first two dogs and place them back in the numerator.

Now, do all of the dogs have an even amount of scoops? Yes.

How many scoops per dog? 2 scoops/1 dog.

How many left over? 2 scoops/3 dogs.

So our answer is two scoops per one dog and two more scoops to be divided among three dogs. We write our answer as $2\frac{2}{3}$.

Independent Practice

It's your turn to try some practice problems on your own. Use your pencil and paper to draw pictures using tallies and groups. Be sure to draw a picture of your answer and give the number answer on your paper.

LESSON 3

Division with Fractional Answers

3.A (abstract only)

Describe/Model

a) $\dfrac{23}{4}$

b) $\dfrac{14}{5}$

Guided Practice

c) $\dfrac{32}{6}$

d) $\dfrac{17}{3}$

e) $\dfrac{16}{4}$

f) $\dfrac{60}{8}$

Word Problem

g) Eighteen slices of pizza are bought for 5 basketball players. The slices are to be shared equally. How many slices of pizza will each player eat? Show your answer using the same abstract steps taught in this lesson.

What does the fraction in the answer mean?

Independent Practice

h) $\dfrac{19}{7}$

i) $\dfrac{55}{9}$

j) $\dfrac{48}{8}$

k) $\dfrac{21}{4}$

Teaching **LESSON 3**

Division with Fractional Answers

3.A (abstract only)

Describe/Model

We are now going to begin working out some division problems with fractional answers just as we have been doing with sticks and tallies; however, now we are going to learn how to find our answers without using those sticks and tallies. I am going to work out a couple of problems for you.

(Problem A: $2\frac{3}{4}$) Our first problem is twenty-three fourths, or 23 divided by 4. This problem is just like asking to separate twenty three tallies among four groups. We want to find how we can put twenty three into four groups. We know that four will go into twenty three evenly five times ($5 \times 4 = 20$). So, now we have five tallies per each group. We have used twenty tallies and have three left over because $23 - 20 = 3$. Therefore, our answer is 5/1 and $\frac{3}{4}$, or $5\frac{3}{4}$.

(Problem B: $\frac{14}{5}$) Our next problem is fourteen fifths, or 14 divided by 5. We want to know how we can separate fourteen into five. The first thing we need to decide is how many times five will evenly go into fourteen. We can use our multiplication facts. Let's try 5×3. Five times three is equal to what? 15. We know this can't work because we only have fourteen in our numerator. Let's back up one number to 5×2. Five times two equals what number? 10. So far we have two tallies in each of our five groups, which means we have used ten tallies. How many do we have left over? Very good, 4. So we have 2/1 and 4/5. We write our answer as $2\frac{4}{5}$.

Guided Practice

Let's try some problems together.

(Problem C: $\frac{32}{6}$) **How do we read this problem?** Thirty-two sixths.

    What is another way to read this problem? 32 divided by 6.

    What number are we trying to separate into groups? 32.

    How many groups are we working with? 6.

    What do we need to do first? Find out how many times six will go into thirty two evenly (5).

    How many tallies have we used in this case? $6 \times 5 = 30$.

    How many are left over? $32 - 30 = 2$. Great job.

    So, the first part of our answer is . . . ? $\frac{5}{1}$.

    The second part of our answer is . . . ? $\frac{2}{6}$.

    We write our answer as $5\frac{2}{6}$.

(Problem D: $\frac{17}{3}$) **How do we read this problem?** Seventeen thirds.

    What is another way to read this problem? 17 divided by 3.

    What number are we trying to separate into groups? 17.

    How many groups are we working with? 3.

    What do we need to do first? Find out how many times three will go into seventeen evenly (5).

    How many tallies have we used in this case? $3 \times 5 = 15$

    How many are left over? $17 - 15 = 2$. Great job.

So, the first part of our answer is . . . ? $\frac{5}{1}$.

The second part of our answer is . . . ? $\frac{2}{3}$.

We write our answer as $5\frac{2}{3}$.

(Problem E: $\frac{16}{4}$) **How do we read this problem?** Sixteen fourths.

What is another way to read this problem? 16 divided by 4.

What number are we trying to separate into groups? 16.

How many groups are we working with? 4.

What do we need to do first? Find out how many times four will go into sixteen evenly (4).

How many tallies have we used in this case? $4 \times 4 = 16$.

How many are left over? $16 - 16 = 0$. **Great job.**

So, the first part of our answer is . . . ? $\frac{4}{1}$.

The second part of our answer is . . . ? There is no second part because there are no tallies left over.

We write our answer as $\frac{4}{1}$, or 4.

(Problem F: $\frac{60}{8}$) **How do we read this problem?** Sixty eighths.

What is another way to read this problem? 60 divided by 8.

What number are we trying to separate into groups? 60.

How many groups are we working with? 8.

What do we need to do first? Find out how many times eight will go into sixty evenly (7).

How many tallies have we used in this case? $8 \times 7 = 56$.

How many are left over? $60 - 56 = 4$. **Great job.**

So, the first part of our answer is . . . ? $\frac{7}{1}$.

The second part of our answer is . . . ? $\frac{4}{8}$.

We write our answer as $7\frac{4}{8}$.

Word Problem

(Problem G) Let's look at this scenario. **Eighteen slices of pizza are bought for 5 basketball players. The slices are to be shared equally. How many slices of pizza will each player eat?** We will show our answer using the same abstract steps taught in this lesson.

What is this problem asking us to do? Divide.

So, let's think about how we would write this division problem as a fraction.

What are we trying to divide? 18 slices of pizza.

Who are we dividing the pizza among? 5 basketball players.

So, we can write this problem as $\frac{18}{5}$.

How do we read this problem? Eighteen fifths.

What is another way to read this problem? 18 divided by 5.

What number are we trying to separate into groups? 18.

How many groups are we working with? 5.

What do we need to do first? Find out how many times five will go into eighteen evenly (3).

How many slices of pizza have we used in this case? $5 \times 3 = 15$.

How many are left over? $18 - 15 = 3$. Great job.

So, the first part of our answer is . . . ? $\frac{3}{1}$.

The second part of our answer is . . . ? $\frac{3}{5}$.

We write our answer as $3\frac{3}{5}$. Each basketball player will eat $3\frac{3}{5}$ slices of pizza.

Independent Practice

Now you are going to try some of these problems on your own. Be sure to use the abstract method just as we have been doing today. If you get stuck on a problem, you can use the tally method to help you.

LESSON 4

Division with Fractional Answers

4.A (generalized)

Describe/Model *(You may use your calculator to show each step using long division.)*

a) $\dfrac{185}{12}$

$$12\overline{)185}$$
$$\underline{12}$$
$$65$$
$$\underline{60}$$
$$5$$

with quotient 15 r.5

b) $\dfrac{65}{9}$ $9\overline{)65}$

Guided Practice

c) $\dfrac{85}{11}$ $\overline{)}$

d) $\dfrac{122}{25}$ $\overline{)}$

Word Problem

e) Before the homecoming dance, there were 84 cars that dropped students off in the first 5 hours. How many cars per hour dropped off students? Show your answer using the same steps taught in this lesson.

What does the fraction in the answer mean?

Independent Practice

f) $\dfrac{77}{10}$

g) $\dfrac{53}{7}$

h) $\dfrac{140}{33}$

i) $\dfrac{98}{21}$

LESSON 5

Division with Fractional Answers

1.C (sticks-only method)

Describe/Model *(Answer is in groups of sticks.)*

a) $\dfrac{14 \text{ sticks}}{2 \text{ sticks}}$

b) $\dfrac{11 \text{ sticks}}{5 \text{ sticks}}$

c) $\dfrac{13 \text{ sticks}}{6 \text{ sticks}}$

d) $\dfrac{4 \text{ sticks}}{8 \text{ sticks}}$

Guided Practice

e) $\dfrac{9 \text{ sticks}}{4 \text{ sticks}}$

f) $\dfrac{3 \text{ sticks}}{9 \text{ sticks}}$

Word Problem

g) Four friends (sticks) are sharing lunch. They could only afford 7 hamburgers (sticks) to be split between the 4 of them. If each person eats the same amount, how many hamburgers does each (÷) person eat? Show your answer using the same concrete format taught in this lesson.

What does the fraction in the answer mean?

Independent Practice

h) $\dfrac{8 \text{ sticks}}{3 \text{ sticks}}$

i) $\dfrac{5 \text{ sticks}}{2 \text{ sticks}}$

j) $\dfrac{12 \text{ sticks}}{3 \text{ sticks}}$

k) $\dfrac{13 \text{ sticks}}{5 \text{ sticks}}$

Teaching **LESSON 5**

Division with Fractional Answers

1.C (sticks-only method)

Describe/Model *(Answer is in groups of sticks.)*

Today we are going to start learning how to reduce fractions to find equivalent fractions. We will be using the same sticks that we used in our first lesson on division with fractional answers. When we reduce fractions we will commonly group the sticks in the numerator and denominator. What separates the numerator from the denominator? Divisor line. Very good.

I am going to work out some of these problems for you. Be sure to follow along so that you are ready to work out some with me and on your own at the end of the lesson.

(Problem A: 14 sticks/2 sticks) We are going to reduce this fraction (fourteen halves) so that our answer is in groups of sticks. We have fourteen sticks in the numerator and two sticks in the denominator. First, we need to figure out how to commonly group the sticks in both the numerator and the denominator. Because there are only two sticks in the denominator, we will try groups of two sticks. Let's see how many groups of two sticks we can make using the fourteen in the numerator ($14 \div 2 = 7$). Do all the groups in this fraction have an equal number of sticks? Yes (2). So we have 7 groups of sticks/ 1 group of sticks, $\frac{7}{1}$. This tells us that the fraction $\frac{14}{2}$ is equal to $\frac{7}{1}$ or 7.

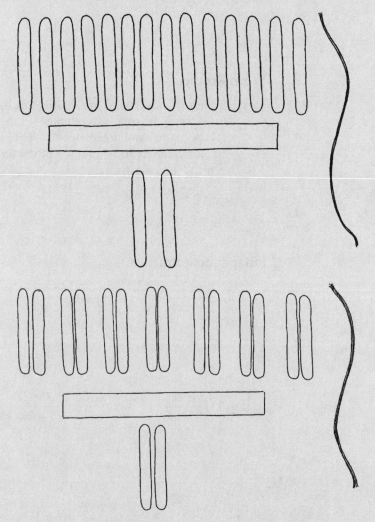

(Problem B: 11 sticks/5 sticks) We are going to reduce this fraction (eleven fifths) so that our answer is in groups of sticks. We have eleven sticks in the numerator and five sticks in the denominator. First, we need to figure out how to commonly group the sticks in both the numerator and the denominator. We need to make sure that all our sticks in the denominator belong to a group. Because our numerator is not even, we know that we cannot separate those sticks evenly; we will have at least one stick in the numerator that does not belong to a group. We will need to use groups of five sticks so that all the sticks in the denominator belong to a group. We know we will have one group of five sticks in the denominator. Let's see how many groups of five sticks we can make using the eleven in the numerator. Two groups with one stick left over. Do all the groups in this fraction have an equal number of sticks? Yes (5). So we have 2 groups of sticks/1 group of sticks and 1 stick/5 sticks, or $2\frac{1}{5}$. This tells us that $\frac{11}{5}$ is also equal to $2\frac{1}{5}$.

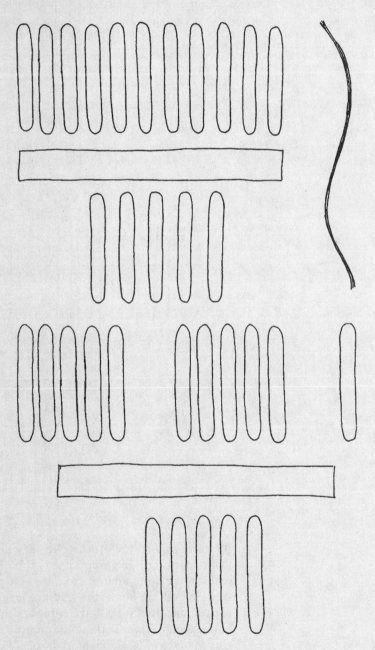

(Problem C: 13 sticks/6 sticks) We are going to reduce this fraction (thirteen sixths) so that our answer is in groups of sticks. We have thirteen sticks in the numerator and six sticks in the denominator. First, we need to figure out how to commonly group the sticks in both the numerator and the denominator. Let's try groups of six. Will that make our denominator so that there will be no sticks left out of a group? Yes. We know that we will have one group of six sticks in the denominator. Let's see how many groups of six sticks we can make using the thirteen in the numerator. Two groups with one stick left over. Do all the groups in this fraction have an equal number of sticks? Yes (6). So we have 2 groups of sticks/1 group of sticks and 1 stick/6 sticks or $2\frac{1}{6}$. This tells us that the fraction $\frac{13}{6}$ is equal to $2\frac{1}{6}$.

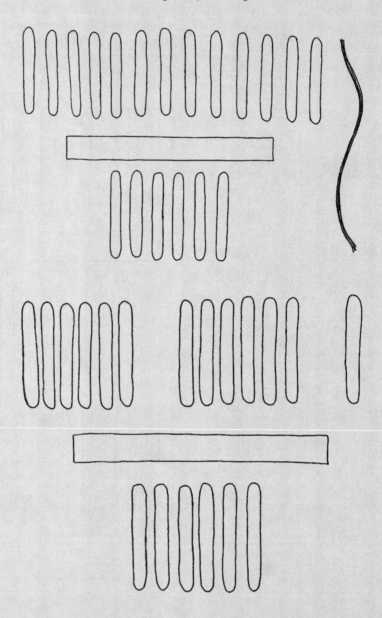

(Problem D: 4 sticks/8 sticks) We are going to reduce this fraction (four eighths) so that our answer is in groups of sticks. We have four sticks in the numerator and eight sticks in the denominator. First, we need to figure out how to commonly group the sticks in both the numerator and the denominator. Because there are only four sticks in the numerator, we will try groups of four sticks. We already know that there will be one group of four sticks in the numerator. Let's see how many groups of four sticks we can make using the eight in the denominator. 2. Do all the groups in this fraction have an equal number of sticks? Yes (4). So we have 1 group of sticks/2 groups of sticks or $\frac{1}{2}$. This tells us that the fraction $\frac{4}{8}$ is equal to $\frac{1}{2}$.

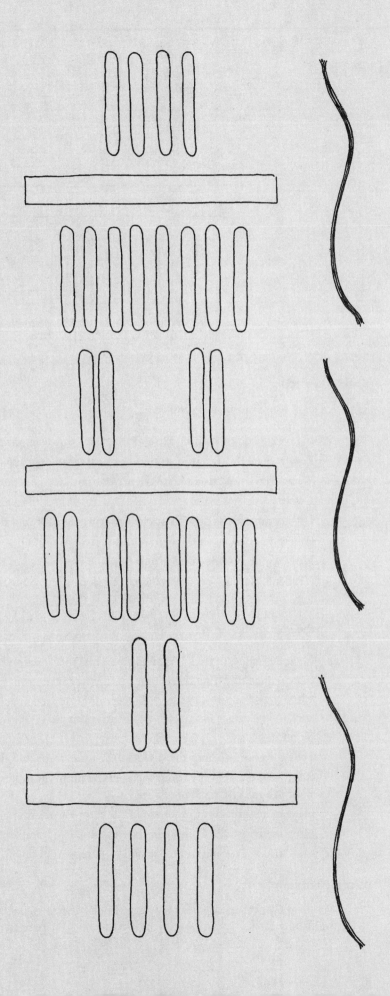

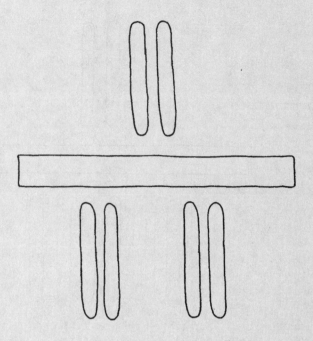

Guided Practice

Let's try some problems together.

(Problem E: 9 sticks/4 sticks) **How do we read this fraction?** Nine fourths.

> **Let's reduce this fraction so that our answer is in groups of sticks.**
>
> **What do we need to do first?** Figure out how we can commonly group the sticks.
> **Good.**
>
> **Let's commonly group the sticks in the numerator and denominator.**
>
> **Group your sticks in the denominator first so that all sticks belong to a group.**
>
> **Now, use that same-sized group to place your sticks in the numerator.**
>
> (Students should get answers of 2 groups/1 group and 1 stick/4 sticks, or 4 groups/2 groups and 1 stick/4 sticks. If students get the second answer, encourage them to reduce the first part of their answer "$\frac{4}{2}$" so that there is 1 group in the denominator.)

(Problem F: 3 sticks/9 sticks) **How do we read this fraction?** Three ninths.

> **Let's reduce this fraction so that our answer is in groups of sticks.**
>
> **What do we need to do first?** Figure out how we can commonly group the sticks.
>
> **Good.**
>
> **Let's commonly group the sticks in the numerator and denominator.**
>
> **Because there are only three sticks in the numerator, how many sticks per group should we try first?** 3
>
> **How many groups of three are in the numerator?** 1
>
> **How many groups of three in the denominator?** 3
>
> **Our answer is going to be 1 group/3 groups or $\frac{1}{3}$.**

Word Problem

(Problem G) **Let's look at this scenario. Four friends (sticks) are sharing lunch. They could only afford 7 hamburgers (sticks) to be split between the 4 of them. If each** person eats the same amount, how many hamburgers does each (÷) person eat? We will show our answer using sticks just as we did in the first part of the lesson.

Let's set this up as a fraction.

What are we trying to divide in this problem? 7 hamburgers.

How many people are we dividing the hamburgers among? 4.

So our fraction would be $\frac{7}{4}$, or . . . ? Seven fourths.

Let's work this problem using 7 sticks/4 sticks so that we can get an answer in groups of sticks.

We only have 4 sticks in the denominator, so how many sticks could we try per group? 4.

How many groups of 4 sticks in the denominator? 1.

How many groups of 4 sticks in the numerator? 1.

What is the first part of our answer? 1 group/1 group.

The second part? 3 sticks/4 sticks.

Our answer is $1\frac{3}{4}$ hamburgers.

Independent Practice

Now you are going to try out some of these problems on your own. Use your sticks to find the answer and then write your answer in numbers on your paper.

LESSON 6

Division with Fractional Answers   *2.R (tallies-only method)*

Describe/Model *(Answer is in groups of sticks.)*

a) $\dfrac{15 \text{ sticks}}{4 \text{ sticks}}$

b) $\dfrac{7 \text{ sticks}}{14 \text{ sticks}}$

c) $\dfrac{17 \text{ sticks}}{6 \text{ sticks}}$

d) $\dfrac{8 \text{ sticks}}{4 \text{ sticks}}$

Guided Practice

e) $\dfrac{9 \text{ sticks}}{3 \text{ sticks}}$

f) $\dfrac{14 \text{ sticks}}{6 \text{ sticks}}$

Word Problem

g) A man paid a group $20 (sticks) for painting a fence. Three boys (sticks) painted the fence together. If each boy earned the same amount, how much did each (÷) receive? Show your answer using the same picture format taught in this lesson.

What does the fraction in the answer mean?

Independent Practice

h) $\dfrac{18 \text{ sticks}}{7 \text{ sticks}}$

i) $\dfrac{15 \text{ sticks}}{9 \text{ sticks}}$

j) $\dfrac{4 \text{ sticks}}{10 \text{ sticks}}$

k) $\dfrac{10 \text{ sticks}}{5 \text{ sticks}}$

Teaching **LESSON 6**

Division with Fractional Answers

2.R (tallies-only method)

Describe/Model *(Answer is in groups of tallies.)*

Today we will continue to learn how to reduce fractions in order to find equivalent fractions. Instead of using sticks today, we will be using tallies.

I am going to work out some of these problems for you. Be sure to follow along so that you are ready to work out some with me and on your own at the end of the lesson.

(Problem A: 15 tallies/4 tallies) We are going to reduce this fraction (fifteen fourths) so that our answer is in groups of tallies. We have fifteen tallies in the numerator and four tallies in the denominator. First, we need to figure out how to commonly group the tallies in both the numerator and the denominator. Because there are only four tallies in the denominator, we will try groups of four tallies. Let's see how many groups of four tallies we can make using the fifteen in the numerator. Three groups with three tallies left over. Do all the groups in this fraction have an equal number of tallies? Yes (4). So we have 3 groups of tallies/1 group of tallies and 3 tallies/4 tallies, or $3\frac{3}{4}$. This tells us that the fraction $\frac{15}{4}$ is equal to $3\frac{3}{4}$.

(Problem B: 7 tallies/14 tallies) We are going to reduce this fraction (seven fourteenths) so that our answer is in groups of tallies. We have seven tallies in the numerator and fourteen tallies in the denominator. First, we need to figure out how to commonly group the tallies in both the numerator and the denominator. Since there are only seven tallies in the numerator, let's use groups of seven tallies. How many groups will that give us in the numerator? 1. How many groups of seven sticks will we have in the denominator? 2. Do all the groups in this fraction have an equal number of tallies? Yes (7). So we have 1 group of tallies/2 groups of tallies, or $\frac{1}{2}$. This tells us that $\frac{7}{14}$ is also equal to $\frac{1}{2}$.

(Problem C: 17 tallies/6 tallies) We are going to reduce this fraction (seventeen sixths) so that our answer is in groups of tallies. We have seventeen tallies in the numerator and six tallies in the denominator. First, we need to figure out how to commonly group the tallies in both the numerator and the denominator. Because there are only six tallies in the denominator, let's try groups of six tallies. Will there be no tallies in the denominator left out of a group? Yes. We know that we will have one group of six tallies in the denominator. Let's see how many groups of six tallies we can make using the seventeen in the numerator. Two groups with four tallies left over. Do all the groups in this fraction have an equal number of tallies? Yes (6). So we have 2 groups of tallies/1 group of tallies and 4 tallies/6 tallies, or $2\frac{4}{6}$. This tells us that the fraction $\frac{17}{6}$ is equal to $2\frac{4}{6}$.

(Problem D: 8 tallies/4 tallies) We are going to reduce this fraction (eight fourths) so that our answer is in groups of tallies. We have eight tallies in the numerator and four tallies in the denominator. First, we need to figure out how to commonly group the tallies in both the numerator and the denominator. Because there are only four tallies in the denominator, let's try groups of four tallies. We know that there will be one group of four tallies in the denominator. Let's see how many groups of four tallies we can make using the eight in the numerator. 2. Do all the groups in this fraction have an equal number of tallies? Yes (4). So we have 2 groups of tallies/1 group of tallies, or 2. This tells us that the fraction $\frac{8}{4}$ is equal to $\frac{2}{1}$, or 2.

a)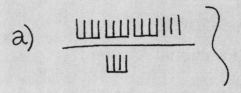

b)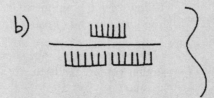

c)

d)

Guided Practice

Let's try some problems together.

(Problem E: 9 tallies/3 tallies) **How do we read this fraction?** Nine thirds.

    Let's reduce this fraction so that our answer is in groups of tallies.

    What do we need to do first? Figure out how we can commonly group the tallies. **Good.**

    Let's commonly group the tallies in the numerator and denominator.

    Because there are only three tallies in the denominator, how many tallies could we try per group? 3. **Good.**

    Group your tallies in your numerator and denominator by groups of three.

    How many groups in the numerator? 3 groups.

    How many groups in the denominator? 1 group.

    Our answer is 3 groups/1 group or . . . ? 3.

(Problem F: 14 tallies/6 tallies) **How do we read this fraction?** Fourteen sixths.

    Let's reduce this fraction so that our answer is in groups of tallies.

    What do we need to do first? Figure out how we can commonly group the tallies. **Good.**

    Let's commonly group the tallies in the numerator and denominator.

Because there are only six tallies in the numerator, how many tallies could we try per group? 6.

Group your tallies in your numerator and denominator by groups of six.

How many groups in the numerator? 2.

How many sticks are left over in the numerator? 2.

How many groups in the denominator? 1.

What is the first part of our answer? 2 groups/1 group.

What is the second part of our answer? 2 sticks/6 sticks.

Our answer is 2 groups/1 group and 2 sticks/6 sticks, or $2\frac{2}{6}$.

Because both numbers in the second part of our answer are even, that tells us that we can reduce the fraction again. Let's reduce 2 sticks/6 sticks.

(Use the same questioning techniques until students arrive at the answer of $\frac{1}{3}$.)

Our final answer is $2\frac{1}{3}$. That tells us that $\frac{14}{6}$ is equal to $2\frac{1}{3}$.

Word Problem

(Problem G) Let's look at this scenario. A man paid a group $20 (tallies for painting a fence). Three boys (tallies) painted the fence together. If each boy earned the same amount, how much did each (÷) receive? We will show our answers using the same picture format with tallies as we did in the first part of this lesson.

Let's set this up as a fraction.

What are we trying to divide in this problem? 20 dollars.

How many people are we dividing the dollars among? 3.

So, our fraction would be $\frac{20}{3}$ or . . . ? Twenty thirds.

Let's work out this problem using 20 tallies/3 tallies so that we can get an answer in groups of tallies.

We only have three tallies in the denominator, so how many tallies could we try per group? 3.

How many groups of three tallies in the denominator? 1.

How many groups of three tallies in the numerator? 6.

How many tallies (dollars) are left over in the numerator? 2.

What is the first part of our answer? 6 groups/1 group.

The second part? 2 tallies/3 tallies.

Our answer is $6\frac{2}{3}$ dollars.

If we use a calculator, we can divide $\frac{2}{3}$ to see that each boy earned about $6.67.

Independent Practice

Now you are going to try some of these problems on your own. Use your tally marks to find the answer and then write your answer in numbers on your paper.

LESSON 7

Division with Fractional Answers

3.A (abstract only)

Describe/Model *(Answer is in groups of sticks.)*

a) $\dfrac{10 \text{ sticks}}{3 \text{ sticks}}$

b) $\dfrac{5 \text{ sticks}}{15 \text{ sticks}}$

Guided Practice

c) $\dfrac{13 \text{ sticks}}{4 \text{ sticks}}$

d) $\dfrac{12 \text{ sticks}}{4 \text{ sticks}}$

e) $\dfrac{21 \text{ sticks}}{5 \text{ sticks}}$

f) $\dfrac{17 \text{ sticks}}{4 \text{ sticks}}$

Word Problem

g) Five girls decided to start walking pets. They made about $12 altogether per hour. If the money was split equally between the 5 girls, how much did each earn per hour? Show your answer using the same format taught in this lesson. What does the fraction in the answer mean?

Independent Practice

h) $\dfrac{25 \text{ sticks}}{6 \text{ sticks}}$

i) $\dfrac{22 \text{ sticks}}{7 \text{ sticks}}$

j) $\dfrac{31 \text{ sticks}}{10 \text{ sticks}}$

k) $\dfrac{16 \text{ sticks}}{5 \text{ sticks}}$

Teaching **LESSON 7**

Division with Fractional Answers

3.A (abstract only)

Describe/Model *(Answer is in groups of sticks.)*

Today we will be working more on reducing fractions. In the past couple of lessons, we have used sticks and tally marks to work out these problems. In this lesson, our problems are going to look exactly the same; however, we will be using our division and multiplication facts to get our answers rather than sticks and tallies.

I will begin by doing a couple problems for you.

(Problem A: 10 sticks/3 sticks) We are going to reduce this fraction (ten thirds) so that our answer is in groups. The first thing we need to do is decide what number will divide into both the numerator and the denominator (that is, decide how we can commonly group the sticks). By thinking about our division and multiplication facts and using divisibility rules, we know that there is not a number that will divide evenly into ten and three—there will be some left over. Because we only have a three in the denominator, let's divide by three. $10 \div 3$ will give us three with one left over in the numerator. The three represents our "groups" and the one represents one "stick." $3 \div 3$ will give us one group in the denominator. Therefore, our answer is $\frac{3}{1}$ and $\frac{1}{3}$ or $9\frac{1}{3}$. This tells us that $\frac{10}{3}$ is also equal to $3\frac{1}{3}$.

(Problem B: 5 sticks/15 sticks) We are going to reduce this fraction (five fifteenths) so that our answer will be in groups. The first thing we need to do is decide what number will divide into both the numerator and the denominator (that is, decide how we can commonly group the sticks). By thinking about our division and multiplication facts and using divisibility rules, we know that five will divide into both five and fifteen. Let's divide the numerator by five. $5 \div 5$ will give us one in the numerator. The one represents our "group." $15 \div 5$ will give us three groups in our denominator. Therefore, our answer is $\frac{1}{3}$. This tells us that $\frac{5}{15}$ is also equal to $\frac{1}{3}$.

Guided Practice

Let's try some problems together.

(Problem C: 13 sticks/4 sticks) How do we read this fraction? Thirteen fourths.

We need to reduce this fraction so that our answer will be in groups.

What is the first thing we need to do? Decide what number will divide into both the numerator and the denominator. Very good.

Think about our divisibility rules and our multiplication and division facts to come up with a number that will divide into thirteen and four. (Allow think time.)

What number did you come up with? There is not a number that will divide evenly into both numbers. There are going to be some left over.

There are only four "sticks" in the denominator, so what number should we try? 4.

Let's divide our numerator by four. 3 groups with 1 stick left over.

Let's divide our denominator by 4. 1 group.

What is the first part of our answer? 3 groups/1 group, or $\frac{3}{1}$.

What is the second part of our answer? 1 stick/4sticks.

Very good. We can write our answer as $3\frac{1}{4}$. We know that $\frac{13}{4}$ is also equal to $3\frac{1}{4}$.

(Problem D: 12 sticks/4 sticks) How do we read this fraction? Twelve fourths.

We need to reduce this fraction so that our answer will be in groups.

What is the first thing we need to do? Decide what number will divide into both the numerator and the denominator. Very good.

Think about our divisibility rules and our multiplication and division facts to come up with a number that will divide into twelve and four. (Allow think time.)

What number did you come up with? 4.

Let's divide our numerator by 4. 3 groups.

Let's divide our denominator by 4. 1 group.

What is our answer? 3 groups/1 group, or $\frac{3}{1}$.

Very good. We can write our answer as $\frac{3}{1}$ or 3. We know that $\frac{12}{4}$ is also equal to 3.

(Problem E: 21 sticks/5 sticks) How do we read this fraction? Twenty-one fifths.

We need to reduce this fraction so that our answer will be in groups.

What is the first thing we need to do? Decide what number will divide into both the numerator and the denominator. Very good.

Think about our divisibility rules and our multiplication and division facts to come up with a number that will divide into twenty one and five. (Allow think time.)

What number did you come up with? There is not a number that will divide evenly into both numbers. There are going to be some left over.

There are only five "sticks" in the denominator, so what number should we try? 5.

Let's divide our numerator by 5. 4 groups with 1 stick left over.

Let's divide our denominator by 5. 1 group.

What is the first part of our answer? 4 groups/1 group, or $\frac{4}{1}$.

What is the second part of our answer? 1 stick/5 sticks.

Very good. We can write our answer as $4\frac{1}{5}$. We know that $\frac{21}{5}$ is also equal to $4\frac{1}{5}$.

(Problem F: 17 sticks/4 sticks) How do we read this fraction? Seventeen fourths.

We need to reduce this fraction so that our answer will be in groups.

What is the first thing we need to do? Decide what number will divide into both the numerator and the denominator. Very good.

Think about our divisibility rules and our multiplication and division facts to come up with a number that will divide into seventeen and four. (Allow think time.)

What number did you come up with? There is not a number that will divide evenly into both numbers. There are going to be some left over.

There are only four "sticks" in the denominator, so what number should we try? 4.

Let's divide our numerator by 4. 4 groups with 1 stick left over.

Let's divide our denominator by 4. 1 group.

What is the first part of our answer? 4 groups/1 group, or $\frac{4}{1}$.

What is the second part of our answer? 1 stick/4 sticks.

Very good. We can write our answer as $4\frac{1}{4}$. We know that $\frac{17}{4}$ is also equal to $4\frac{1}{4}$.

Word Problem

(Problem G) Let's look at this scenario. Five girls decided to start walking pets. They made about $12 altogether per hour. If the money was split equally between the 5 girls, how much does each earn per hour? We will show our answer using the same format as in the first part of this lesson.

Let's start by setting this problem up as a fraction.

What is the problem asking us to do? Divide.

What are we trying to separate? 12 dollars.

How many groups are we separating the $12 into? 5.

So, our fraction would look like this: $\frac{12}{5}$.

How do we read that fraction? Twelve fifths.

We need to reduce this fraction so that our answer will be in groups.

What is the first thing we need to do? Decide what number will divide into both the numerator and the denominator. **Very good.**

Think about our divisibility rules and our multiplication and division facts to come up with a number that will divide into twelve and five. (Allow think time.)

What number did you come up with? There is not a number that will divide evenly into both numbers. There are going to be some left over.

There are only five girls in the denominator, so what number should we try? 5.

Let's divide our numerator by five. 2 groups with 2 sticks left over.

Let's divide our denominator by five. 1 group.

What is the first part of our answer? 2 groups/1 group, or $\frac{2}{1}$.

What is the second part of our answer? 2 sticks/5 sticks.

Very good. We can write our answer as $2\frac{2}{5}$. Each girl would earn $2\frac{2}{5}$ dollars. If we divide $\frac{2}{5}$ on a calculator, we can find that each girl would receive $2.40.

Independent Practice

Now you are going to try some of these problems on your own. Use the same method we have been using in this lesson and give your answer in numbers on your paper. If you get stuck, you may use tally marks to help find the answer.

Note: To review division with fractional answers, see Cumulative Review A starting on page 150.

LESSON 8

Multiplication of Fractions   *1.C (cups and sticks method)*

Describe/Model *(Answer is in groups of sticks.)*

a) $\left(\dfrac{2}{1}\right)$ cups of $\left(\dfrac{1}{3}\right)$ sticks

b) $\left(\dfrac{1}{3}\right)$ cups of $\left(\dfrac{3}{4}\right)$ sticks

c) $\left(\dfrac{1}{4}\right)$ cups of (5) sticks

d) (2) cups of $\left(\dfrac{2}{3}\right)$ sticks

Guided Practice

e) $\left(\dfrac{2}{3}\right)$ cups of $\left(\dfrac{1}{2}\right)$ sticks

f) (3) cups of $\left(\dfrac{2}{5}\right)$ sticks

Word Problem

g) A young man wants to make $\frac{1}{2}$ (cups) of (multiply) the usual pancake batter. A pancake mix calls for $\frac{2}{3}$ cup of water. How much water is needed in the batter? Show your problem solving using concrete materials.

What does the fraction in the answer mean?

Independent Practice

h) $\left(\dfrac{3}{1}\right)$ cups of $\left(\dfrac{3}{1}\right)$ sticks

i) $\left(\dfrac{1}{5}\right)$ cups of $\left(\dfrac{2}{3}\right)$ sticks

j) $\left(\dfrac{2}{4}\right)$ cups of $\left(\dfrac{3}{5}\right)$ sticks

k) $\left(\dfrac{1}{4}\right)$ cups of $\left(\dfrac{1}{4}\right)$ sticks

Teaching **LESSON 8**

Multiplication of Fractions

1.C (cups and sticks method)

Describe/Model *(Answer is in sticks.)*

Today we will be using cups and sticks again to learn how to multiply fractions. I will start by working out some of these problems for you. Be sure to pay very close attention so that you are ready to work out some of these with me and then try some on your own at the end of the lesson.

(Problem A: $\left(\frac{2}{1}\right)$ cups of $\left(\frac{1}{3}\right)$ sticks) This is a multiplication problem. The word "of" tells us to multiply. This problem would look like: $\frac{2}{1} \times \frac{1}{3}$. To set this up with cups and sticks, our first fraction will have two cups in the numerator and one cup in the denominator. What separates the two? A divisor line. In our second fraction we will have one stick in the numerator and three sticks in the denominator. What separates the two? A divisor line. In between our two fractions we need to place a multiplication symbol ($\times$). When we multiply fractions, we multiply the numerators and then the denominators. Let's start by multiplying the numerators. One stick in the numerator of our second fraction tells us that we need to place one stick in each of the two cups in the numerator of our first fraction. This will give use two groups of one in our numerator. Now, let's multiply the denominators. Three sticks in the denominator of our second fraction tells us that we need to place three sticks in each cup in the denominator of our first fraction. This gives us one group of three. Now we will count the total number of sticks to find our final answer. There are two in the numerator and three in the denominator, so we write our answer as 2 sticks/3 sticks, or $\frac{2}{3}$.

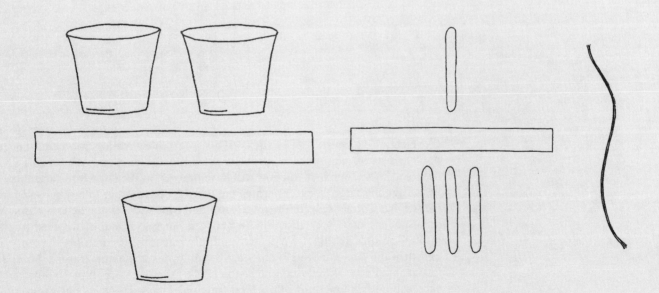

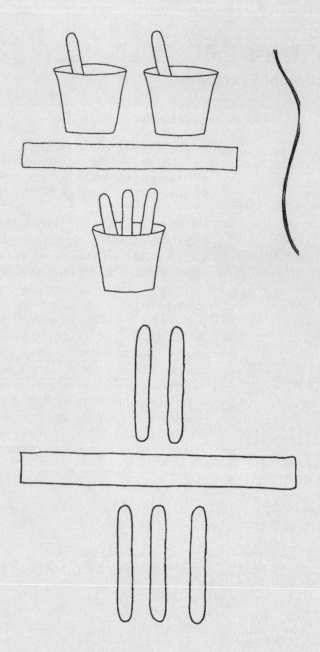

(Problem B: $\left(\frac{1}{3}\right)$ cups of $\left(\frac{3}{4}\right)$ sticks) This is a multiplication problem. The word "of" tells us to multiply. This problem would look like: $\frac{1}{3} \times \frac{3}{4}$. To set this up with cups and sticks, our first fraction will have one cup in the numerator and three cups in the denominator. What separates the two? A divisor line. In our second fraction we will have three sticks in the numerator and four sticks in the denominator. What separates the two? A divisor line. In between our two fractions we need to place a multiplication symbol (×). When we multiply fractions, we multiply the numerators and then the denominators. Let's start by multiplying the numerators. Three sticks in the numerator of our second fraction tells us that we need to place three sticks in each cup in the numerator of our first fraction. This will give us one group of three in the numerator. Now, let's multiply the denominators. Four sticks in the denominator of our second fraction tells us that we need to place four sticks in each cup in the denominator of our first fraction. This gives us three groups of four. Now we will count the total number of sticks to find our final answer. There are three in the numerator and twelve in the denominator, so we write our answer as 3 sticks/12 sticks, or $\frac{3}{12}$.

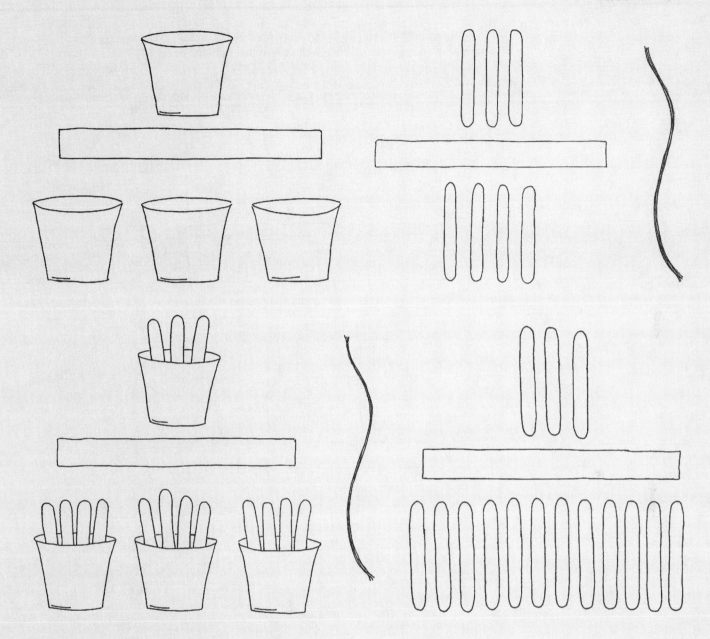

(Problem C: $\left(\frac{1}{4}\right)$ cups of (5) sticks) This is a multiplication problem. The word "of" tells us to multiply. This problem is a little different because there is a whole number where the second fraction usually is. To make this whole number a fraction, all we need to do is put a one in the denominator because $5 \div 1$ is equal to 5. Our fraction will look like $\frac{5}{1}$. This problem would look like: $\frac{1}{4} \times \frac{5}{1}$. To set this up with cups and sticks, our first fraction will have one cup in the numerator and four cups in the denominator. What separates the two? A divisor line. In our second fraction we will have five sticks in the numerator and one stick in the denominator. What separates the two? A divisor line. In between our two fractions we need to place a multiplication symbol ($\times$). When we multiply fractions, we multiply the numerators and then the denominators. Let's start by multiplying the numerators. Five sticks in the numerator of our second fraction tells us that we need to place one stick in each cup in the numerator of our first fraction. This will give us one group of five in our numerator. Now, let's multiply the denominators. One stick in the denominator of our second fraction tells us that we need to place one stick in each cup in the denominator of our first fraction. This gives us four groups of one. Now we will count the total number of sticks to find our final answer. There are five in the numerator and four in the denominator, so we write our answer as 5 sticks/4 sticks, or $\frac{5}{4}$.

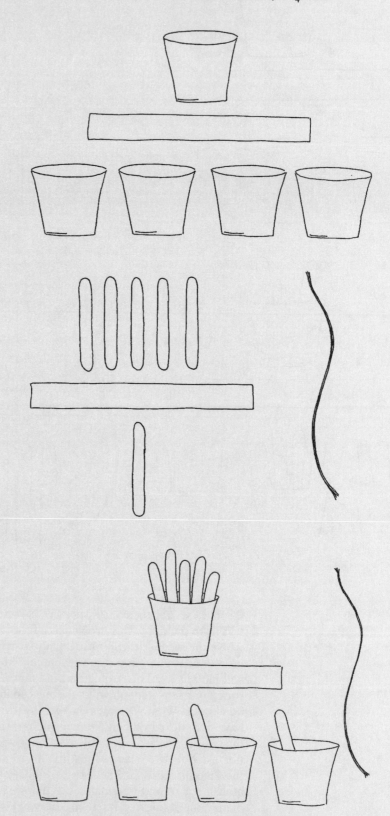

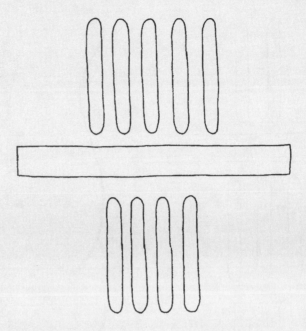

(Problem D: (2) cups of $\left(\frac{2}{3}\right)$ sticks) **This is a multiplication problem. The word "of" tells us to multiply. This problem is a little different because there is a whole number (2) where the first fraction usually is. What do we have to do to make this whole number a fraction? Place a one in the denominator. That is correct because 2 ÷ 1 is equal to 2. This problem would look like: $\frac{2}{1} \times \frac{2}{3}$. To set this up with cups and sticks, our first fraction will have two cups in the numerator and one cup in the denominator. What separates the two? A divisor line. In our second fraction, we will have two sticks in the numerator and three sticks in the denominator. What separates the two? A divisor line. In between our two fractions we need to place a multiplication symbol (×). When we multiply fractions, we multiply the numerators and then the denominators. Let's start by multiplying the numerators. Two sticks in the numerator of our second fraction tells us that we need to place one stick in each of the two cups in the numerator of our first fraction. This will give us two groups of two in our numerator. Now, let's multiply the denominators. Three sticks in the denominator of our second fraction tells us that we need to place three sticks in each cup in the denominator of our first fraction. This gives us one group of three. Now we will count the total number of sticks to find our final answer. There are four in the numerator and three in the denominator, so we write our answer as 4 sticks/3 sticks, or $\frac{4}{3}$.**

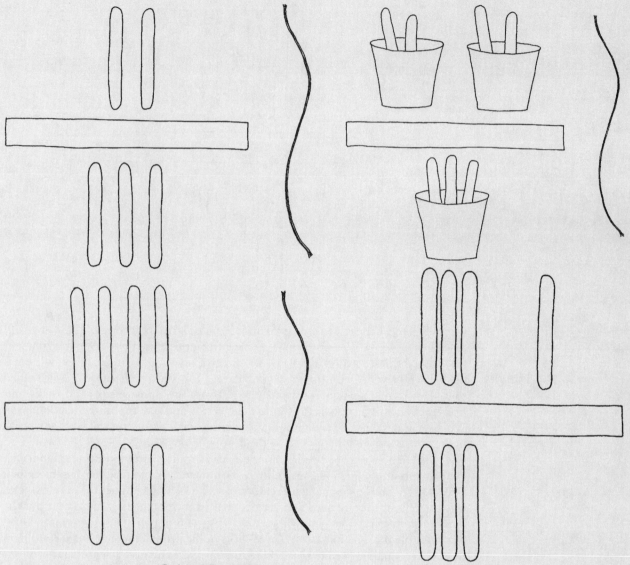

Guided Practice

Let's try some problems together.

(Problem E: $\left(\frac{2}{3}\right)$ cups of $\left(\frac{1}{2}\right)$ sticks) **Let's begin by writing this as a multiplication problem using numbers only.** $\frac{2}{3} \times \frac{1}{2}$.

Now let's set this problem up using cups and sticks. First fraction: 2 cups over 3 cups; second fraction: 1 stick over 2 sticks.

What should we multiply first? Numerators.

How many sticks do we need to place in each cup in the numerator of the first fraction? 1.

Now we have two groups of one stick in our numerator.

What should we do next? Multiply the denominators.

How many sticks should we place in each cup in the denominator of our first fraction? 3.

Now we have three groups of two sticks in our denominator.

What do we do to find our final answer? Count the total number of sticks.

How many in the numerator? 2.

How many in the denominator? 6.

Our answer is 2 sticks/6 sticks, or $\frac{2}{6}$.

(Problem F: (3) cups of $\left(\frac{2}{5}\right)$ sticks) Let's begin by writing this as a multiplication problem using numbers only. $\frac{3}{1} \times \frac{2}{5}$.

What did you have to do to make the first whole number a fraction? Put a one in the denominator.

Now let's set this problem up using cups and sticks. First fraction: 3 cups over 1 cup; second fraction: 2 sticks over 5 sticks.

What should we multiply first? Numerators.

How many sticks do we need to place in each cup in the numerator of the first fraction? 2.

Now we have three groups of two sticks in our numerator.

What should we do next? Multiply the denominators.

How many sticks should we place in each cup in the denominator of our first fraction? 5.

Now we have one group of five sticks in our denominator.

What do we do to find our final answer? Count the total number of sticks.

How many in the numerator? 6.

How many in the denominator? 5.

Our answer is 6 sticks/5 sticks, or $\frac{6}{5}$.

Word Problem

(Problem G) Let's look at this scenario. A young man wants to make $\frac{1}{2}$ (cups) of (multiply) the usual pancake batter. A pancake mix calls for $\frac{2}{3}$ cup of water. How much water is needed in the batter? We will show our answer using cups and sticks.

Let's begin by setting this up as a multiplication problem.

What is our first fraction? $\frac{1}{2}$. So we will let that represent $\left(\frac{1}{2}\right)$ cups.

What is our second fraction? $\frac{2}{3}$. So we will let that represent $\left(\frac{2}{3}\right)$ sticks.

Our problem will look like this: $\frac{1}{2} \times \frac{2}{3}$.

Now let's set this problem up using cups and sticks. First fraction: 1 cup over 2 cups; second fraction: 2 sticks over 3 sticks.

What should we multiply first? Numerators.

How many sticks do we need to place in each cup in the numerator of the first fraction? 2.

Now we have one group of two sticks in our numerator.

What should we do next? Multiply the denominators.

How many sticks should we place in each cup in the denominator of our first fraction? 3.

Now we have two groups of three sticks in our denominator.

What do we do to find our final answer? Count the total number of sticks.

How many in the numerator? 2.

How many in the denominator? 6.

Our answer is 2 sticks/6 sticks, or $\frac{2}{6}$.

The young man needs to use $\frac{2}{6}$. cups of water for his pancakes.

Independent Practice

Now you are going to try some of these multiplication problems on your own. Use cups and sticks to find your answers and then make sure to write your answer in numbers on your paper.

LESSON 9

Multiplication of Fractions   *2.R (groups and tallies method)*

Describe/Model *(Answer is in tallies.)*

a) $\left(\dfrac{3}{2}\right)$ cups of $\left(\dfrac{2}{3}\right)$ sticks   b) $\left(\dfrac{1}{4}\right)$ cups of $\left(\dfrac{1}{4}\right)$ sticks

c) (1) cups of $\left(\dfrac{3}{5}\right)$ sticks   d) $\left(\dfrac{4}{5}\right)$ cups of (2) sticks

Guided Practice

e) $\left(\dfrac{1}{3}\right)$ cups of $\left(\dfrac{3}{4}\right)$ sticks   f) (2) cups of $\left(\dfrac{3}{6}\right)$ sticks

Word Problem

g) While making formula to help a new mother next door, a young girl must mix $\frac{1}{4}$ (groups) of (multiply) a can of formula with pure water in the baby bottle. If the can holds $\frac{2}{3}$ cup (tallies) of formula, how much formula (cups) is mixed in the can? Use the pictorial steps in this lesson to solve the problem.

What does the fraction in the answer mean?

Independent Practice

h) $\left(\dfrac{1}{2}\right)$ cups of $\left(\dfrac{1}{6}\right)$ sticks   i) $\left(\dfrac{2}{3}\right)$ cups of $\left(\dfrac{1}{5}\right)$ sticks

j) $\left(\dfrac{1}{4}\right)$ cups of $\left(\dfrac{4}{5}\right)$ sticks   k) $\left(\dfrac{2}{5}\right)$ cups of $\left(\dfrac{1}{3}\right)$ sticks

Teaching **LESSON 9**

Multiplication of Fractions

2.R (groups and tallies method)

Describe/Model *(Answer is in tallies.)*

Today we will be working out more problems in which we multiply fractions. However, we will be using groups and tallies again to find our answer. Everyone remembers using tally marks and groups (or circles) when we worked on division with fractional answers. I will begin by working out some problems for you. Be sure to pay close attention so that you will be able to do some of these with me and eventually on your own at the end of the lesson.

(Problem A: $\left(\frac{3}{2}\right)$ groups of $\left(\frac{2}{3}\right)$ tallies) This is a multiplication problem. The word "of" tells us to multiply. This problem would look like: $\frac{3}{2} \times \frac{2}{3}$. To set this up with groups and tallies, our first fraction will have three groups in the numerator and two groups in the denominator. What separates the two? A divisor line. In our second fraction, we will have two tallies in the numerator and three tallies in the denominator. What separates the two? A divisor line. In between our two fractions we need to place a multiplication symbol (×). When we multiply fractions, we multiply the numerators and then the denominators. Let's start by multiplying the numerators. Two tallies in the numerator of our second fraction tells us that we need to place two tallies in each of the three groups in the numerator of our first fraction. This will give us three groups of two in our numerator. Now, let's multiply the denominators. Three tallies in the denominator of our second fraction tells us that we need to place three tallies in each group in the denominator of our first fraction. This gives us two groups of three. Now we will count the total number of tallies to find our final answer. There are six in the numerator and six in the denominator so our answer is 6 tallies/6 tallies, or $\frac{6}{6}$.

(Problem B: $\left(\frac{1}{4}\right)$ groups of $\left(\frac{1}{4}\right)$ tallies) This is a multiplication problem. The word "of" tells us to multiply. This problem would look like: $\frac{1}{4} \times \frac{1}{4}$. To set this up with groups and tallies, our first fraction will have one group in the numerator and four groups in the denominator. What separates the two? A divisor line. In our second fraction, we will have one tally in the numerator and four tallies in the denominator. What separates the two? A divisor line. In between our two fractions we need to place a multiplication symbol (×). When we multiply fractions, we multiply the numerators and then the denominators. Let's start by multiplying the numerators. One tally in the numerator of our second fraction tells us that we need to place one tally in each group in the numerator of our first fraction. This will give use one group of one in our numerator. Now, let's multiply the denominators. Four tallies in the denominator of our second fraction tells us that we need to place four tallies in each group in the denominator of our first fraction. This gives us four groups of four. Now we will count the total number of tallies to find our final answer. There is one in the numerator and sixteen in the denominator so our answer is 1 tally/16 tallies, or $\frac{1}{16}$.

(Problem C: (1) group of $\left(\frac{3}{5}\right)$ tallies) This is a multiplication problem. The word "of" tells us to multiply. This problem is a little different because there is a whole number where the first fraction usually is. To make this whole number a fraction all we need to do is put a one in the denominator because $1 \div 1$ is equal to one. Our fraction will look like $\frac{1}{1}$. This problem would look like: $\frac{1}{1} \times \frac{3}{5}$. To set this up with groups and tallies, our first fraction will have one group in the numerator and one group in the denominator. What separates the two? A divisor line. In our second fraction, we will have three tallies in the numerator and five tallies in the denominator. What separates the two? A divisor line. In between our two fractions we need to place a multiplication symbol (×). When we multiply fractions, we multiply the numerators and then the denominators. Let's start by multiplying the numerators. Three tallies in the numerator of our second fraction tells us that we need to place three tallies in each group in the numerator of our first fraction. This will give us one group of three in our numerator. Now, let's multiply the denominators. Five tallies in the denominator of our second fraction tells us that we need to place five tallies in each group in the denominator of our first fraction. This gives us one group of five. Now we will count the total number of tallies to find our final answer. There are three in the numerator and five in the denominator so our answer is 3 tallies/5 tallies, or $\frac{3}{5}$.

(Problem D: $\left(\frac{4}{5}\right)$ groups of (2) tallies) This is a multiplication problem. The word "of" tells us to multiply. This problem is a little different because there is a whole number where the second fraction usually is. What do we have to do to make this whole number a fraction? Place a one in the denominator. That is correct because $2 \div 1$ is equal to 2. This problem would look like: $\frac{4}{5} \times \frac{2}{1}$. To set this up with groups and tallies, our first fraction will have four groups in the numerator and five groups in the denominator. What separates the two? A divisor line. In our second fraction, we will have two tallies in the numerator and one tally in the denominator. What separates the two? A divisor line. In between our two fractions we need to place a multiplication symbol (×). When we multiply fractions we multiply the numerators and then the denominators. Let's start by multiplying the numerators. Two tallies in the numerator of our second fraction tells us that we need to place two tallies in each of the groups in the numerator of our first fraction. This will give us four groups of two in our numerator. Now, let's multiply the denominators. One tally in the denominator of our second fraction tells us that we need to place one tally in each group in the denominator of our first fraction. This gives us five groups of one. Now we will count the total number of tallies to find our final answer. There are eight in the numerator and five in the denominator so our answer is 8 tallies/5 tallies, or $\frac{8}{5}$.

Guided Practice

Let's try some problems together.

(Problem E: $\left(\frac{1}{3}\right)$ groups of $\left(\frac{3}{4}\right)$ tallies) Let's begin by writing this as a multiplication problem using numbers only. $\frac{1}{3} \times \frac{3}{4}$.

Now let's set this problem up using groups and tallies. First fraction: 1 group over 3 groups; second fraction: 3 tallies over 4 tallies.

What should we multiply first? Numerators.

How many tallies do we need to place in each group in the numerator of the first fraction? 3.

Now we have one group of three tallies in our numerator.

What should we do next? Multiply the denominators.

How many tallies should we place in each group in the denominator of our first fraction? 4.

Now we have three groups of four tallies in our denominator.

What do we do to find our final answer? Count the total number of tallies.

How many in the numerator? 3.

How many in the denominator? 12.

Our answer is 3 tallies/12 tallies, or $\frac{3}{12}$.

(Problem F: (2) groups of $\left(\frac{3}{6}\right)$ tallies) Let's begin by writing this as a multiplication problem using numbers only. $\frac{2}{1} \times \frac{3}{6}$.

What did you have to do to make the first whole number a fraction? Put a one in the denominator.

Now let's set this problem up using groups and tallies. First fraction: 2 groups over 1 group; second fraction: 3 tallies over 6 tallies.

What should we multiply first? Numerators.

How many tallies do we need to place in each group in the numerator of the first fraction? 3.

Now we have two groups of three tallies in our numerator.

What should we do next? Multiply the denominators.

How many tallies should we place in each group in the denominator of our first fraction? 6.

Now we have one group of six tallies in our denominator.

What do we do to find our final answer? Count the total number of tallies.

How many in the numerator? 6.

How many in the denominator? 6.

Our answer is 6 tallies/6 tallies, or $\frac{6}{6}$.

Word Problem

(Problem G) Let's look at this scenario. While making formula to help a new mother next door, a young girl must mix $\frac{1}{4}$ (groups) of (multiply) a can of formula with pure water in the baby bottle. If the can holds $\frac{2}{3}$ cup (tallies) of formula, how much formula (cups) is mixed in the can? We will use pictures to find our answer just as we did in the first part of this lesson.

Let's begin by setting this up as a multiplication problem.

What is our first fraction? $\frac{1}{4}$. So we will let that represent $\left(\frac{1}{4}\right)$ groups.

What is our second fraction? $\frac{2}{3}$. So we will let that represent $\left(\frac{2}{3}\right)$ tallies.

Our problem will look like this: $\frac{1}{4} \times \frac{2}{3}$.

Now let's set this problem up using groups and tallies. **First fraction: 1 group over 4 groups; second fraction: 2 tallies over 3 tallies.**

What should we multiply first? Numerators.

How many tallies do we need to place in each group in the numerator of the first fraction? 2.

Now we have one group of two tallies in our numerator.

What should we do next? Multiply the denominators.

How many tallies should we place in each group in the denominator of our first fraction? 3.

Now we have four groups of three tallies in our denominator.

What do we do to find our final answer? Count the total number of tallies.

How many in the numerator? 2.

How many in the denominator? 12.

Our answer is 2 tallies/12 tallies, or $\frac{2}{12}$.

$\frac{2}{12}$ cups of formula needs to be mixed.

Independent Practice

Now you are going to try some of these multiplication problems on your own. Use groups and tallies to find your answers and then make sure to write your answer in numbers on your paper.

LESSON 10

Multiplication of Fractions

3.A (abstract only)

Describe/Model *(Answer is in groups of sticks.)*

a) $\left(\dfrac{5}{6}\right)\left(\dfrac{1}{2}\right)$

b) $\left(\dfrac{2}{4}\right)\left(\dfrac{3}{5}\right)$

Guided Practice

c) $\left(\dfrac{1}{4}\right)(3)$

d) $\left(\dfrac{3}{2}\right)\left(\dfrac{1}{6}\right)$

e) $\left(\dfrac{3}{4}\right)\left(\dfrac{1}{2}\right)$

f) $(2)\left(\dfrac{2}{5}\right)$

Word Problem

g) Your mom tells you to share the milkshake with your two brothers. The three of you have to split the $\frac{3}{2}$ cup of milkshake equally. Set up the multiplication problem using fractions. How much milkshake will each person receive? Show your problem solving abstractly.

What does the fraction in the answer mean?

Independent Practice

h) $(3)\left(\dfrac{3}{5}\right)$

i) $\left(\dfrac{1}{2}\right)\left(\dfrac{4}{3}\right)$

j) $\left(\dfrac{1}{6}\right)\left(\dfrac{1}{3}\right)$

k) $\left(\dfrac{2}{5}\right)\left(\dfrac{2}{3}\right)$

Teaching **LESSON 10**

Multiplication of Fractions

3.A (abstract only)

Describe/Model *(Answer is in sticks.)*

Today we are going to continue multiplying fractions. We have been using a couple of different methods to find our answers. First, we used cups and sticks; second, we used groups and tallies. In this lesson we will be using our knowledge of basic multiplication facts to find our answer. I will work out a couple of these problems for you before we try some together. At the end of the lesson you will work out some of these on your own.

(Problem A: $\left(\frac{5}{6}\right)\left(\frac{1}{2}\right)$) When we see two numbers or fractions in parentheses like this we should multiply. Going back to our other methods of multiplying fractions, what do we do first? Multiply the numerators. Very good. So, $5 \times 1 = ?$ *5*. On the other side of our equal sign we will now put a five in the numerator of a new fraction. What do we do next? Multiply the denominators. Very good. So, $6 \times 2 = ?$ *12*. On the other side of our equal sign in our new fraction, we will place a twelve in the denominator. Let's read our new fraction. *Five twelfths.* So, five sixths times one half is equal to five twelfths.

(Problem B: $\left(\frac{2}{4}\right)\left(\frac{3}{5}\right)$) When we see two numbers or fractions in parentheses like this we should multiply. What do we need to do first? Multiply the numerators. Very good. So, $2 \times 3 = ?$ *6*. On the other side of our equal sign we will now put a six in the numerator of a new fraction. What do we do next? Multiply the denominators. Very good. So, $4 \times 5 = ?$ *20*. On the other side of our equal sign in our new fraction, we will place a twenty in the denominator. Let's read our new fraction. *Six twentieths.* So, two fourths times three fifths is equal to six twentieths.

Guided Practice

Let's try some problems together.

(Problem C: $\left(\frac{1}{4}\right)(3)$) When we see two fractions (or numbers) in parentheses like this what should we do? *Multiply.*

> What do we need to do to make the second number a fraction? *Put a one in the denominator.*
>
> What do we do first when multiplying these fractions? *Multiply the numerators.*
>
> What is one times three? *3.*
>
> Where do we place the three? *On the other side of the equal sign in the numerator of a new fraction.*
>
> What do we do next? *Multiply the denominators.*
>
> What is four times one? *4.*
>
> Where do we place the four? *On the other side of the equal sign in the denominator of the new fraction.*
>
> Let's read our new fraction. *Three fourths.*
>
> One fourth times three is equal to three fourths.

(Problem D: $\left(\frac{3}{2}\right)\left(\frac{1}{6}\right)$) **When we see two fractions (or numbers) in parentheses like this what should we do?** Multiply.

What do we do first when multiplying these fractions? Multiply the numerators.

What is three times one? 3.

Where do we place the three? On the other side of the equal sign in the numerator of a new fraction.

What do we do next? Multiply the denominators.

What is two times six? 12.

Where do we place the twelve? On the other side of the equal sign in the denominator of the new fraction.

Let's read our new fraction. Three twelfths.

Three halves times one sixth is equal to three twelfths.

(Problem E: $\left(\frac{3}{4}\right)\left(\frac{1}{2}\right)$) **When we see two fractions (or numbers) in parentheses like this what should we do?** Multiply.

What do we do first when multiplying these fractions? Multiply the numerators.

What is three times one? 3.

Where do we place the three? On the other side of the equal sign in the numerator of a new fraction.

What do we do next? Multiply the denominators.

What is four times two? 8.

Where do we place the eight? On the other side of the equal sign in the denominator of the new fraction.

Let's read our new fraction. Three eighths.

Three fourths times one half is equal to three eighths.

(Problem F: $(2)\left(\frac{2}{5}\right)$) **When we see two fractions (or numbers) in parentheses like this what should we do?** Multiply.

What do we need to do to make the first number a fraction? Put a one in the denominator.

What do we do first when multiplying these fractions? Multiply the numerators.

What is two times two? 4.

Where do we place the four? On the other side of the equal sign in the numerator of a new fraction.

What do we do next? Multiply the denominators.

What is one times five? 5.

Where do we place the five? On the other side of the equal sign in the denominator of the new fraction.

Let's read our new fraction. Four fifths.

Two times two fifths is equal to four fifths.

Word Problem

(Problem G) **Let's look at this scenario. Your mom tells you to share the milkshake with your two brothers. The three of you have to split the $\frac{3}{2}$ cup of milkshake equally. Set up the multiplication problem using fractions. How much milkshake will each** person receive? We will show our answer using numbers only as we did during this lesson.

Let's begin by setting this up as a multiplication problem.

How many people are splitting the milkshake? 3.

How much milkshake are they splitting? $\frac{3}{2}$ cup.

Our multiplication problem will be $(3)\frac{3}{2}$.

What do we need to do to make the first number a fraction? Put a one in the denominator.

What do we do first when multiplying these fractions? Multiply the numerators.

What is three times three? 9.

Where do we place the nine? On the other side of the equal sign in the numerator of a new fraction.

What do we do next? Multiply the denominators.

What is one times two? 2.

Where do we place the two? On the other side of the equal sign in the denominator of the new fraction.

Let's read our new fraction. Nine halves.

Each of you will get $\frac{9}{2}$ cups of the milkshake.

Independent Practice

Now you are going to try some of these problems on your own. Be sure to use your basic multiplication facts to get your answer and show your work on paper.

Note: To review multiplication of fractions, see Cumulative Review B starting on page 151.

LESSON 11

Multiplication of Fractions

4.A (generalized)

Describe/Model *(Answer is in groups of sticks.)*

a) $(2)\left(\dfrac{6}{7}\right)\left(\dfrac{1}{4}\right)$

b) $\left(\dfrac{4}{5}\right)\left(\dfrac{2}{3}\right)(3)$

Guided Practice

c) $\left(\dfrac{1}{2}\right)\left(\dfrac{2}{3}\right)\left(\dfrac{1}{2}\right)$

d) $\left(\dfrac{2}{3}\right)\left(\dfrac{9}{10}\right)$

e) $\left(\dfrac{1}{4}\right)(3)\left(\dfrac{2}{5}\right)$

f) $\left(\dfrac{1}{2}\right)\left(\dfrac{4}{7}\right)\left(\dfrac{7}{2}\right)$

Word Problem

g) At home, a mother wants to make $\frac{1}{3}$ cup of hot chocolate for her daughter. To make 1 cup, the mix calls for $\frac{3}{2}$ tablespoon of cocoa and $\frac{1}{4}$ teaspoon vanilla. To make the daughter's drink, how much cocoa mix and vanilla will the mother need?

What does the fraction in the answer mean?

Independent Practice

h) $(5)\left(\dfrac{3}{2}\right)\left(\dfrac{3}{5}\right)$

i) $\left(\dfrac{5}{6}\right)\left(\dfrac{2}{3}\right)\left(\dfrac{1}{2}\right)$

j) $\left(\dfrac{1}{4}\right)\left(\dfrac{1}{6}\right)\left(\dfrac{1}{5}\right)$

k) $\left(\dfrac{2}{4}\right)\left(\dfrac{3}{4}\right)\left(\dfrac{1}{3}\right)$

LESSON 12

Division of Fractions

1.A (abstract only)

Describe/Model

a) $\left(\dfrac{3}{1}\right) \div \left(\dfrac{1}{4}\right)$

b) $\left(\dfrac{1}{2}\right) \div \left(\dfrac{1}{3}\right)$

c) $\left(\dfrac{3}{5}\right) \div \left(\dfrac{1}{2}\right)$

d) $\left(\dfrac{1}{3}\right) \div \left(\dfrac{1}{3}\right)$

Guided Practice

e) $\left(\dfrac{2}{3}\right) \div \left(\dfrac{1}{5}\right)$ sticks

f) $\left(\dfrac{4}{1}\right) \div \left(\dfrac{1}{2}\right)$ sticks

Word Problem

g) A boy is making breakfast for his family on Saturday. He scrambles 3 $\left(\dfrac{3}{1}\right)$ cups of eggs but will divide ($\div$) the eggs into $\left(\dfrac{1}{2}\right)$ cups. How many servings of eggs will he make? Show your problem solving using abstract notation.

What happened with the division in this problem?

Independent Practice

h) $\left(\dfrac{2}{1}\right) \div \left(\dfrac{1}{3}\right)$

i) $\left(\dfrac{1}{4}\right) \div \left(\dfrac{1}{2}\right)$

j) $\left(\dfrac{2}{3}\right) \div \left(\dfrac{1}{5}\right)$

k) $\left(\dfrac{2}{5}\right) \div \left(\dfrac{1}{4}\right)$

Teaching **LESSON 12**

Division of Fractions

1.A (abstract only)

Describe/Model

Today were going to be starting something new; however, we will still be working with fractions. We will be learning how to divide fractions. We will not start with sticks and cups like we did with multiplication, rather, will go straight to the abstract method and use, believe it or not, multiplication facts to solve these division problems. I am going to tell you how. What is $\frac{4}{1}$? Yes, 4. What is $\frac{63.3}{1}$? Yes, 63.3. What is any number divided by one? That's right, itself. We are going to divide fractions using this same concept. First, we must learn about reciprocals. A reciprocal is a flipped fraction. For example, the reciprocal of $\frac{3}{7}$ is $\frac{7}{3}$. We flipped the numerator and denominator. Another example is that the reciprocal of $\frac{3}{2}$ is $\frac{2}{3}$. I want all of you to practice finding the reciprocal of some fractions. (Give three to four fractions for students to find reciprocals.) Now I am going to work out some division problems for you. Watch carefully so that you are able to help me do some problems later, and then work out some problems on your own.

(Problem A: $\left(\frac{3}{1}\right) \div \left(\frac{1}{4}\right)$) We have three over one divided by one fourth. Let's divide these fractions. First, we write $\frac{3}{1}$. Then we will draw another divisor line and under that the $\frac{1}{4}$. Because we know anything divided by one is itself, we want to turn that $\frac{1}{4}$ into a 1 so that the answer is only the top fraction. In order to do that, we must multiply both top and bottom fractions by the reciprocal of $\frac{1}{4}$. What is the reciprocal of $\frac{1}{4}$? $\frac{4}{1}$. Now we have four multiplication problems. (Write down the multiplication problems.) From the top they are 3 × 4 and 1 × 1 over 4 × 1 and

1 × 4. (Write an equal sign.) What is our answer? $\frac{\frac{12}{1}}{\frac{4}{4}}$. Because $\frac{4}{4}$ is 1, the answer is

$\frac{12}{1}$. Because any number divided by 1 is itself, $\frac{12}{1}$ is 12. So our answer is $\frac{12}{1}$ or 12.

$\frac{3}{1} \div \frac{1}{4} = 12$.

(Problem B: $\left(\frac{1}{2}\right) \div \left(\frac{1}{3}\right)$) We have one half divided by one third. Let's divide these fractions. First, we write $\frac{1}{2}$. Then we will draw another divisor line and under that the $\frac{1}{3}$. Because we know anything divided by one is itself, we want to turn that $\frac{1}{3}$ into a 1 so that the answer is only the top fraction. In order to do that we must multiply both top and bottom fractions by the reciprocal of $\frac{1}{3}$. What is the reciprocal of $\frac{1}{3}$? $\frac{3}{1}$. Now we have four multiplication problems. (Write down the multiplication problems.) From the top they are 1 × 3 and 2 × 1 over 1 × 3 and 3 × 1. (Write an equal sign.) What is our answers? $\frac{\frac{3}{2}}{\frac{3}{3}}$ Because $\frac{3}{3}$ is 1, the answer is $\frac{\frac{3}{2}}{1}$. Because any number divided by 1 is itself, $\frac{\frac{3}{2}}{1}$ is $\frac{3}{2}$. So our answer is $\frac{3}{2}$. $\frac{1}{2} \div \frac{1}{3} = \frac{3}{2}$.

(Problem C: $\left(\frac{3}{5}\right) \div \left(\frac{1}{2}\right)$) We have three fifths divided by one half. Let's divide these fractions. First, we write $\frac{3}{5}$. Then we will draw another divisor line and under that the $\frac{1}{2}$. Because we know anything divided by one is itself, we want to turn that $\frac{1}{2}$ into a 1 so that the answer is only the top fraction. In order to do that we must multiply both top and bottom fractions by the reciprocal of $\frac{1}{2}$. What is the reciprocal of $\frac{1}{2}$? $\frac{2}{1}$. Now we have four multiplication problems. (Write down the multiplication problems.) From the top they are 3 × 2 and 5 × 1 over 1 × 2 and 2 × 1. (Write an equal sign.) What is our answer? $\frac{\frac{6}{5}}{\frac{2}{2}}$. Because $\frac{2}{2}$ is 1, the answer is $\frac{\frac{6}{5}}{1}$. Because any number divided by 1 is itself, $\frac{\frac{6}{5}}{1}$ is $\frac{6}{5}$. So our answer is $\frac{6}{5} \cdot \frac{3}{5} \div \frac{1}{2} = \frac{6}{5}$. To reduce this as we did in earlier lessons, we divide the numerator and denominator by 5. We are left with $1\frac{1}{5}$.

(Problem D: $\left(\frac{1}{3}\right) \div \left(\frac{1}{3}\right)$) We have one third divided by one third. Let's divide these fractions. First, we write $\frac{1}{3}$. Then we will draw another divisor line and under that the $\frac{1}{3}$. Because we know anything divided by one is itself, we want to turn that $\frac{1}{3}$ into a 1 so that the answer is only the top fraction. In order to do that we must multiply both top and bottom fractions by the reciprocal of $\frac{1}{3}$. What is the reciprocal of $\frac{1}{3}$? $\frac{3}{1}$. Now we have four multiplication problems. (Write down the multiplication problems.) From the top they are 1 × 3 and 3 × 1 over 1 × 3 and 3 × 1. (Write an equal sign.)

What is our answer? $\frac{\frac{3}{3}}{\frac{3}{3}}$. Because $\frac{3}{3}$ is 1, the answer is $\frac{\frac{3}{3}}{1}$. Wait, there is another $\frac{3}{3}$?

So our answer is $\frac{3}{3}$, or 1. $\frac{1}{3} \div \frac{1}{3} = 1$.

Guided Practice

Let's try some problems together.

(Problem E: $\left(\frac{2}{3}\right) \div \left(\frac{1}{5}\right)$) **Let's read our problem.** Two thirds divided by one fifth.
  Let's divide these fractions.
  What do we need to do first? Write $\frac{2}{3}$, a divisor line, and then $\frac{1}{5}$.
  What do we need to do second? Set up multiplication of both fractions by the reciprocal of the denominator fraction, $\frac{5}{1}$.
  What do we need to do third? Multiply four problems.
  Let's multiply these fractions from the top.
  What is 2 × 5? 10.
  What do we multiply second?
  What is 3 × 1? 3.
  What do we multiply third?
  What is 1 × 5? 5.
  What do we multiply fourth?
  What is 5 × 1? 5.
  What are we left with? $\frac{\frac{10}{3}}{\frac{5}{5}}$.
  What do we do with $\frac{5}{5}$? Make it a 1.
  What is the answer? $\frac{\frac{10}{3}}{1}$, or $\frac{10}{3}$.

(Problem F: $\left(\frac{4}{1}\right) \div \left(\frac{1}{2}\right)$) **Let's read our problem.** Four over one divided by one half.
  Let's divide these fractions.
  What do we need to do first? Write $\frac{4}{1}$, a divisor line, and then $\frac{1}{2}$.
  What do we need to do second? Set up multiplication of both fractions by the reciprocal of the denominator fraction, $\frac{2}{1}$.
  What do we need to do third? Multiply four problems.
  Let's multiply these fractions from the top.
  What is 4 × 2? 8.
  What do we multiply second?

What is 1×1? 1.

What do we multiply third?

What is 1×2? 2.

What do we multiply fourth?

What is 2×1? 2.

What are we left with? $\dfrac{\frac{8}{1}}{\frac{2}{2}}$.

What do we do with $\frac{2}{2}$? Make it a 1.

What is the answer? $\dfrac{\frac{8}{1}}{1}$, or 8.

Word Problem

(Problem G) Let's look at this scenario. A boy is making breakfast for his family on Saturday. He scrambles $3 \left(\frac{1}{2}\right)$ cups of eggs but will divide ($\div$) the eggs into $\frac{1}{2}$ cups. How many servings of eggs will he make? We will show our answer using the same abstract method we have been using in this lesson.

Let's begin by setting this up as a division problem.

What is our first fraction? $\frac{3}{1}$.

What is our second fraction? $\frac{1}{2}$.

So our division problem is $\frac{3}{1} \div \frac{1}{2}$.

Let's divide these fractions.

What do we need to do first? Write $\frac{3}{1}$, a divisor line, and then $\frac{1}{2}$.

What do we need to do second? Set up multiplication of both fractions by the reciprocal of the denominator fraction, $\frac{2}{1}$.

What do we need to do third? Multiply four problems.

Let's multiply these fractions from the top.

What is 3×2? 6.

What do we multiply second?

What is 1×1? 1.

What do we multiply third?

What is 1×2? 2.

What do we multiply fourth?

What is 2×1? 2.

What are we left with? $\dfrac{\frac{6}{1}}{\frac{2}{2}}$.

What do we do with $\frac{2}{2}$? Make it a 1.

What is the answer? $\dfrac{\frac{6}{1}}{1}$ or 5.

What is $\frac{3}{1} \div \frac{1}{2}$? $\frac{6}{1}$, or 6.

The boy will make 6 servings of eggs.

Independent Practice

Now you are going to try some of these on your own. Use the same method we have been using throughout this lesson and be sure to show all your work and steps on paper.

LESSON 13

Division of Fractions

2.A (abstract only)

Describe/Model

a) $(2) \div \left(\dfrac{1}{3}\right)$

b) $\left(\dfrac{2}{5}\right) \div \left(\dfrac{2}{4}\right)$

Guided Practice

c) $\left(\dfrac{3}{1}\right) \div \left(\dfrac{2}{3}\right)$

d) $\left(\dfrac{2}{3}\right) \div (3)$

e) $\left(\dfrac{2}{3}\right) \div \left(\dfrac{1}{2}\right)$

f) $\left(\dfrac{4}{1}\right) \div \left(\dfrac{3}{4}\right)$

Word Problem

g) A software company had $4 \left(\dfrac{4}{1}\right)$ crates of videogames to distribute to stores. Each store bought $\dfrac{2}{3}$ of a crate. How many stores bought crates? Show your problem solving using abstract notation.

What happened with the division in this problem?

Independent Practice

h) $(3) \div \left(\dfrac{1}{4}\right)$

i) $\left(\dfrac{1}{4}\right) \div \left(\dfrac{3}{5}\right)$

j) $\left(\dfrac{2}{3}\right) \div \left(\dfrac{2}{4}\right)$

k) $\left(\dfrac{2}{5}\right) \div (4)$

Teaching **LESSON 13**

Division of Fractions

2.A (abstract only)

Describe/Model

Today we are going to continue dividing fractions. Remember, when we divide fraction we multiply by the . . .? Reciprocal. Good. What is the reciprocal of $\frac{1}{4}$? $\frac{4}{1}$. Did you notice a pattern in using the reciprocal? Did you notice that every time we did, we ended with a denominator fraction of one? The answer was always in the numerator fraction. We are going to shorten our steps to solving division problems this time. We are not changing what we do, just saving some time. I am going to work out a couple problems for you before you join me in working out some together. At the end of the lesson, you will have another opportunity to work out some problems on your own.

(Problem A: $(2) \div \left(\frac{1}{3}\right)$) We have two divided by one third. What should we do to make the two a fraction? Place a one in the denominator. Let's divide these fractions. First, write $\frac{2}{1}$. Then we will draw another divisor line and under that the $\frac{1}{3}$. To make that denominator fraction $\frac{1}{3}$ a 1, what must we multiply by? Yes, the reciprocal; $\frac{3}{1}$. Now we are going to multiply $\frac{2}{1}$ by $\frac{3}{1}$. (Write down the two multiplication problems.) From the top they are 2 × 3 and 1 × 1. (Write an equal sign.) The answer is $\frac{6}{1}$, or 6. What did we do differently? Yes, we did not write the $\frac{1}{3}$ by $\frac{3}{1}$ because that would equal one, which will not affect the answer. So our answer is $\frac{6}{1}$, or 6. $\frac{2}{1} \div \frac{1}{3} = 6$.

(Problem B: $\left(\frac{2}{5}\right) \div \left(\frac{2}{4}\right)$) We have two fifths divided by two fourths. Let's divide these fractions. First, write $\frac{2}{5}$. Then we will draw another divisor line and under that the $\frac{2}{4}$. To make that denominator fraction $\frac{2}{4}$ a 1, what must we multiply by? Yes, the reciprocal; $\frac{4}{2}$. Now we are going to multiply $\frac{2}{5}$ by $\frac{4}{2}$. (Write down the two multiplication problems.) From the top they are 2 × 4 and 5 × 2. (Write an equal sign.) The answer is $\frac{8}{10}$. As in the first example, what did we do differently from the previous lesson? Yes, we did not write the $\frac{2}{4}$ by $\frac{4}{2}$ because that would equal one, which will not affect the answer. So our answer is $\frac{8}{10}$. $\frac{2}{5} \div \frac{2}{4} = \frac{8}{10}$.

Guided Practice

Let's try some problems together.

(Problem C: $\left(\frac{3}{1}\right) \div \left(\frac{2}{3}\right)$) **Let's read our problem.** Three over one divided by two thirds.

Let's divide these fractions.

What do we need to do first? Write down $\frac{3}{1}$ to start a new problem.

What do we need to do second? Change the sign to multiply.

What do we need to do third? Find the reciprocal of the second fraction and write it as the second fraction in the new multiplication problem.

What is the reciprocal of the second fraction? $\frac{3}{2}$.

What do we put at the end of our new multiplication problem? =.

Let's multiply these fractions.

What do we multiply first? Numerators.

What is 3 × 3? 9.

What do we multiply second? Denominators.

What is 1 × 2? 2.

What is $\frac{3}{1} \div \frac{2}{3}$? $\frac{9}{2}$.

(Problem D: $\left(\frac{2}{3}\right) \div (3)$) **Let's read our problem.** Two thirds divided by three.

What should we do to make the three a fraction? Place a one in the denominator.

Let's divide these fractions.

What do we need to do first? Write down $\frac{2}{3}$ to start a new problem.

What do we need to do second? Change the sign to multiply.

What do we need to do third? Find the reciprocal of the second fraction and write it as the second fraction in the new multiplication problem.

What is the reciprocal of the second fraction? $\frac{1}{3}$.

What do we put at the end of our new multiplication problem? =.

Let's multiply these fractions.

What do we multiply first? Numerators.

What is 2 × 1? 2.

What do we multiply second? Denominators.

What is 3 × 3? 9.

What is $\frac{2}{3} \div 3$? $\frac{2}{9}$.

(Problem E: $\left(\frac{2}{3}\right) \div \left(\frac{1}{2}\right)$) **Let's read our problem.** *Two* thirds divided by one half.

Let's divide these fractions.

What do we need to do first? Write down $\frac{2}{3}$ to start a new problem.

What do we need to do second? Change the sign to multiply.

What do we need to do third? Find the reciprocal of the second fraction and write it as the second fraction in the new multiplication problem.

What is the reciprocal of the second fraction? $\frac{2}{1}$.

What do we put at the end of our new multiplication problem? =.

Let's multiply these fractions.

What do we multiply first? Numerators.

What is 2 × 2? 4.

What do we multiply second? Denominators.

What is 3 × 1? 3.

What is $\frac{2}{3} \div \frac{1}{2}$? $\frac{4}{3}$.

(Problem F: $\left(\frac{4}{1}\right) \div \left(\frac{3}{4}\right)$) **Let's read our problem.** Four over one divided by three fourths.

Let's divide these fractions.

What do we need to do first? Write down $\frac{4}{1}$ to start a new problem.

What do we need to do second? Change the sign to multiply.

What do we need to do third? Find the reciprocal of the second fraction and write it as the second fraction in the new multiplication problem.

What is the reciprocal of the second fraction? $\frac{4}{3}$.

What do we put at the end of our new multiplication problem? =.

Let's multiply these fractions.

What do we multiply first? Numerators.

What is 4 × 4? 16.

What do we multiply second? Denominators.

What is 1 × 3? 3.

What is $\frac{4}{1} \div \frac{3}{4}$? $\frac{16}{3}$.

Word Problem

(Problem G) **Let's look at this scenario. A software company had** $4\left(\frac{4}{1}\right)$ **crates of videogames to distribute to stores. Each store bought** $\frac{2}{3}$ **of a crate. How many stores bought crates? We will show our answer using the same method we have been using in this lesson.**

Let's begin by setting this up as a division problem.

What is our first fraction? $\frac{4}{1}$.

What is our second fraction? $\frac{2}{3}$.

So our division problem is $\frac{4}{1} \div \frac{2}{3}$.

Let's divide these fractions.

What do we need to do first? Write down $\frac{4}{1}$ to start a new problem.

What do we need to do second? Change the sign to multiply.

What do we need to do third? Find the reciprocal of the second fraction and write it as the second fraction in the new multiplication problem.

What is the reciprocal of the second fraction? $\frac{3}{2}$.

What do we put at the end of our new multiplication problem? $=$.

Let's multiply these fractions.

What do we multiply first? Numerators.

What is 4×3? 12.

What do we multiply second? Denominators.

What is 1×2? 2.

What is $\frac{4}{1} \div \frac{2}{3}$? $\frac{12}{2}$.

$\frac{12}{2}$, **or 6 stores bought crates.**

Independent Practice

Now you are going to try some of these on your own. Use the same method we have been using throughout this lesson and be sure to show all your work and steps on paper.

LESSON 14

Division of Fractions

3.A (abstract only)

Describe/Model

a) $\left(\dfrac{5}{2}\right) \div \left(\dfrac{2}{5}\right)$

b) $\left(\dfrac{3}{4}\right) \div \left(\dfrac{4}{5}\right)$

Guided Practice

c) $\left(\dfrac{1}{5}\right) \div \left(\dfrac{8}{3}\right)$

d) $\left(\dfrac{4}{3}\right) \div \left(\dfrac{2}{9}\right)$

e) $\frac{8}{3}$ of a ton of bricks is to be delivered to repair companies. Each repair company will receive $\frac{2}{3}$ of a ton. How many companies will receive bricks? Show your problem solving using abstract notation.

What happened with the division in this problem?

Word Problem

f) $\left(\dfrac{1}{5}\right) \div \left(\dfrac{7}{2}\right)$

g) $\left(\dfrac{5}{6}\right) \div (3)$

Independent Practice

h) $(6) \div \left(\dfrac{1}{2}\right)$

i) $\left(\dfrac{3}{5}\right) \div \left(\dfrac{2}{5}\right)$

j) $\left(\dfrac{5}{3}\right) \div \left(\dfrac{8}{5}\right)$

k) $\left(\dfrac{2}{7}\right) \div \left(\dfrac{2}{4}\right)$

Teaching **LESSON 14**

Division of Fractions

3.A (abstract only)

Describe/Model

Today we are going to wrap up our work on dividing fractions. Remember, when we divide fractions we multiply by the . . .? Reciprocal. Good. What is the reciprocal of $\frac{1}{4}$? $\frac{4}{1}$. I am going to work out a couple problems for you before you join me in working out some together. At the end of the lesson, you will have another opportunity to work out some problems on your own.

(Problem A: $\left(\frac{5}{2} \div \frac{2}{5}\right)$) We have five halves divided by two fifths. Let's divide these fractions. First, we are going to write down $\frac{5}{2}$ to start a new problem. Second, we will change the sign to multiply ($\times$). Third, we need to find the reciprocal of the second fraction and write it as the second fraction in the new multiplication problem. What is the reciprocal of $\frac{2}{5}$? $\frac{5}{2}$. Very good. Now we are going to put an equal sign at the end of our second fraction, and then we can multiply. Our new multiplication problem is $\frac{5}{2} \times \frac{5}{2}$. What do we multiply first? The numerators. What is 5×5? 25. What do we multiply next? The denominators. What is 2×2? 4. Our answer is $\frac{25}{4}$. $\frac{5}{2} \div \frac{2}{5} = \frac{25}{4}$.

(Problem B: $\left(\frac{3}{4} \div \frac{4}{5}\right)$) We have three fourths divided by four fifths. Let's divide these fractions. First, we are going to write down $\frac{3}{4}$ to start a new problem. Second, we will change the sign to multiply ($\times$). Third, we need to find the reciprocal of the second fraction and write it as the second fraction in the new multiplication problem. What is the reciprocal of $\frac{4}{5}$? $\frac{5}{4}$. Very good. Now we are going to put an equal sign at the end of our second fraction, and then we can multiply. Our new multiplication problem is $\frac{3}{4} \times \frac{5}{4}$. What do we multiply first? The numerators. What is 3×5? 15. What do we multiply next? The denominators. What is 4×4? 16. Our answer is $\frac{15}{16}$. $\frac{3}{4} \div \frac{4}{5} = \frac{15}{16}$.

Guided Practice

Let's try some problems together.

(Problem C: $\left(\frac{1}{5} \div \frac{8}{3}\right)$) **Let's read our problem.** One fifth divided by eight thirds.

Let's divide these fractions.

What do we need to do first? Write down $\frac{1}{5}$ to start a new problem.

What do we need to do second? Change the sign to multiply.

What do we need to do third? Find the reciprocal of the second fraction and write it as the second fraction in the new multiplication problem.

What is the reciprocal of the second fraction? $\frac{3}{8}$.

What do we put at the end of our new multiplication problem? =.

Let's multiply these fractions.

What do we multiply first? Numerators.

What is 1×3? 3.

What do we multiply second? Denominators.

What is 5×8? 40.

What is $\frac{1}{5} \div \frac{8}{3}$? $\frac{3}{40}$.

(Problem D: $\left(\frac{4}{3} \div \frac{2}{9}\right)$) **Let's read our problem.** Four thirds divided by two ninths.

    Let's divide these fractions.

    What do we need to do first? Write down $\frac{4}{3}$ to start a new problem.

    What do we need to do second? Change the sign to multiply.

    What do we need to do third? Find the reciprocal of the second fraction and write it as the second fraction in the new multiplication problem.

    What is the reciprocal of the second fraction? $\frac{9}{2}$.

    What do we put at the end of our new multiplication problem? $=$.

    Let's multiply these fractions.

    What do we multiply first? Numerators.

    What is 4 × 9? 36.

    What do we multiply second? Denominators.

    What is 3 × 2? 6.

    What is $\frac{4}{3} \div \frac{2}{9}$? $\frac{36}{6}$.

Word Problem

(Problem E) **Let's look at this scenario.** $\frac{8}{3}$ of a ton of bricks is to be delivered to repair companies. Each repair company will receive $\frac{2}{3}$ of a ton. How many companies will receive bricks? We will show our answer using the same method we have been using throughout this lesson.

    Let's begin by setting this up as a division problem.

    What is our first fraction? $\frac{8}{3}$.

    What is our second fraction? $\frac{2}{3}$.

    So our division problem is $\frac{8}{3} \div \frac{2}{3}$.

    Let's divide these fractions.

    What do we need to do first? Write down $\frac{8}{3}$ to start a new problem.

    What do we need to do second? Change the sign to multiply.

    What do we need to do third? Find the reciprocal of the second fraction and write it as the second fraction in the new multiplication problem.

    What is the reciprocal of the second fraction? $\frac{3}{2}$.

    What do we put at the end of our new multiplication problem? $=$.

    Let's multiply these fractions.

    What do we multiply first? Numerators.

    What is 8 × 3? 24.

    What do we multiply second? Denominators.

    What is 3 × 2? 6.

    What is $\frac{8}{3} \div \frac{2}{3}$? $\frac{24}{6}$.

    $\frac{24}{6}$, or 4 companies will receive bricks.

Independent Practice

Now you are going to try some of these on your own. Use the same method we have been using throughout this lesson and be sure to show all your work and steps on paper.

Note: To review division of fractions, see Cumulative Review C starting on page 152.

LESSON 15

Finding Equivalent Fractions   *1.C (sticks-only method)*

Describe/Model

a) $\dfrac{1}{3} = \dfrac{2}{6} =$ _____ $=$ _____

b) What was multiplied in the numerator and denominator to find the last equivalent fraction?

Guided Practice

c) $\dfrac{3}{4} = \dfrac{6}{8} =$ _____ $=$ _____ $=$ _____

d) What was multiplied in the numerator and denominator to find the last equivalent fraction?

e) Circle the fractions in a) and c) that have the same denominator.

Which one has the larger numerator?

Word Problem

f) Your friend says that a recipe calls for $\frac{4}{8}$ cup of flour. You have already poured $\frac{1}{2}$ cup. Are these the same or different? Use equivalent fractions to find if $\frac{1}{2}$ is the same as $\frac{4}{8}$. Show your problem solving using concrete materials.
How did you find the equivalent fraction?

Independent Practice

g) $\dfrac{1}{2} = \dfrac{2}{4} =$ _____ $=$ _____ $=$ _____

h) What was multiplied in the numerator and denominator to find the last equivalent fraction?

i) $\dfrac{2}{3} = \dfrac{4}{6} =$ _____

j) What was multiplied in the numerator and denominator to find the last equivalent fraction?

k) Circle the fractions in g) and i) that have the same denominator.

Which one has the larger numerator?

Teaching **LESSON 15**

Finding Equivalent Fractions

1.C (sticks-only method)

Describe/Model

Today we are going to start learning how to find equivalent fractions using sticks. For example, $\frac{1}{2}$ is equivalent to $\frac{2}{4}$. As you complete this lesson, you will be able to use sticks and your basic multiplication facts to find more equivalent fractions of other common fractions like $\frac{1}{2}$. I will begin by showing you how to work out some of these.

(Problem A: $\frac{1}{3} = \frac{2}{6} = $ _____ = _____) & (Problem B: What was multiplied in the numerator and denominator to find the last equivalent fraction?)

We will start by setting up our first fraction with sticks and a divisor line. In our numerator we will have how many sticks? One. In our denominator we will have how may sticks? Three. What separates the numerator and denominator? Divisor line. Our second fraction, two sixths, is an equivalent fraction of one third. We will insert more groups of sticks to the first fraction that we set up using sticks to form our second equivalent fraction. To form two sixths we will need to add one stick to the numerator and another group of three sticks to the denominator. We now have 2 sticks/6 sticks, which is equivalent to one third. Let's find another equivalent fraction of one third and two sixths. To do this we will need to insert one more group of sticks to the numerator and one to the denominator that are the same size as the first groups we added. So, add one stick to the numerator and another group of three sticks to the denominator. We now have 3 sticks/9 sticks, or 3 groups of 1 stick over 3 groups of 3 sticks, which is equivalent to $\frac{1}{3}$ and $\frac{2}{6}$. Let's find one more equivalent fraction. We will need to add one stick to the numerator and another group of three sticks to the denominator. We now have 4 sticks/12 sticks, which is equal to $\frac{1}{3}$, $\frac{2}{6}$, and $\frac{3}{9}$. Now we want to figure out what number we could multiply by in both the numerator and denominator of the first fraction to get the numerator and denominator of the last fraction. We are going to stack up the sticks in each group. We have four groups in the numerator and four groups in the denominator. This shows us that we can multiply $\frac{1}{3}$ by $\frac{4}{4}$ to find the equivalent fraction of $\frac{4}{12}$.

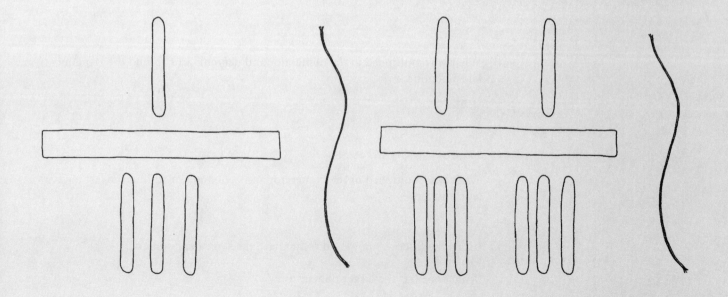

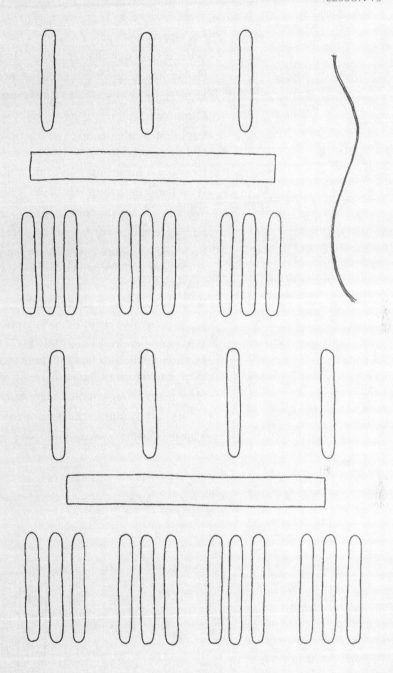

Guided Practice

Now you are going to use your own sticks to start finding equivalent fractions with me before you have a chance to find some equivalent fractions on your own.

(Problem C: $\frac{3}{4} = \frac{6}{8} =$ _____ = _____) & (Problem D: What was multiplied in the numerator and denominator to find the last equivalent fraction?)

Begin by setting up the first fraction using your sticks. What is the first fraction? Three fourths.

How many sticks are in the numerator? 3.

How many sticks are in the denominator? 4.

What separates the numerator and denominator? Divisor line.

Let's insert more groups to form our equivalent fraction.

What is our equivalent fraction? Six eighths.

How many groups of three do we need in the numerator? One.

How many groups of four do we need in the denominator? One.

Our new fraction, $\frac{6}{8}$, is also equal to what fraction? $\frac{3}{4}$.

Let's find another equivalent fraction by adding more groups to the numerator and denominator. We will add one more group to each.

How big is the group we should multiply in the numerator? 3 sticks.

How big is the group we should multiply in the denominator? 4 sticks.

What is our new fraction? $\frac{9}{12}$.

So, $\frac{9}{12}$ is equal to what other two fractions? $\frac{3}{4}$ and $\frac{6}{8}$.

Let's find one more equivalent fraction. Go ahead and add one group to the numerator and denominator. Make sure your groups have the correct number of sticks.

What is your new fraction? $\frac{12}{16}$.

So, $\frac{12}{16}$ is equal to what other three fractions? $\frac{3}{4}$, $\frac{6}{8}$, and $\frac{9}{12}$.

What number can we multiply by in both the numerator and denominator of our first fraction to find the numerator and denominator of our last fraction? What can we do to figure this out? Stack our sticks according to their groups.

How many groups in the numerator? 4.

How many groups in the denominator? 4.

This tells us that we can multiply $\frac{3}{4}$ by $\frac{4}{4}$ to find the equivalent fraction of $\frac{12}{16}$.

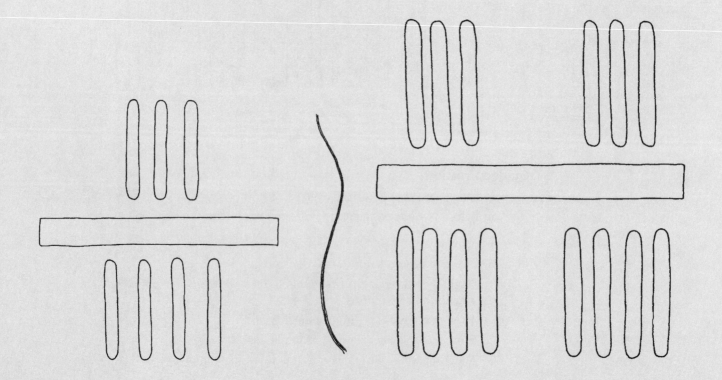

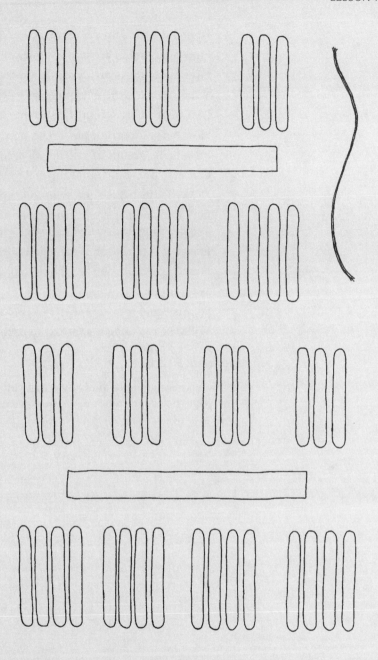

(Problem E: Circle the fractions in problems A and C that have the same denominator.)
Which number is the denominator? The number below the divisor line.

What does the denominator represent? The total number in the whole.

Let's look at the four fractions we have worked with so far. Which fractions have the same denominator? $\frac{4}{12}$ and $\frac{9}{12}$. **Which one has the largest numerator?** $\frac{9}{12}$. **That is the larger of the two fractions.**

Word Problem

(Problem F) **Let's look at this scenario. Your friend says that a recipe calls for** $\frac{4}{8}$ **cup of flour. You have already poured** $\frac{1}{2}$ **cup. Are these the same or different? We will use equivalent fractions (and sticks) to find out if** $\frac{1}{2}$ **is the same as** $\frac{4}{8}$. **We will show our answer using the concrete method and will write our answer and show our work on paper.**

Let's start with $\frac{1}{2}$ **because it is the fraction with the smallest numerator and denominator.**

Begin by setting up the first fraction using your sticks.

How many sticks are in the numerator? 1.

How many sticks are in the denominator? 2.

What separates the numerator and denominator? Divisor line.

Let's insert more groups to form our equivalent fraction.

How many groups of one do we need to insert in the numerator? 1.

How many groups of two do we need to insert in the denominator? 1.

Our new fraction, $\frac{2}{4}$, is also equal to what fraction? $\frac{1}{2}$.

Do we know if $\frac{4}{8}$ is equivalent to $\frac{1}{2}$? No. Let's keep working.

Let's find another equivalent fraction by adding more groups to the numerator and denominator. We will add one group to each.

How big is the group we should multiply in the numerator? 1 stick.

How big is the group we should multiply in the denominator? 2 sticks.

What is our new fraction? $\frac{4}{8}$.

So, $\frac{4}{8}$ is equal to what other two fractions? $\frac{1}{2}$ and $\frac{2}{4}$.

Will it be the same if your friend uses $\frac{1}{2}$ cup of flour? Yes.

Independent Practice

Now you are going to find some equivalent fractions on your own. You will be using your sticks and the same method we used during the first part of the lesson. You will also be showing all your work on paper.

LESSON 16

Finding Equivalent Fractions

2.R (tallies-only method)

Describe/Model

a) $\dfrac{2}{5} = \dfrac{}{10} = \underline{\quad} = \underline{\quad}$

b) What was multiplied in the numerator and denominator to find the last equivalent fraction?

Guided Practice

c) $\dfrac{1}{2} = \dfrac{2}{} = \underline{\quad} = \underline{\quad} = \underline{\quad}$

d) What was multiplied in the numerator and denominator to find the last equivalent fraction?

e) Circle the fractions in a) and c) that have the same denominator.
   Which one has the larger numerator?

Word Problem

f) You notice your sandwich looks small. Your friend tells you it is only $\frac{1}{3}$ of a foot long. You measure 5 inches on a 12-inch ruler. Is $\frac{1}{3}$ the same or different from $\frac{5}{12}$? Use equivalent fractions to find if $\frac{1}{3}$ is the same as $\frac{5}{12}$. Show your problem solving using tallies.

   How did you find the equivalent fraction?

Independent Practice

g) $\dfrac{1}{3} = \dfrac{2}{} = \underline{\quad} = \underline{\quad} = \underline{\quad}$

h) What was multiplied in the numerator and denominator to find the last equivalent fraction?

i) $\dfrac{5}{6} = \dfrac{10}{} = \underline{\quad} = \underline{\quad} = \underline{\quad}$

j) What was multiplied in the numerator and denominator to find the last equivalent fraction?

k) Circle the fractions in g) and i) that have the same denominator.
   Which one has the larger numerator?

Teaching **LESSON 16**

Finding Equivalent Fractions

2.R (tallies-only method)

Describe/Model

Today we are going to continue finding equivalent fractions. However, in this lesson we will be using tallies on notebook paper to replace the sticks that we used yesterday. I will begin by working out some of these with you.

(Problem A: $\frac{2}{5} = \frac{}{10} = \underline{} = \underline{}$) & (Problem B: What was multiplied in the numerator and denominator to find the last equivalent fraction?)

We will start by drawing our tallies to set up the first fraction. In our numerator we will have how many tallies? Two. In our denominator we will have how may tallies? Five. What separates the numerator and denominator? Divisor line. Our second fraction looks a little different than our second fractions did yesterday. We have to figure out what number goes in the numerator. We will include an equal number of groups to the numerator and denominator of the first fraction using tallies to form our second equivalent fraction and figure out what will be in our numerator. To form a ten in the denominator of the second fraction we will need to insert one group of five tallies. To find our numerator we will also add one group to it. What size will this group be? Two tallies. What will our numerator be? Four. We now have 4 tallies/10 tallies, which is the same as $\frac{2}{5}$. Let's find another equivalent fraction of two fifths and four tenths. To do this, we will add one more group of tallies to the numerator and one to the denominator that are the same size as the first groups we added. So, add a group of two tallies to the numerator and a group of five tallies to the denominator. We now have 6 tallies/15 tallies, which is equal to $\frac{2}{5}$ and $\frac{4}{10}$. Let's find one more equivalent fraction. We will add another group of two tallies to the numerator and another group of five tallies to the denominator. We now have 8 tallies/20 tallies, which is equal to $\frac{2}{5}$, $\frac{4}{10}$, and $\frac{6}{15}$. Now we want to figure out what number we could multiply by in both the numerator and denominator of the first fraction to get the numerator and denominator of the last fraction. Let's ask ourselves, what number could we multiply two by to get eight? The answer is four. If we also multiply five by four will we get the correct denominator? Yes, twenty. So we can multiply $\frac{2}{5}$ by $\frac{4}{4}$ to get the equivalent fraction of $\frac{8}{20}$.

Guided Practice

Now you are going to make tallies to start finding equivalent fractions with me before you have a chance to find some equivalent fractions on your own.

(Problem C: $\frac{1}{2} = \frac{2}{} = \underline{} = \underline{}$) & (Problem D: What was multiplied in the numerator and denominator to find the last equivalent fraction?)

Begin by setting up the first fraction using your tallies. What is the first fraction? One half.

How many tallies are in the numerator? 1.

How many tallies are in the denominator? 2.

What separates the numerator and denominator? Divisor line.

Let's insert groups to form our equivalent fraction. We are going to have to figure out what number goes in the denominator of our second fraction.

How many groups of one do we need to add to the numerator? 1.

How many groups should we add to the denominator? 1.

What size is this group? 2 tallies What is our denominator? 4.

Our new fraction, $\frac{2}{4}$, is also equivalent to what fraction? $\frac{1}{2}$.

Let's find another equivalent fraction by adding more groups to the numerator and denominator. We will add one group to each.

How big is the group we should add to the numerator? 1 tally.

How big is the group we should add to the denominator? 2 tallies.

What is our new fraction? $\frac{3}{6}$.

So, $\frac{3}{6}$ is equal to what other two fractions? $\frac{1}{2}$ and $\frac{2}{4}$.

Let's find one more equivalent fraction. Go ahead and add one group to the numerator and denominator. Make sure your groups have the correct number of tallies.

What is your new fraction? $\frac{4}{8}$.

So, $\frac{4}{8}$ is equivalent to what other three fractions? $\frac{1}{2}$, $\frac{2}{4}$, and $\frac{3}{6}$.

What number can we multiply by in both the numerator and denominator of our first fraction to find the numerator and denominator of our last fraction? 4.

So this tells us that we can multiply $\frac{1}{2}$ by $\frac{4}{4}$ to find the equivalent fraction of $\frac{4}{8}$.

(Problem E: Circle the fractions in problems A and C that have the same denominator.)

Which number is the denominator? The number below the divisor line.

What does the denominator represent? The total number in the whole.

Let's look at the four fractions we have worked with so far. Which fractions have the same denominator? $\frac{4}{10}$ and $\frac{5}{10}$.

Which one has a larger numerator? $\frac{5}{10}$. $\frac{5}{10}$ is the larger fraction.

Word Problem

(Problem F) Let's look at this scenario. You notice your sandwich looks small. Your friend tells you it is only $\frac{1}{3}$ of a foot long. You measure 5 inches on a 12-inch ruler. Is $\frac{1}{3}$ the same or different from $\frac{5}{12}$? We will use equivalent fractions to find if $\frac{1}{3}$ is the same as $\frac{5}{12}$. We will show our answer using the tallies method.

Let's start with $\frac{1}{3}$ because it is the fraction with the smallest numerator and denominator.

Begin by setting up the first fraction using your tallies.

How many tallies are in the numerator? 1.

How many tallies are in the denominator? 3.

What separates the numerator and denominator? Divisor line.

Now let's add groups to form our equivalent fraction.

How many groups of one do we need to add to the numerator? 1.

How many groups of three do we need to add to the denominator? 1.

Our new fraction, $\frac{2}{6}$, is also equal to what fraction? $\frac{1}{3}$.

Do we know yet if $\frac{5}{12}$ is equivalent to $\frac{1}{3}$? No. Let's keep working.

Let's find another equivalent fraction by adding more groups to the numerator and denominator. We will add one group to each.

How big is the group we should add to the numerator? 1 tally.

How big is the group we should add to the denominator? 3 tallies.

What is our new fraction? $\frac{3}{9}$.

So, $\frac{3}{9}$ is equal to what other two fractions? $\frac{1}{3}$ and $\frac{2}{6}$.

Do we know yet if $\frac{5}{12}$ is equivalent to $\frac{1}{3}$? No. Let's keep working.

Let's find another equivalent fraction by adding more groups to the numerator and denominator. We will add one group to each.

How big is the group we should add to the numerator? 1 tally.

How big is the group we should add to the denominator? 3 tallies.

What is our new fraction? $\frac{4}{12}$.

So, $\frac{4}{12}$ is equal to what other three fractions? $\frac{1}{3}$, $\frac{2}{6}$, and $\frac{3}{9}$.

We now know that the fraction equivalent to $\frac{1}{3}$ with a 12 in the denominator is $\frac{4}{12}$, not $\frac{5}{12}$.

Will it be the same to have a sandwich that is $\frac{1}{3}$ of a foot as it is to have a sandwich that is $\frac{5}{12}$ of a foot? No.

Independent Practice

Now you are going to find some equivalent fractions on your own. You will be using your tallies and the same method we have used during the first part of the lesson. Show all your work on paper.

LESSON 17

Finding Equivalent Fractions

3.A   (abstract only)

Describe/Model

a) $\dfrac{5}{12} = \dfrac{10}{} = \underline{} = \underline{}$

b) What was multiplied in the numerator and denominator to find the last equivalent fraction?

Guided Practice

c) $\dfrac{1}{4} = \dfrac{2}{} = \underline{} = \underline{} = \underline{}$

d) What was multiplied in the numerator and denominator to find the last equivalent fraction?

e) Circle the fractions in a) and c) that have the same denominator.

Which one has the larger numerator?

Word Problem

f) Sherita says she jogs $\dfrac{9}{12}$ mile every day before practice. Your coach makes you run $\dfrac{1}{2}$ mile. Are these the same or different? Use equivalent fractions to find if $\dfrac{1}{2}$ is the same as $\dfrac{9}{12}$. Show your problem solving using abstract notation.

How did you find the equivalent fraction?

Independent Practice

g) $\dfrac{2}{9} = \dfrac{}{18} = \underline{} = \underline{} = \underline{}$

h) What was multiplied in the numerator and denominator to find the last equivalent fraction?

i) $\dfrac{1}{6} = \dfrac{2}{} = \underline{} = \underline{} = \underline{}$

j) What was multiplied in the numerator and denominator to find the last equivalent fraction?

k) Circle the fractions in g) and i) that have the same denominator.

Which one has the larger numerator?

Teaching **LESSON 17**

Finding Equivalent Fractions

3.A (abstract only)

Describe/Model

Today we are going to continue finding equivalent fractions. However, in this lesson we will not be using pictures or sticks. We will be using our basic addition, multiplication, and division facts to find equivalent fractions using an abstract method. I will do some of these with you first.

(Problem A: $\frac{5}{12} = \frac{10}{} = \underline{\qquad}$) & (Problem B: What was multiplied in the numerator and denominator to find the last equivalent fraction?)

Our original fraction is five twelfths. The first thing we are going to do in this problem is find an equivalent fraction with ten as the numerator. We will add one group of five to the numerator to get ten because $5 + 5 = 10$. Then, we will also add one group to the denominator. What size is this group? 12. So, $12 + 12 = ?$ 24. Ten twenty-fourths is equal to five twelfths. Now let's find another equivalent fraction. We will add another group to the numerator and denominator. How many are we adding to the numerator? 5. So, $10 + 5 = ?$ 15. How many are we adding to the denominator? 12. So, $24 + 12 = ?$ 36. Our new fraction is $\frac{15}{36}$. Fifteen thirtysixths is also equal to five twelfths and ten twentyfourths. Now we want to find out what number we can multiply by in the numerator and denominator of the original fraction to find the last fraction. What number times five is equal to fifteen? Three. If we multiply three by the denominator of the first fraction, do we get the denominator of the last fraction? Yes. That tells us that we can multiply $\frac{5}{12}$ by $\frac{3}{3}$ to find the equivalent fraction $\frac{15}{36}$.

Guided Practice

Let's try some problems together.

(Problem C: $\frac{1}{4} = \frac{2}{} = \underline{\qquad} = \underline{\qquad} = \underline{\qquad}$) & (Problem D: What was multiplied in the numerator and denominator to find the last equivalent fraction?)

What is the first fraction? One fourth.

Now let's add groups to form our equivalent fraction. We are going to have to figure out what number goes in the denominator of our second fraction.

How many groups of one do we need to add to the numerator? 1.

How many groups should we add to the denominator? 1.

What size is this group? 4. What is our denominator? 8.

Our new fraction, $\frac{2}{8}$, is also equal to what fraction? $\frac{1}{4}$.

Let's find another equivalent fraction by adding more groups to the numerator and denominator. We will add one group to each.

How big is the group we should add to the numerator? 1.

How big is the group we should add to the denominator? 4.

What is our new fraction? $\frac{3}{12}$.

So, $\frac{3}{12}$ is equal to what other two fractions? $\frac{1}{4}$ and $\frac{2}{8}$.

Let's find another equivalent fraction. Go ahead and add one group to the numerator and denominator. Make sure your groups are the correct size.

What is your new fraction? $\frac{4}{16}$.

So, $\frac{4}{16}$ is equal to what other three fractions? $\frac{1}{4}$, $\frac{2}{8}$, and $\frac{3}{12}$.

We are going to find one more equivalent fraction of $\frac{1}{4}$, although we could find many.

Insert another group to the numerator and denominator of our last fraction.

What is our new equivalent fraction? $\frac{5}{20}$.

What number can we multiply by in both the numerator and denominator of our first fraction to find the numerator and denominator of our last fraction? 5.

This tells us that we can multiply $\frac{1}{4}$ by $\frac{5}{5}$ to find the equivalent fraction of $\frac{5}{20}$.

(Problem E: Circle the fractions in problems A and C that have the same denominator.)

Which number is the denominator? The number below the divisor line.

And what does the denominator represent? The total number in the whole.

Let's look at the fractions we have worked with so far. Which fractions have the same denominator? $\frac{5}{12}$ and $\frac{3}{12}$.

Which one has the larger numerator? $\frac{5}{12}$. That is the larger fraction.

Word Problem

(Problem F) Let's look at this scenario. Sherita says she jogs $\frac{9}{12}$ mile everyday before practice. Your coach makes you run $\frac{1}{2}$ mile. Are these the same or different? We will use equivalent fractions to find out if $\frac{1}{2}$ is the same as $\frac{9}{12}$. The method we will use is the same abstract method we have been using throughout this lesson.

Let's start with $\frac{1}{2}$ because it is the fraction with the smallest numerator and denominator.

Add groups to form our equivalent fraction.

How many groups of one do we need to insert to the numerator? 1.

How many groups of two do we need to insert to the denominator? 1.

Our new fraction, $\frac{2}{4}$, is also equal to what fraction? $\frac{1}{2}$.

Do we know yet if $\frac{9}{12}$ is equivalent to $\frac{1}{2}$? No. Let's keep working.

Let's find another equivalent fraction by adding more groups to the numerator and denominator. We will add one group to each.

How big is the group we should add to the numerator? 1.

How big is the group we should add to the denominator? 2.

What is our new fraction? $\frac{3}{6}$.

So, $\frac{3}{6}$ is equal to what other two fractions? $\frac{1}{2}$ and $\frac{2}{4}$.

Do we know yet if $\frac{9}{12}$ is equivalent to $\frac{1}{2}$? No. Let's keep working.

Let's find another equivalent fraction by adding more groups to the numerator and denominator. We will add one group to each.

How big is the group we should add to the numerator? 1.

How big is the group we should add to the denominator? 2.

What is our new fraction? $\frac{4}{8}$.

So, $\frac{4}{8}$ is equal to what other three fractions? $\frac{1}{2}$, $\frac{2}{4}$, and $\frac{3}{6}$.

Do we know yet if $\frac{9}{12}$ is equivalent to $\frac{1}{2}$? No. Let's keep working.

Let's find another equivalent fraction by adding more groups to the numerator and denominator. We will add one group to each.

How big is the group we should add to the numerator? 1.

How big is the group we should add to the denominator? 2.

What is our new fraction? $\frac{5}{10}$.

So, $\frac{5}{10}$ is equal to what other four fractions? $\frac{1}{2}$, $\frac{2}{4}$, $\frac{3}{6}$, and $\frac{4}{8}$.

Do we know yet if $\frac{9}{12}$ is equivalent to $\frac{1}{2}$? No. Let's keep working.

Let's find another equivalent fraction by adding more groups to the numerator and denominator. We will add one group to each.

How big is the group we should add to the numerator? 1.

How big is the group we should add to the denominator? 2.

What is our new fraction? $\frac{6}{12}$.

So, $\frac{6}{12}$ is equal to what other five fractions? $\frac{1}{2}$, $\frac{2}{4}$, $\frac{3}{6}$, $\frac{4}{8}$, and $\frac{5}{10}$.

We now know that the fraction equivalent to $\frac{1}{2}$ with a **12** in the denominator is $\frac{6}{12}$, not $\frac{9}{12}$.

Will it be the same to run $\frac{1}{2}$ mile as it is to run $\frac{9}{12}$ mile? No.

Independent Practice

Now you are going to find some equivalent fractions on your own. You will be using the same abstract method to show your answers on paper.

LESSON 18

Finding Equivalent Fractions

4. A (generalized)

Describe/Model

a) $\dfrac{3}{8}$ = ____ = ____ = ____

b) What was multiplied in the numerator and denominator to find the last equivalent fraction?

Guided Practice

c) $\dfrac{1}{6}$ = ____ = ____ = ____

d) What was multiplied in the numerator and denominator to find the last equivalent fraction?

e) Circle the fractions in a) and c) that have the same denominator.

Word Problem

f) Your neighbor is driving you to the store. She says that it is $\frac{1}{4}$ mile away. The car's odometer reads $\frac{3}{10}$ when you get there. Are these the same or different? Use equivalent fractions to find if $\frac{1}{4}$ is the same as $\frac{3}{10}$. Show your problem solving using abstract notation.

How did you find the equivalent fraction?

Independent Practice

g) $\dfrac{3}{10}$ = ____ = ____ = ____ = ____

h) What was multiplied in the numerator and denominator to find the last equivalent fraction?

i) $\dfrac{2}{7}$ = ____ = ____ = ____ = ____

j) What was multiplied in the numerator and denominator to find the last equivalent fraction?

k) Circle the fractions in g) and i) that have the same denominator. If none, what would you do to find fractions with the same denominator?

Note: To review finding equivalent fractions, see Cumulative Review D starting on page 153.

LESSON 19

Reducing and Comparing Fractions

1.C (sticks-only method)

Describe/Model

a) $\dfrac{8}{12} = $ _____

b) What was divided equally in the numerator and denominator to find the fraction in its simplest form?

c) $\dfrac{3}{9} = $ _____

d) What was divided equally in the numerator and denominator to find the fraction in its simplest form?

e) Which fraction is larger, a) or c)? How do you know?

Guided Practice

Use concrete objects to reduce these fractions to their simplest form. (LCM)

f) $\dfrac{6}{10} = $ _____

g) $\dfrac{6}{15} = $ _____

h) What did you divide in the numerator and denominator of f) and g)? Which one is larger?

Word Problem

i) A recipe calls for $\dfrac{9}{12}$ cup of milk. You have two different measuring cups: a $\dfrac{1}{3}$-cup and a $\dfrac{1}{4}$-cup measure. Which measuring cup has the same denominator as $\dfrac{9}{12}$? Reduce $\dfrac{9}{12}$ to its simplest form to determine which cup to use. Show your problem solving using concrete materials.

Independent Practice

Use concrete objects to reduce these fractions to their simplest form.

j) $\dfrac{12}{16} = $ _____

k) $\dfrac{2}{8} = $ _____

l) What did you divide in the numerator and denominator for j) and k)?

m) $\dfrac{3}{6} = $ _____

n) $\dfrac{7}{14} = $ _____

o) What did you divide in the numerator and denominator for m) and n)?

Teaching **LESSON 19**

Reducing and Comparing Fractions

1.C (sticks-only method)

Describe/Model *(Answer in groups.)*

Today we will be using sticks again as we work with fractions. We will learn how to reduce fractions to their simplest forms. For example, we just finished learning about equivalent fractions, and we found that $\frac{1}{2}$ is equal to $\frac{4}{8}$. $\frac{1}{2}$ is the simplest (or most reduced) form of $\frac{4}{8}$. I will work out some of these problems for you first and then you will work out some with me. At the end of this lesson, you will be able to use sticks to reduce fractions on your own.

(Problem A: $\frac{8}{12}$ = _____) & (Problem B: What was divided equally in the numerator and denominator to find the fraction in its simplest form?)

What is the fraction here that we want to reduce, or put into simplest form? Eight twelfths. Very good. We will begin by setting this problem up using our sticks. How many sticks do we place in the numerator? 8. How many sticks do we place in the denominator? 12. What separates the two? Divisor line. To reduce this fraction we need to divide it by the same number of sticks. We will try to divide by two first. (Move sticks together in groups of two.) Are all the sticks in equal groups? Yes. To show our reduced fraction we are going to stack the sticks according to their group. We are left with 4 groups/6 groups. Is there another way we can divide the groups of sticks left into a smaller number of groups? Yes. Right, because four and six are both divisible by two. So let's divide these groups by two groups. (Put the groups into groups of two—two groups left in the numerator and three groups left in the denominator.) We are now left with 2 groups/3 groups. We cannot divide these groups any further so we will stack all the sticks according to groups again to show the fraction in its simplest form. The simplest form of $\frac{8}{12}$ is . . .? $\frac{2}{3}$. What was divided equally in the numerator and denominator to find the fraction in its simplest form? 4.

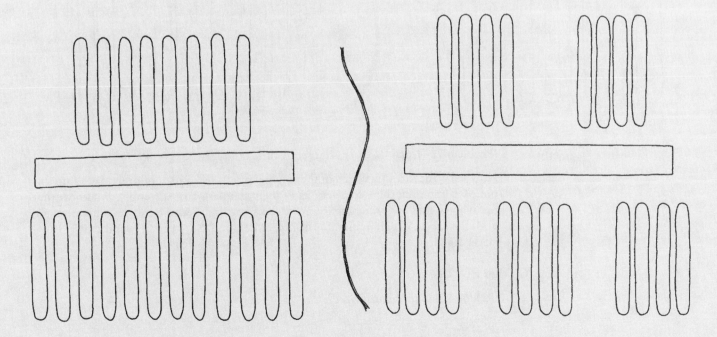

(Problem C: $\frac{3}{9}$ = _____) & (Problem D: What was divided equally in the numerator and denominator to find the fraction in its simplest form?)

What is the fraction here that we want to reduce, or put into simplest form? Three ninths. Very good. We will begin by setting this problem up using our sticks. How many sticks do we place in the numerator? 3. How many sticks do we place in the denominator? 9. What separates the two? Divisor line. To reduce this fraction we need to divide it by the same number of sticks. We will try to divide by two first. (Move sticks together in groups of two.) Are all the sticks in equal groups? No. Then, we will divide by a different number. We will try three. (Place the sticks in groups of three.) Now, are all the sticks in equally sized groups? Yes. To show our reduced fraction, we are going to stack the sticks according to their group. We are left with 1 group/3 groups. Is there another way we can divide the groups of sticks left into a smaller number of groups? No. The simplest form of $\frac{3}{9}$ is . . .? $\frac{1}{3}$. What was divided equally in the numerator and denominator to find the fraction in its simplest form? 3.

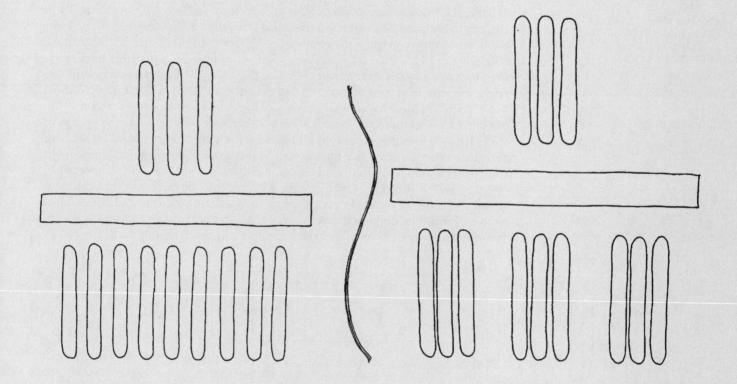

(Problem E: Which fraction is larger, A or C, and how do you know?)

Now we want to know which of the original fractions, $\frac{8}{12}$ or $\frac{3}{9}$, is larger. Let's find this out by comparing the two fractions in their simplest forms, $\frac{2}{3}$ and $\frac{1}{3}$. We know that the wholes that we are comparing are the same size because the denominators are both the same. Which numerator is larger? 2. Good. So we have found that $\frac{8}{12}$ is the larger fraction.

Guided Practice

Let's try some problems together.

(Problem F: $\frac{6}{10}$ = _____)

What is the fraction here that we want to reduce, or put into simplest form? Six tenths.

Let's begin by setting this problem up using our sticks.

How many sticks do we place in the numerator? 6.

How many sticks do we place in the denominator? 10.

What separates the two? Divisor line.

What do we need to do to reduce this fraction? Divide the numerator and denominator by the same number of sticks.

What can we try to divide by first? 2.

Are all the sticks in equal groups? Yes.

Let's stack the sticks to show our reduced fraction.

What is the new fraction? $\frac{3}{5}$.

Is there another way we can divide the groups of sticks left into a smaller number of groups? No.

The simplest form of $\frac{6}{10}$ is . . .? $\frac{3}{5}$.

(Problem G: $\frac{6}{15}$ = _____)

What is the fraction here that we want to reduce, or put into simplest form? Six fifteenths.

Let's begin by setting this problem up using our sticks.

How many sticks do we place in the numerator? 6.

How many sticks do we place in the denominator? 15.

What separates the two? Divisor line.

What do we need to do to reduce this fraction? Divide the numerator and denominator by the same number of sticks.

What can we try to divide by first? 2.

Are all the sticks in equal groups? No.

Then what do we need to do? Try to divide by another number.

What should we try next? 3.

Are all the sticks in equal groups? Yes.

Let's stack the sticks to show our reduced fraction.

What is the new fraction? $\frac{2}{5}$.

Is there another way we can divide the groups of sticks left into a smaller number of groups? No.

The simplest form of $\frac{6}{15}$ is . . .? $\frac{2}{5}$.

(Problem H: What did you divide in the numerator and denominator of F and G? Which fraction is larger?)

Let's look at the original problem in F, $\frac{6}{10}$. What did we divide in the numerator and denominator of $\frac{6}{10}$ to find the fraction in its simplest form, $\frac{3}{5}$? 2.

Let's look at the original problem in G, $\frac{6}{15}$. What did we divide in the numerator and denominator of $\frac{6}{15}$ to find the fraction in its simplest form, $\frac{2}{5}$? 3.

Now we want to find out which of these fractions is larger. What should we compare? The two fractions in their simplest forms.

Are the sizes of the whole the same for both fractions? Yes.

Why? Because the denominators are both 5.

Which has the larger numerator? $\frac{3}{5}$.

So, which of the original fractions is larger? $\frac{6}{10}$.

Word Problem

(Problem I) Let's look at this scenario. A recipe calls for $\frac{9}{12}$ cup of milk. You have two different measuring cups: a $\frac{1}{3}$-cup and a $\frac{1}{4}$-cup measure. Which measuring cup is the same as $\frac{9}{12}$? Reduce $\frac{9}{12}$ to its simplest form to determine which cup to use. We will show our problem using concrete materials (sticks).

What is the fraction here that we want to reduce, or put into simplest form? Nine twelfths.

Let's begin by setting this problem up using our sticks.

How many sticks do we place in the numerator? 9.

How many sticks do we place in the denominator? 12.

What separates the two? Divisor line.

What do we need to do to reduce this fraction? Divide the numerator and denominator by the same number of sticks.

What can we try to divide by first? 2.

Are all the sticks in equal groups? No.

Then what do we need to do? Try to divide by another number.

What should we try next? 3.

Are all the sticks in equal groups? Yes.

Let's stack the sticks to show our reduced fraction.

What is the new fraction? $\frac{3}{4}$.

Is there another way we can divide the groups of sticks left into a smaller number of groups? No.

The simplest form of $\frac{9}{12}$ is . . .? $\frac{3}{4}$. Therefore, we need to use the $\frac{1}{4}$-cup measuring cup 3 times.

Independent Practice

Now you are going to reduce some fractions on your own. Use concrete models (sticks) to show your answers and put your work on paper. Make sure your final answers are in simplest form.

LESSON 20

Reducing and Comparing Fractions

2.R (tallies-only method)

Describe/Model

a) $\dfrac{5}{20} = $ _____

b) What was divided equally in the numerator and denominator to find the fraction in its simplest form?

Guided Practice

c) $\dfrac{12}{16} = $ _____

d) What was divided equally in the numerator and denominator to find the fraction in its simplest form?

e) Which fraction is larger, a) or c)? How do you know?

Use tallies to reduce these fractions to their simplest forms.

f) $\dfrac{6}{10} = $ _____   g) $\dfrac{8}{14} = $ _____

h) What did you divide in the numerator and denominator of f) and g)?

Word Problem

i) An ad reads that 8 out of 10 dentists recommend a new toothpaste. The toothpaste you use says that 4 out of 5 dentists recommend it. Which toothpaste is more highly recommended by dentists: $\frac{8}{10}$ or $\frac{4}{5}$? Reduce $\frac{8}{10}$ to its simplest form to determine the answer. Show your problem solving using tallies.

Independent Practice

Use tallies to reduce these fractions to their simplest forms.

j) $\dfrac{3}{6} = $ _____   k) $\dfrac{6}{12} = $ _____

l) What did you divide in the numerator and denominator of j) and k)?

Which one is larger?

m) $\dfrac{6}{9} = $ _____   n) $\dfrac{12}{15} = $ _____

o) What did you divide in the numerator and denominator of m) and n)?

Teaching **LESSON 20**

Reducing and Comparing Fractions

2.R (tallies-only method)

Describe/Model *(Answer is in groups.)*

Yesterday we started learning how to reduce fractions to their simplest forms. Today we will continue reducing fractions; however, we will be using tallies to work out our problems rather than sticks. I am going to do some of these for you first. Then, you will work out some with me. At the end of the lesson, you will have the opportunity to reduce some fractions on your own using the tally method.

(Problem A: $\frac{5}{20} =$ _____) & (Problem B: What was divided equally in the numerator and denominator to find the fraction in its simplest form?)

What is the fraction that we want to reduce or put into simplest form? Five twentieths. Very good. We will begin by setting up this problem using tallies. How many tallies do we place in the numerator? 5. How many tallies do we place in the denominator? 20. What separates the two? Divisor line. To reduce this fraction we need to divide the numerator and denominator by the same number of tallies. We will try to divide by two first. (Draw lines under the tallies in groups of two.) Are all the tallies in equal groups? No. Now we need to try to divide by a different number. Let's look at the two numbers we are working with, five and twenty. Using your divisibility rules, what number is five and twenty commonly divisible by? 5. Very good. So, let's divide the numerator and denominator by five tallies. (Group numerator and denominator by five.) Are all the tallies now in equally sized groups? Yes. To find our reduced fraction we are going to count the number of groups. We are left with 1 group/4 groups. Is there another way we can divide the groups of tallies left into a smaller number of groups? No. The simplest form of $\frac{5}{20}$ is . . .? $\frac{1}{4}$. What was divided equally in the numerator and denominator to find the fraction in its simplest form? 5.

(Problem C: $\frac{12}{16} =$ _____) & (Problem D: What was divided equally in the numerator and denominator to find the fraction in its simplest form?)

What is the fraction that we want to reduce or put into simplest form? Twelve sixteenths. Very good. We will begin by setting up this problem using tallies. How many tallies do we place in the numerator? 12. How many tallies do we place in the denominator? 16. What separates the two? Divisor line. To reduce this fraction we need to divide the numerator and denominator by the same number of tallies. We will try to divide by two first. (Underline tallies together in groups of two.) Are all the tallies in equal groups? Yes. Let's count the number of groups to find our reduced fraction. We have 6 groups/8 groups. Is there another way we can divide the groups of tallies into smaller amounts of groups? Yes. What number is six and eight both divisible by? 2. So, let's put the groups into groups of two. [Circle two groups at a time in the numerator (left with three groups) and circle two groups at a time in the denominator (left with four groups)]. Now we are left with 3 groups/4 groups. Can we divide these groups into smaller groups? No. The simplest form of $\frac{12}{16}$ is . . .? $\frac{3}{4}$. What was divided equally in the numerator and denominator to find the fraction in its simplest form? 4.

a) $\dfrac{\text{IIIII}}{\text{IIIIIIIIIIIIIIIIIIII}}$ } $\dfrac{\text{IIII}}{\text{IIII IIII IIII IIII}}$

c) $\dfrac{\text{IIII IIII IIII}}{\text{IIII IIII IIII IIII}}$

(Problem E: Which fraction is larger, A or C, and how do you know?)

Now we want to know which of the original fractions, $\frac{5}{20}$ or $\frac{12}{16}$, is larger. Let's find this out by comparing the two fractions in their simplest forms, $\frac{1}{4}$ and $\frac{3}{4}$. We know that the wholes we are comparing are the same size because the denominators are both the same. Which numerator is larger? 3. Good. So we have found that $\frac{12}{16}$ is the larger fraction.

Guided Practice

Let's try some problems together.

(Problem F: $\frac{6}{10}$ = _____)

What is the fraction that we want to reduce or put into simplest form? Six tenths.

Let's begin by setting up this problem using tallies.

How many tallies do we place in the numerator? 6.

How many tallies do we place in the denominator? 10.

What separates the two? Divisor line.

What do we need to do to reduce this fraction? Group, or divide, the numerator and denominator by the same number of tallies.

What can we try to divide by first? Two.

Are all the sticks in equal groups? Yes.

Let's count the groups to find our reduced fraction.

What is the new fraction? $\frac{3}{5}$.

Is there another way we can divide the groups of tallies left into a smaller number of groups? No.

The simplest form of $\frac{6}{10}$ is . . .? $\frac{3}{5}$.

(Problem G: $\frac{8}{14}$ = _____)

What is the fraction that we want to reduce or put into simplest form? Eight fourteenths.

Let's begin by setting up this problem using tallies.

How many tallies do we place in the numerator? 8.

How many tallies do we place in the denominator? 14.

What separates the two? Divisor line.

What do we need to do to reduce this fraction? Group, or divide, the numerator and denominator by the same number of tallies.

What can we try to divide by first? Two.

Are all the tallies in equal groups? Yes.

Let's count the groups to find our reduced fraction. What is the reduced fraction? $\frac{4}{7}$.

Is there another way we can divide the groups of tallies left into a smaller number of groups? No.

The simplest form of $\frac{8}{14}$ is . . .? $\frac{4}{7}$.

(Problem H: What did you divide in the numerator and denominator of F and G?)

Let's look at the original fraction in F, $\frac{6}{10}$. What did we divide in the numerator and denominator of $\frac{6}{10}$ to find the fraction in its simplest form, $\frac{3}{5}$? 2.

Let's look at the original fraction in G, $\frac{8}{14}$. What did we divide in the numerator and denominator of $\frac{8}{14}$ to find the fraction in its simplest form, $\frac{4}{7}$? 2.

Word Problem

(Problem I) Let's look at this scenario. An ad reads that 8 out of 10 dentists recommend a new toothpaste. The toothpaste you use now says that 4 out of 5 dentists recommend it. Which toothpaste is more highly recommended by dentists: $\frac{8}{10}$ or $\frac{4}{5}$? Reduce $\frac{8}{10}$ to its simplest form to determine the answer. We will show our problem solving using tallies.

What is the fraction here that we want to reduce or put into simplest form? Eight tenths.

Let's begin by setting up this problem up using tallies.

How many tallies do we place in the numerator? 8.

How many tallies do we place in the denominator? 10.

What separates the two? Divisor line.

What do we need to do to reduce this fraction? Group, or divide, the numerator and denominator by the same number of tallies.

What can we try to divide by first? Two.

Are all the tallies in equal groups? Yes.

Let's count the groups to show our reduced fraction.

What is the new fraction? $\frac{4}{5}$.

Is there another way we can divide the groups of tallies left into a smaller number of groups? No.

The simplest form of $\frac{8}{10}$ is . . .? $\frac{4}{5}$. Therefore, both types of toothpaste are equally recommended.

Independent Practice

Now you are going to reduce some fractions on your own. Use representational pictures (tallies) to show your answers. Be sure that your final answers are in their simplest forms.

LESSON 21

Reducing and Comparing Fractions

3.A (abstract only)

Describe/Model

a) $\dfrac{7}{21} = $ _____

b) What was divided equally in the numerator and denominator to find the fraction in its simplest form?

Guided Practice

c) $\dfrac{12}{18} = $ _____

d) What was divided equally in the numerator and denominator to find the fraction in its simplest form?

e) Which fraction is larger, a) or c)? How do you know?

Use division to reduce these fractions to their simplest forms.

f) $\dfrac{10}{15} = $ _____   (g) $\dfrac{5}{20} = $ _____

h) What did you divide in the numerator and denominator of f) and g)?

Word Problem

i) The map shows that you have traveled 4 out of 10 miles on your trip. Your friend tells you that you are $\frac{3}{5}$ of the way there. Is your friend correct? Show why or why not using abstract notation.

Independent Practice

Use division to reduce these fractions to their simplest forms.

j) $\dfrac{8}{32} = $ _____   k) $\dfrac{12}{40} = $ _____

l) What did you divide in the numerator and denominator of j) and k)?

m) $\dfrac{27}{36} = $ _____   n) $\dfrac{9}{27} = $ _____

o) What did you divide in the numerator and denominator of m) and n)?

Teaching **LESSON 21**

Reducing and Comparing Fractions

3.A *(abstract only)*

Describe/Model *(Answer is in groups.)*

During the past couple of days we have been learning how to reduce fractions. At first, we used sticks to find fractions in their simplest forms and then we moved to using tallies. Today, we are going to begin reducing fractions using only the abstract method. In other words, we will strictly be using our basic facts to find fractions in their simplest forms. I will work out some of these for you at first and then you will work out some with me. At the end of the lesson, you will have the opportunity to use the abstract method to reduce some fractions on your own.

(Problem A: $\frac{7}{21} =$ _____) & (Problem B: What was divided equally in the numerator and denominator to find the fraction in its simplest form?)

What is the fraction that we want to reduce or put into simplest form? $\frac{7}{21}$. Very good. Let's begin by thinking about our divisibility rules. Normally we start with dividing by two. Are seven and twenty one divisible by two? No. Are seven and twenty one both divisible by three? No. Are seven and twenty one both divisible by four? No. Are seven and twenty one both divisible by five? No. Are seven and twenty one both divisible by six? No. Are seven and twenty one both divisible by seven? Yes. Let's divide our numerator and denominator by seven. $7 \div 7$ is . . .? 1. $21 \div 7$ is . . .? 3. Our new reduced fraction is $\frac{1}{3}$. Is there another number that we can divide by in both the numerator and denominator to form smaller groups? No. So, $\frac{7}{21}$ in simplest form is . . .? $\frac{1}{3}$. What was divided equally in the numerator and denominator to find the fraction in its simplest form? 7.

(Problem C: $\frac{12}{18} =$ _____) & (Problem D: What was divided equally in the numerator and denominator to find the fraction in its simplest form?)

What is the fraction that we want to reduce or put into simplest form? Twelve eighteenths. Very good. Let's begin by thinking about our divisibility rules. Are twelve and eighteen divisible by two? Yes. Let's divide our numerator and denominator by two. $12 \div 2$ is . . .? 6. $18 \div 2$ is . . .? 9. Our new reduced fraction is $\frac{6}{9}$. Think about your divisibility rules again. Is there another number that we can divide by in both the numerator and denominator to form smaller groups? Yes. What number? 3. Let's divide our new fraction by $\frac{3}{3}$. $6 \div 3$ is . . .? 2. $9 \div 3$ is . . .? 3. Our new reduced fraction is $\frac{2}{3}$. Think about your divisibility rules again. Is there another number that we can divide by in both the numerator and denominator to form smaller groups? No. So, $\frac{12}{18}$ in simplest form is . . .? $\frac{2}{3}$. What was divided equally in the numerator and denominator to find the fraction in its simplest form? 6.

(Problem E: Which fraction is larger, A or C, and how do you know?)

Now we want to know which of our original fractions, $\frac{7}{21}$ or $\frac{12}{18}$, is larger. Let's find this out by comparing the two fractions in their simplest forms, $\frac{1}{3}$ and $\frac{2}{3}$. We know that the wholes that we are comparing are the same size because the denominators are both the same. Which numerator is larger? 2. Good. So we have found that $\frac{12}{18}$ is the larger fraction.

Guided Practice

Let's try some of problems together.

(Problem F: $\frac{10}{15} =$ _____) What is the fraction that we want to reduce or put into simplest form? Ten fifteenths.

Let's start by thinking about our divisibility rules.

Are both numbers divisible by two? No.

By three? No.

By four? No.

By five? Yes.

Let's divide our numerator and denominator by five.

$10 \div 5$ is 2.

$15 \div 5$ is 3.

What is our reduced fraction? $\frac{2}{3}$.

Think about our divisibility rules again. Is there another number that we can divide by in both the numerator and denominator to form smaller groups? No.

So, $\frac{10}{15}$ in simplest form is . . .? $\frac{2}{3}$.

(Problem G: $\frac{5}{20} =$ _____) What is the fraction that we want to reduce or put into simplest form? Five twentieths.

Let's start by thinking about our divisibility rules.

Are both numbers divisible by two? No.

By three? No.

By four? No.

By five? Yes.

Let's divide our numerator and denominator by five.

$5 \div 5$ is 1.

$20 \div 5$ is 4.

What is our reduced fraction? $\frac{1}{4}$.

Think about our divisibility rules again. Is there another number that we can divide by in both the numerator and denominator to form smaller groups? No.

So, $\frac{5}{20}$ in simplest form is . . .? $\frac{1}{4}$.

(Problem H: What did you divide in the numerator and denominator of F and G?)

Let's look at the original fraction in F, $\frac{10}{15}$. What did we divide in the numerator and denominator to find the fraction in its simplest form, $\frac{2}{3}$? 5.

Let's look at the original fraction in G, $\frac{5}{20}$. What did we divide in the numerator and denominator to find the fraction in its simplest form, $\frac{1}{4}$? 5.

Word Problem

(Problem I) Let's look at this scenario. The map shows that you have traveled 4 out of 10 miles on your trip. Your friend tells you that you are $\frac{3}{5}$ of the way there? Is your friend correct? Show why or why not using abstract notation. We will show our problem solving using the abstract method.

What is the fraction that we want to reduce or put into simplest form? Eight tenths.

Let's begin by thinking about our divisibility rules.

Are both these numbers divisible by two? Yes.

Let's divide our numerator and denominator by two.

$8 \div 2 = 4$.

$10 \div 2 = 5$.

What is our reduced fraction? $\frac{4}{5}$.

Think about our divisibility rules again. Is there another number that we can divide by in both the numerator and denominator to form smaller groups? No. So, $\frac{8}{10}$ in simplest form is . . .? $\frac{4}{5}$.

Therefore, both types of toothpaste are equally recommended.

Independent Practice

Now you are going to reduce some fractions on your own. Use the abstract method to show your work on paper. Be sure that all your final fractions are in their simplest forms.

LESSON 22

Reducing and Comparing Fractions

4.A (generalized abstract)

Describe/Model

Fill in the blank with $>$, $=$, or $<$ after reducing and finding equivalent fractions to find equal denominators.

a) $\left(\dfrac{2}{9}\right)\underline{\quad}\left(\dfrac{6}{9}\right)$ b) $\left(\dfrac{1}{4}\right)\underline{\quad}\left(\dfrac{1}{2}\right)$

c) $\left(\dfrac{8}{40}\right)\underline{\quad}\left(\dfrac{6}{15}\right)$ d) $\left(\dfrac{2}{8}\right)\underline{\quad}\left(\dfrac{1}{4}\right)$

Guided Practice

e) $\left(\dfrac{2}{3}\right)\underline{\quad}\left(\dfrac{1}{5}\right)$ f) $\left(\dfrac{8}{12}\right)\underline{\quad}\left(\dfrac{7}{21}\right)$

Word Problem

g) Harold wants to buy $\frac{1}{2}$ carton of eggs. Instead, the store owner gives him $\frac{5}{12}$ carton. Which is bigger? How do you know? Use abstract computation to explain your answer.

Independent Practice

h) $\left(\dfrac{2}{1}\right)\underline{\quad}\left(\dfrac{1}{3}\right)$ i) $\left(\dfrac{12}{15}\right)\underline{\quad}\left(\dfrac{6}{10}\right)$

j) $\left(\dfrac{20}{30}\right)\underline{\quad}\left(\dfrac{1}{3}\right)$ k) $\left(\dfrac{2}{5}\right)\underline{\quad}\left(\dfrac{1}{4}\right)$

Note: To review reducing and comparing fractions, see Cumulative Review E starting on page 154.

LESSON 23

Adding and Subtracting Fractions with Like Denominators   *1.C (concrete only)*

Describe/Model

a) $\dfrac{1}{3} + \dfrac{1}{3} =$ b) $\dfrac{3}{4} + \dfrac{1}{4} =$

c) $\dfrac{3}{4} - \dfrac{1}{4} =$ d) $\dfrac{2}{5} - \dfrac{2}{5} =$

Guided Practice

e) $\dfrac{1}{4} + \dfrac{2}{4} =$ f) $\dfrac{3}{5} - \dfrac{1}{5} =$

Word Problem

g) You bought $\frac{3}{4}$ carton of cards. You give $(-)\frac{1}{4}$ of them to your friend. How much of a carton do you have left? Show your problem solving using concrete materials.

Independent Practice

h) $\dfrac{1}{5} + \dfrac{3}{5} =$ i) $\dfrac{3}{4} - \dfrac{2}{4} =$

j) $\dfrac{3}{3} - \dfrac{1}{3} =$ k) $\dfrac{2}{2} + \dfrac{1}{2} =$

Teaching **LESSON 23**

Adding and Subtracting Fractions with Like Denominators   *1.C (concrete only)*

Describe/Model

Today we will begin learning how to add and subtract fractions. We will be using sticks to work out our problems. All the problems that we work out today will have like denominators; for example, $\frac{2}{3} + \frac{1}{3}$. I will work out some problems for you first before you have a chance to work out some with me. At the end of the lesson, you will have the opportunity to add and subtract some fractions using sticks on your own.

(Problem A: $\frac{1}{3} + \frac{1}{3} =$) When we add fractions, we add the numerators but the denominators stay the same. This is because we are adding parts of an equally cut pie. Therefore, before we begin adding, we have to be sure that we have common (or like) denominators. Let's read our problem. One third plus one third. Set up this problem using sticks. On one side of the plus sign, we have 1 stick/3 sticks. On the other side of the plus sign, we have 1 stick/3 sticks. We will put an equal sign at the end of the problem. Do we have common denominators? Yes. On the other side of the equal sign we will also place three sticks in the denominator. Something is missing. We must identify that the first fraction is a positive number. So, we place a plus sign to the left of that fraction. Remember, we discussed that when adding fractions, the common denominator stays the same. To help remember this, we will move both plus signs in front of the numerators. Now we can add the sticks in the numerators. To do this, we will simply move the sticks from the numerators in both original fractions to the numerator on the right side of the equal sign. What is our new fraction? 2 sticks/ 3 sticks. Very good. So, $\frac{1}{3} + \frac{1}{3} = \frac{2}{3}$.

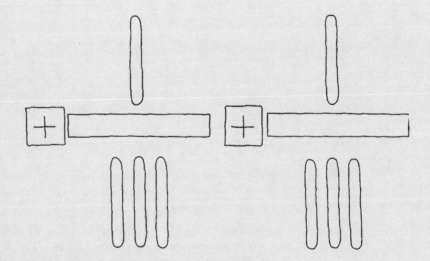

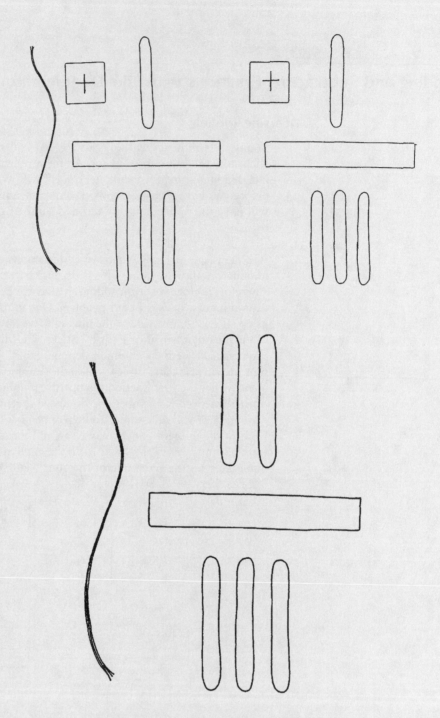

(Problem B: $\frac{3}{4} + \frac{1}{4} =$) Remember, when we add fractions we add the numerators and the denominators stay the same. Let's read our problem. Three fourths plus one fourth. Let's set up this problem using sticks. On one side of the plus sign, we have 3 sticks/4 sticks. On the other side of the plus sign, we have 1 stick/4 sticks. We will put an equal sign at the end of the problem. Do we have common denominators? Yes. On the other side of the equal sign we will also place four sticks in the denominator. We must identify that the first fraction is a positive number. So, we place a plus sign to the left of that fraction. Remember, we discussed that when adding fractions, the common denominator stays the same. Now we can add the sticks in the numerators. Move the plus signs in front of the numerators and move the sticks from the numerators in both original fractions to the numerator on the right side of the equal sign. What is our new fraction? 4 sticks/4 sticks. Very good. So, $\frac{3}{4} + \frac{1}{4} = \frac{4}{4}$.

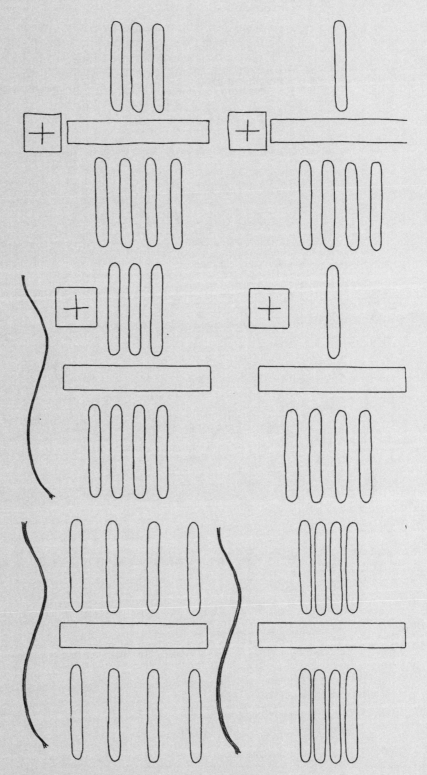

(Problem C: $\frac{3}{4} - \frac{1}{4} =$) Now we are going to subtract these fractions. Just as in adding fractions, when we subtract fractions, our common denominator stays the same in our answer and we subtract the second numerator from the first. Let's read our problem. Three fourths minus one fourth. Let's set up this problem using sticks. On one side of the minus sign, we have 3 sticks/4 sticks. On the other side of the minus sign, we have 1 stick/4 sticks. We will put an equal sign at the end of the problem. Do we have common denominators? Yes. On the other side of the equal sign we will also place four sticks in the denominator. We must identify that the first fraction is a positive number. So, we place a plus sign to the left of that fraction. Remember, we discussed that when subtracting fractions the common denominator stays the same. We move the plus and minus signs in front of their corresponding numerators. Now we can subtract one stick from three. First, we are going to place the same number of sticks in the numerator of our new fraction as there are in the numerator of our original fraction (3). Then, we want to subtract one stick from three sticks, which will leave us with two sticks. What is our new fraction? 2 sticks/4 sticks. Very good. So, $\frac{3}{4} - \frac{1}{4} = \frac{2}{4}$.

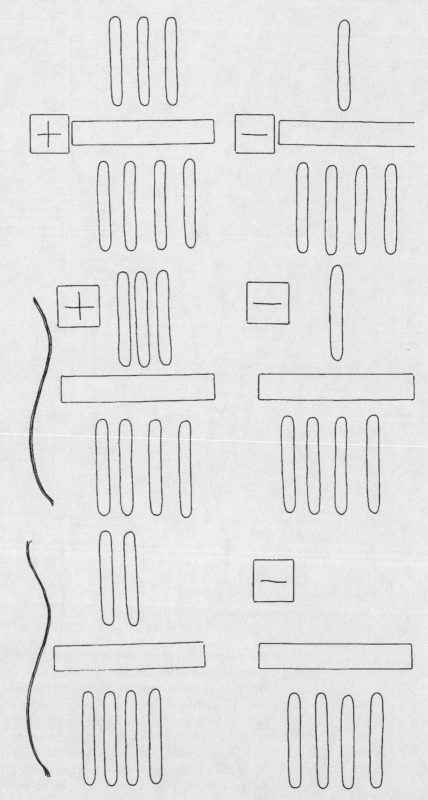

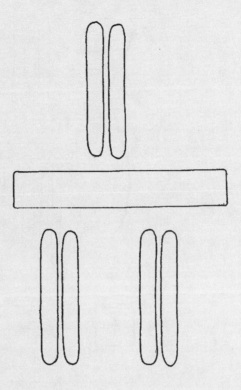

(Problem D: $\frac{2}{5} + \frac{2}{5} =$) Let's read our problem. Two fifths minus two fifths. Let's set up this problem using sticks. On one side of the minus sign, we have 2 sticks/ 5 sticks. On the other side of the minus sign, we have 2 sticks/5 sticks. We will put an equal sign at the end of the problem. Do we have common denominators? Yes. On the other side of the equal sign we will place five sticks in the denominator. We must identify that the first fraction is a positive number. So, we place a plus sign to the left of that fraction. Remember, we discussed that when subtracting fractions the common denominator stays the same. So, let's first move the signs in front of their corresponding numerator. Now we can subtract two sticks from two. First, we are going to place the same number of sticks in the numerator of our new fraction as there are in the numerator of our original fraction (2). Then, we want to subtract two sticks from the two sticks, which will leave us with zero sticks. What is our new fraction? 0 sticks/4 sticks. Very good. So, $\frac{2}{5} - \frac{2}{5} = \frac{0}{5}$. Anytime we have a zero in the numerator of a fraction (0 ÷ 5), that fraction is equal to zero.

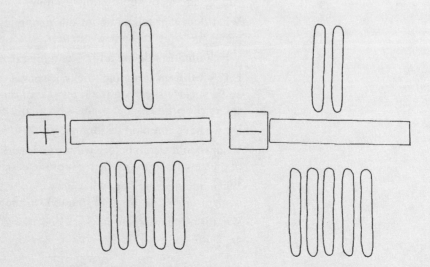

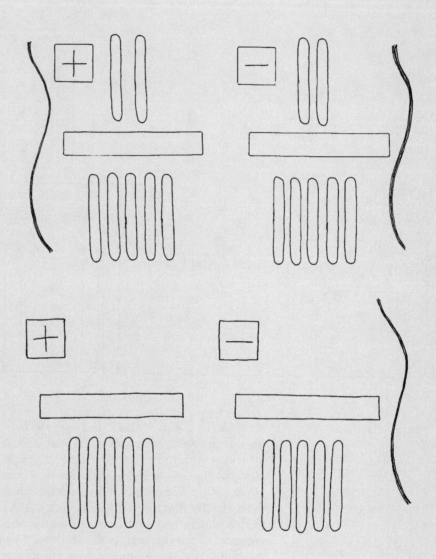

Guided Practice

Let's try some problems together.

(Problem E: $\frac{1}{4} + \frac{2}{4} =$) **Let's read our problem.** One fourth plus two fourths.

Are we adding or subtracting? Adding.

What does that tell us about our denominator? The common denominator remains the same in the new fraction.

Which numbers do we add? The numerators.

Let's set this up using our sticks. 1 stick/4 sticks on the left side of the plus sign and 2 sticks/4 sticks on the right side of the plus sign. Place an equal sign at the end of the problem and a plus sign before the first fraction.

Do we have common denominators? Yes, so move the signs up.

What should we do before we start adding? Place four sticks in the denominator of the new fraction on the right of the equal sign. **Good. Now we can add.**

When adding fractions, what do we do with our sticks? Move all sticks in the numerators of our original fractions to the numerator of our new fraction.

What is our new fraction? 3 sticks/4 sticks.

So, $\frac{1}{4} + \frac{2}{4}$ **is . . .?** $\frac{3}{4}$.

(Problem F: $\frac{3}{5} - \frac{1}{5} =$) **Let's read our problem.** Three fifths minus one fifth.

Are we adding or subtracting? Subtracting.

What does that tell us about our denominator? The common denominator remains the same in the new fraction.

Which numbers do we subtract? The second numerator from the first numerator.

Let's set this up using our sticks. 3 sticks/5 sticks on the left side of the minus sign and 1 stick/5 sticks on the right side of the minus sign. Place an equal sign at the end of the problem and a plus sign before the first fraction.

Do we have common denominators? Yes, so move the signs up.

What should we do before we start subtracting? Place five sticks in the denominator of the new fraction on the right of the equal sign. **Good. Now we can subtract.**

When subtracting fractions, what do we do with our sticks? Place the same number of sticks in the numerator of our new fraction as there are in the numerator of our original fraction (3).

Good. Now how many sticks do we need to take away? One.

What is our new fraction? 2 sticks/5 sticks.

So, $\frac{3}{5} - \frac{1}{5}$ **is . . .?** $\frac{2}{5}$.

Word Problem

(Problem G) **Let's look at this scenario. You bought** $\frac{3}{4}$ **carton of cards. You give (−)** $\frac{1}{4}$ **of them to your friend. How much of a carton do you have left? We will show our answer using concrete materials (sticks).**

Let's start by setting this up as a subtraction problem.

What size carton of cards did we buy? $\frac{3}{4}$.

How much of those cards did we give away? $\frac{1}{4}$.

Our subtraction problem will look like this: $\frac{3}{4} - \frac{1}{4} =$

Let's read our problem. Three fourths minus one fourth.

What does that tell us about our denominator? The common denominator remains the same in the new fraction.

Which numbers do we subtract? The second numerator from the first numerator.

Let's set this up using our sticks. 3 sticks/4 sticks on the left side of the minus sign and 1 stick/4 sticks on the right side of the minus sign. Place an equal sign at the end of the problem and a plus sign before the first fraction.

Do we have common denominators? Yes, so move the signs up.

What should we do before we start subtracting? Place four sticks in the denominator of the new fraction on the right of the equal sign. **Good. Now we can subtract.**

When subtracting fractions, what do we do with our sticks? Place the same number of sticks in the numerator of our new fraction as there are in the numerator of our original fraction (3).

Good. Now how many sticks do we need to take away? One.

What is our new fraction? 2 sticks/4 sticks.

How much of the carton of cards do we have left? $\frac{2}{4}$.

Independent Practice

Now you are going to add and subtract some fractions on your own. Remember, you will be showing your answer using sticks. Make sure that you write your answers on paper.

LESSON 24

Adding and Subtracting Fractions with Like Denominators   *2.R (representational only)*

Describe/Model

a) $\dfrac{1}{4} + \dfrac{2}{4} =$

b) $\dfrac{3}{5} + \dfrac{1}{5} =$

c) $\dfrac{2}{3} - \dfrac{1}{3} =$

d) $\dfrac{5}{4} - \dfrac{3}{4} =$

Guided Practice

e) $\dfrac{1}{3} + \dfrac{2}{3} =$

f) $\dfrac{3}{5} - \dfrac{2}{5} =$

Word Problem

g) You bought $\frac{2}{3}$ case of soda for a party. Your friend brings another $\frac{2}{3}$ case of soda. How much of a case of soda do you have for your party? Show your problem solving using pictorial representations.

Word Problem

h) $\dfrac{2}{4} + \dfrac{2}{4} =$

i) $\dfrac{3}{4} - \dfrac{1}{4} =$

j) $\dfrac{3}{3} - \dfrac{2}{3} =$

k) $\dfrac{1}{2} + \dfrac{0}{2} =$

Teaching **LESSON 24**

Adding and Subtracting Fractions with Like Denominators 2.R *(representational only)*

Describe/Model

Today we will continue adding and subtracting fractions. Yesterday, we worked out these same types of problems using sticks. Today we will let tally marks replace our sticks. All our problems will still have common denominators. I will work out some problems for you first before you have a chance to work out some with me. At the end of the lesson, you will have the opportunity to add and subtract some fractions on your own using tallies.

(Problem A: $\frac{1}{4} + \frac{2}{4} =$) When we add fractions, we add the numerators and the denominators stay the same. Therefore, before we begin adding, we have to be sure that we have common (or like) denominators. Let's read our problem. One fourth plus two fourths. Let's set up this problem using tallies. On one side of the plus sign, we have 1 tally/4 tallies. On the other side of the plus sign, we have 2 tallies/4 tallies. We will put an equal sign at the end of the problem. Do we have common denominators? Yes. On the other side of the equal sign we will also place four tallies in the denominator. Write a positive sign in front of the first fraction. Remember, we discussed that when adding fractions, the common denominator stays the same. Now we can add the tallies in the numerators. To do this, we will simply move the tallies in the numerators from both original fractions to the numerator on the right side of the equal sign. What is our new fraction? 3 tallies/4 tallies. Very good. So, $\frac{1}{4} + \frac{2}{4} = \frac{3}{4}$.

(Problem B: $\frac{3}{5} + \frac{1}{5} =$) Remember, when we add fractions we add the numerators and the denominators stay the same. Let's read our problem. Three fifths plus one fifth. Let's set up this problem using tallies. On one side of the plus sign, we have 3 tallies/5 tallies. On the other side of the plus sign, we have 1 tally/5 tallies. We will put an equal sign at the end of the problem. Do we have common denominators? Yes. On the other side of the equal sign we will also place five tallies in the denominator. Write a positive sign in front of the first fraction. Remember, we discussed that when adding fractions, the common denominator stays the same. Now we can add the tallies in the numerators. To do this, we will simply move the tallies from both numerators in the original fractions to the numerator on the right side of the equal sign. What is our new fraction? 4 tallies/5 tallies. Very good. So, $\frac{3}{5} + \frac{1}{5} = \frac{4}{5}$.

(Problem C: $\frac{2}{3} - \frac{1}{3} =$) Now we are going to subtract fractions. Just as when we are adding fractions, when we subtract fractions our common denominator stays the same in our answer and we subtract the second numerator from the first. Let's read our problem. Two thirds minus one third. Let's set up this problem using tallies. On one side of the minus sign, we have 2 tallies/3 tallies. On the other side of the minus sign, we have 1 tally/3 tallies. We will put an equal sign at the end of the problem. Do we have common denominators? Yes. On the other side of the equal sign we will also place three tallies in the denominator. Write a positive sign in front of the first fraction. Remember, we discussed that when subtracting fractions, the common denominator stays the same. Now we can subtract one tally from two tallies. First, place the same number of tallies in the numerator of our new fraction as there are in the numerator of our original fraction (2). Then, subtract one tally from the two tallies (cross out one tally), which will leave one tally. What is our new fraction? 1 tally/ 3 tallies. Very good. So, $\frac{2}{3} - \frac{1}{3} = \frac{1}{3}$.

(Problem D: $\frac{5}{4} - \frac{3}{4} =$) **Let's read our problem.** Five fourths minus three fourths. **Let's set up this problem using tallies.** On one side of the minus sign, we have 5 tallies/4 tallies. On the other side of the minus sign, we have 3 tallies/4 tallies. We will put an equal sign at the end of the problem. **Do we have common denominators?** Yes. On the other side of the equal sign we will also place four tallies in the denominator. Write a positive sign in front of the first fraction. **Remember, we discussed that when subtracting fractions, the common denominator stays the same. Now we can subtract three tallies from five tallies.** First, place the same number of tallies in the numerator of our new fraction as there are in the numerator of our original fraction (5). Then, subtract three tallies from five tallies (cross out three tallies), which will leave two tallies. **What is our new fraction?** 2 tallies/4 tallies. **Very good.** So, $\frac{5}{4} - \frac{3}{4} = \frac{2}{4}$.

Guided Practice

Let's try some problems together.

(Problem E: $\frac{1}{3} + \frac{2}{3} =$) **Let's read our problem.** One third plus two thirds.

Are we adding or subtracting? Adding.

What does that tell us about our denominator? The common denominator remains the same in the new fraction.

Which numbers do we add? The numerators.

Let's set this up using our tallies. 1 tally/3 tallies on the left side of the plus sign and 2 tallies/3 tallies on the right side of the plus sign. Place an equal sign at the end of the problem and a plus sign before the first fraction.

Do we have common denominators? Yes.

What should we do before we start adding? Place three tallies in the denominator of the new fraction on the right of the equal sign. **Good. Now we can add.**

When adding fractions, what do we do with our tallies? Move all tallies in the numerators of our original fractions to the numerator of our new fraction.

What is our new fraction? 3 tallies/3 tallies.

$\frac{1}{3} + \frac{2}{3}$ is . . .? $\frac{3}{3}$.

(Problem F: $\frac{3}{5} - \frac{2}{5} =$) **Let's read our problem.** Three fifths minus two fifths.

Are we adding or subtracting? Subtracting.

What does that tell us about our denominator? The common denominator remains the same in the new fraction.

Which numbers do we subtract? The second numerator from the first numerator.

Let's set this up using our tallies. 3 tallies/5 tallies on the left side of the minus sign and 2 tallies/5 tallies on the right side of the minus sign. Place an equal sign at the end of the problem and a plus sign before the first fraction.

Do we have common denominators? Yes.

What should we do before we start subtracting? Place five tallies in the denominator of the new fraction on the right of the equal sign. **Good. Now we can subtract.**

When subtracting fractions, what do we do with our tallies? Place the same number of tallies in the numerator of our new fraction as there are in the numerator of our original fraction (3).

Good. How many tallies do we need to take away? Two.

What is our new fraction? 1 tally/5 tallies.

$\frac{3}{5} - \frac{2}{5}$ is . . .? $\frac{1}{5}$.

Word Problem

(Problem G) Let's look at this scenario. You bought $\frac{2}{3}$ case of soda for a party. Your friend brings another $\frac{2}{3}$ case of soda. How much of a case of soda do you have for your party? We will show our problem solving using pictorial representations.

Let's start by setting this up as an addition problem.

What size case did you buy? $\frac{2}{3}$.

How much more did your friend bring? $\frac{2}{3}$.

Our addition problem will look like this: $\frac{2}{3} + \frac{2}{3} =$

Let's read our problem. Two thirds plus two thirds.

What does that tell us about our denominator? The common denominator remains the same in the new fraction.

Which numbers do we add? The numerators.

Let's set this up using our tallies. 2 tallies/3 tallies on the left side of the plus sign and 2 tallies/3 tallies on the right side of the plus sign. Place an equal sign at the end of the problem and a plus sign before the first fraction.

Do we have common denominators? Yes.

What should we do before we start adding? Place three tallies in the denominator of the new fraction on the right of the equal sign. **Good. Now we can add.**

When adding fractions, what do we do with our tallies? Move all the tallies from the numerators of the original two fractions to the numerator of the new fraction on the right side of the equal sign.

What is our new fraction? 4 tallies/3 tallies.

What size case do we have for the party? $\frac{4}{3}$.

Independent Practice

Now you are going to add and subtract some fractions on your own. Remember, you will be showing your answer on paper using tallies.

LESSON 25

Adding and Subtracting Fractions with Like Denominators *3.A (abstract only)*

Describe/Model

a) $\dfrac{1}{7} + \dfrac{2}{7} =$ b) $\dfrac{3}{4} + \dfrac{1}{4} =$

c) $\dfrac{4}{5} - \dfrac{1}{5} =$ d) $\dfrac{5}{6} - \dfrac{2}{6} =$

Guided Practice

e) $\dfrac{1}{3} + \dfrac{2}{3} =$ f) $\dfrac{3}{5} - \dfrac{1}{5} =$

Word Problem

g) The temperature outside reads $\frac{1}{3}$ degree above freezing. The next time you check, it reads $\frac{2}{3}$ degree above freezing. What is the change in temperature? Show your problem solving using abstract notation.

Independent Practice

h) $\dfrac{4}{4} + \dfrac{1}{4} =$ i) $\dfrac{3}{6} - \dfrac{1}{6} =$

j) $\dfrac{4}{5} - \dfrac{1}{5} =$ k) $\dfrac{1}{8} + \dfrac{5}{8} =$

Teaching **LESSON 25**

Adding and Subtracting Fractions with Like Denominators   *3.A (abstract only)*

Describe/Model

Today we will continue adding and subtracting fractions. During the past couple of days we have been adding and subtracting fractions using sticks and tallies. The only difference today is that we will not be using either; we will be using only our basic addition and subtraction facts to work out these problems. All our problems will still have common denominators. I will work out some problems for you first before you have a chance to work out some with me. At the end of the lesson, you will have the opportunity to add and subtract some fractions on your own using the abstract method.

(Problem A: $\frac{1}{7} + \frac{2}{7} =$) Write a plus sign before the first fraction. When we add fractions, we add the numerators and the denominators stay the same. Therefore, before we begin adding, we have to be sure that we have common (or like) denominators. Let's read our problem. One seventh plus two sevenths. Do we have common denominators? Yes. Now we can add. We know that the denominator in our answer will also be seven. So we will write seven under the divisor line on the right side of the equal sign. Then, we will add the numerators. One plus two is . . .? 3. $\frac{1}{7} + \frac{2}{7} = \frac{3}{7}$.

(Problem B: $\frac{3}{4} + \frac{1}{4} =$) Write a plus sign before the first fraction. We are adding here so the denominator will stay the same. Let's read our problem. Three fourths plus one fourth. Do we have common denominators? Yes. Now we can add. We know that the denominator in our answer will be four. So we will write four under the divisor line on the right side of the equal sign. Then, we will add the numerators. Three plus one is . . .? 4. $\frac{3}{4} + \frac{1}{4} = \frac{4}{4}$.

(Problem C: $\frac{4}{5} - \frac{1}{5} =$) Write a plus sign before the first fraction. Now we are going to subtract these fractions. Just as when we are adding fractions, when we subtract fractions our common denominator stays the same in our answer and we subtract the second numerator from the first. Let's read our problem. Four fifths minus one fifth. Do we have common denominators? Yes. Now we can subtract. We know that the denominator in our answer will also be five. So we will write five under the divisor line on the right side of the equal sign. Then, we will subtract the second numerator from the first numerator. Four minus one is . . .? 3. $\frac{4}{5} - \frac{1}{5} = \frac{3}{5}$.

(Problem D: $\frac{5}{6} - \frac{2}{6} =$) Let's read our problem. Five sixths minus two sixths. Write a plus sign before the first fraction. Do we have common denominators? Yes. Now we can subtract. We know that the denominator in our answer will also be six. So we will write six under the divisor line on the right side of the equal sign. Then, we will subtract the second numerator from the first numerator. Five minus two is . . .? 3. $\frac{5}{6} - \frac{2}{6} = \frac{3}{6}$.

Guided Practice

Let's try some problems together.

(Problem E: $\frac{1}{3} + \frac{2}{3} =$) **Let's read our problem.** One third plus two thirds.

Are we adding or subtracting? Adding.

What does that tell us about our denominator? The common denominator remains the same in the new fraction.

Which numbers do we add? The numerators.

Do we have common denominators? Yes.

What will the denominator be in our answer? 3.

Now we can add. One plus two is . . .? 3.

What is our new fraction? $\frac{3}{3}$.

$\frac{1}{3} + \frac{2}{3}$ is . . .? $\frac{3}{3}$.

(Problem F: $\frac{3}{5} - \frac{1}{5} =$) Let's read our problem. Three fifths minus one fifth.

Are we adding or subtracting? Subtracting.

What does that tell us about our denominator? The common denominator remains the same in the new fraction.

Which numbers do we subtract? The second numerator from the first numerator.

Do we have common denominators? Yes.

What will the denominator be in our answer? 5.

Now we can subtract. Three minus 1 is . . .? 2.

What is our new fraction? $\frac{2}{5}$.

$\frac{3}{5} - \frac{1}{5}$ is . . .? $\frac{2}{5}$.

Word Problem

(Problem G) Let's look at this scenario. The temperature outside reads $\frac{1}{3}$ degree above freezing. The next time you check, it reads $\frac{2}{3}$ degree above freezing. What is the change in temperature? We will use the same abstract method to solve this problem.

Let's start by setting this up as a subtraction problem to find the change in temperature.

Our problem will be $\frac{2}{3} - \frac{1}{3}$.

Let's read our problem. Two thirds minus one third.

Are we adding or subtracting? Subtracting.

What does that tell us about our denominator? The common denominator remains the same in the new fraction.

Which numbers do we subtract? The second numerator from the first numerator.

Do we have common denominators? Yes.

What will the denominator be in our answer? 3.

Now we can subtract. Two minus one is . . .? 1.

What is our new fraction? $\frac{1}{3}$.

The temperature went up by $\frac{1}{3}$ degree.

Independent Practice

Now you are going to add and subtract some fractions on your own. Remember, you will be showing your answer on paper using the same abstract method we used throughout this lesson.

LESSON 26

Adding and Subtracting Fractions with Like Denominators   *4.A (generalized)*

Describe/Model

a) $2\frac{1}{3} + \frac{2}{3} =$ b) $\frac{3}{4} + 1\frac{1}{4} =$

Guided Practice

c) $3\frac{4}{5} - 1\frac{1}{5} =$ d) $1\frac{1}{6} + \frac{5}{6} =$

Word Problem

e) Your bookshelf is $\frac{5}{7}$ full. Your neighbor brings more books, enough to fill another $\frac{3}{7}$ of your shelf. How full is your bookshelf now? Show your problem solving using abstract notation. What does the answer mean?

Independent Practice

f) $2\frac{1}{7} + \frac{5}{7} =$ g) $1\frac{1}{6} - \frac{5}{6} =$

h) $\frac{2}{4} + \frac{3}{4} =$ i) $\frac{5}{6} + 3\frac{2}{6} =$

j) $1\frac{4}{5} - \frac{3}{5} =$ k) $1\frac{2}{8} - \frac{10}{8} =$

Note: To review adding and subtracting fractions with like denominators, see Cumulative Review F starting on page 155

LESSON 27

Adding and Subtracting Fractions with Unlike Denominators   *1.C (concrete only)*

Describe/Model

a) $\frac{1}{3} + \frac{2}{9} =$ b) $\frac{3}{8} + \frac{1}{2} =$

c) $\frac{3}{4} - \frac{1}{4} =$ d) $\frac{2}{3} - \frac{1}{6} =$

Guided Practice

e) $\frac{1}{4} + \frac{1}{8} =$ f) $\frac{5}{6} - \frac{2}{3} =$

Word Problem

g) You borrow $\frac{1}{2}$ cup milk from your neighbor to add to the $\frac{2}{8}$ cup you already have. If you combine the milk, how much will you have? Show your problem solving using concrete materials.

Independent Practice

h) $\frac{1}{2} + \frac{5}{8} =$ i) $\frac{1}{3} - \frac{1}{9} =$

j) $\frac{3}{4} - \frac{1}{2} =$ k) $\frac{5}{6} + \frac{1}{3} =$

Teaching **LESSON 27**

Adding and Subtracting Fractions with Unlike Denominators   *1.C (concrete only)*

Describe/Model

Today we are going to continue adding and subtracting fractions. All the fractions that we have added or subtracted so far have had the same denominators. Remember, before we add or subtract fractions the denominators have to be . . .? Common. Very good. Today, the fractions that we add and subtract will have different denominators, so before we work out the problems we will have to find a common denominator. Today we will learn how to work out these problems using sticks. I will work out some for you first and then you will work out some with me. At the end of the lesson, you will have the opportunity to work out some of these addition and subtraction problems on your own.

(Problem A: $\frac{1}{3} + \frac{2}{9} =$) Let's read this problem together. One third plus two ninths. We are going to set up this problem using sticks. On the left side of the plus sign, we will have one stick in the numerator and three sticks in the denominator. On the right side of the plus sign, we will have two sticks in the numerator and nine sticks in the denominator. At the end of the problem, put an equal sign. We also need to identify that the first fraction is positive, so let's place a plus sign in front of it. Do we have common denominators? No. So before adding we must find a common denominator. To do this we will use our basic multiplication facts to find common multiples of the original denominator(s). Let's look at the denominators we have now. Let's look at the smallest denominator (3). Is there a way that we can use multiplication to get from three to nine, our other denominator? Yes, we can multiply by three. Very good. Three sticks times three groups will be nine sticks in the denominator of the first fraction. It is very important to remember that whatever we do to the denominator of a fraction we must also do to the numerator. So, what should we do here in the numerator? Multiply by three groups. Good. So, one stick times three groups will be three sticks in the numerator of our first fraction. What is our new addition problem? Three ninths plus two ninths. Do we have common denominators now? Yes. Now we can add, so let's move the signs up to the numerators. Remember, when we add fractions using the stick method, we begin by placing the common denominator (9) on the right side of the equal sign. Then, we move all the sticks in both numerators of the original fractions to the numerator of the new fraction on the right side of the equal sign. Now we can count the sticks in the new numerator to find our answer. What is our new fraction? $\frac{5}{9}$.

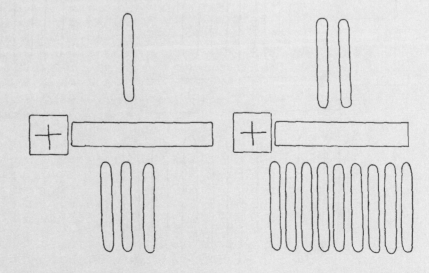

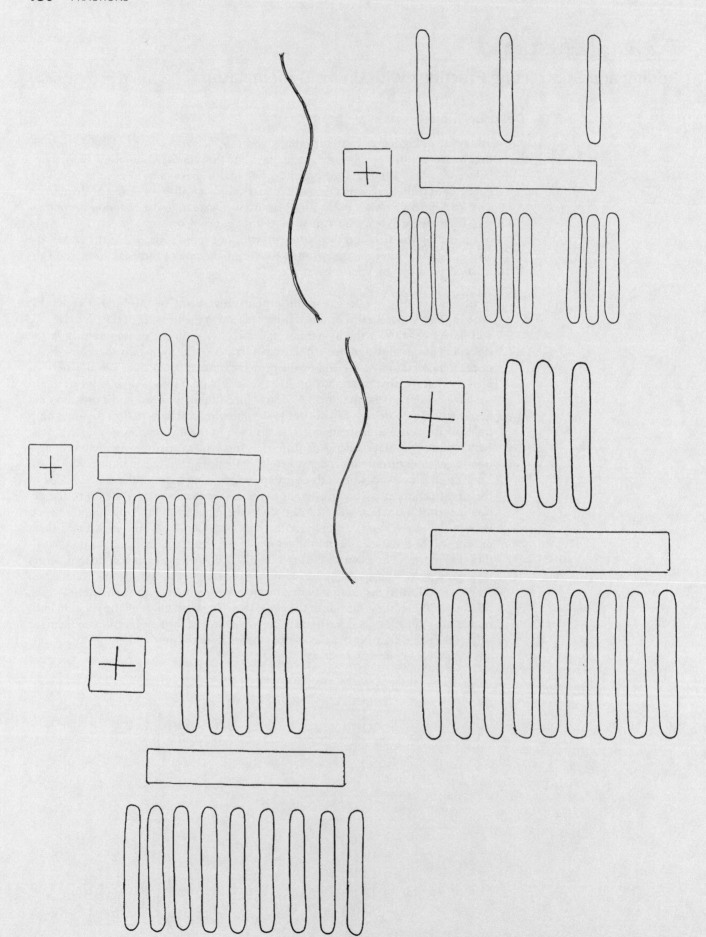

(Problem B: $\frac{3}{8} + \frac{1}{2} = $) Let's read this problem together. Three eighths plus one half. We are going to set up this problem using sticks. On the left side of the plus sign, we will have three sticks in the numerator and eight sticks in the denominator. On the right side of the plus sign, we will have one stick in the numerator and two sticks in the denominator. At the end of the problem we are going to put an equal sign. We also need to identify that the first fraction is positive, so let's place a plus sign in front of it. Do we have common denominators? No. So before adding, we must find a common denominator. To do this, we will use our basic multiplication facts to find common multiples of the original denominator(s). Let's look at the denominators we have now. Let's look at the smallest denominator (2). Is there a way that we can use multiplication to get from two to eight, our other denominator? Yes, we can multiply by four. Very good. Two sticks times four groups will be eight sticks in the denominator of the second fraction. It is very important to remember that whatever we do to the denominator of a fraction, we must also do to the numerator. So, what should we do here in the numerator? Multiply by four groups. Good. So, one stick times four groups will be four sticks in the numerator of our second fraction. What is our new addition problem? Three eighths plus four eighths. Do we have common denominators now? Yes. Now we can add, so let's move the signs up to the numerators. Remember, when we add fractions using the stick method, we begin by placing the common denominator (8) on the right side of the equal sign. Then, we move all the sticks in both numerators of the original fractions to the numerator of the new fraction on the right side of the equal sign. Now we can count the sticks in the new numerator to find our answer. What is our new fraction? $\frac{7}{8}$.

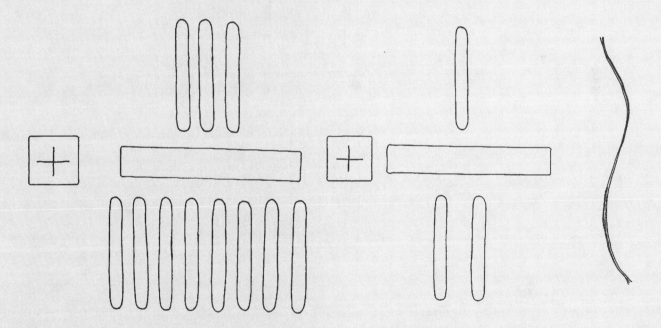

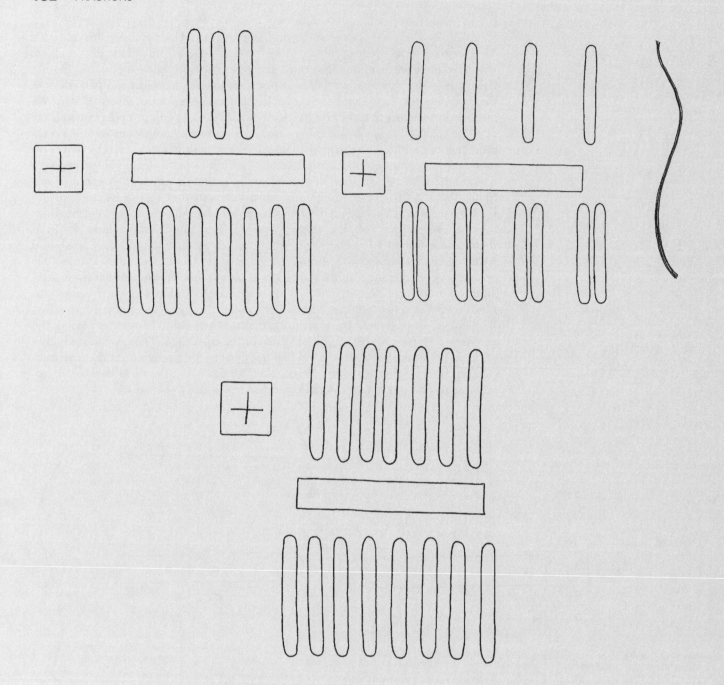

(Problem C: $\frac{3}{4} - \frac{1}{4} =$) Let's read this problem together. Three fourths minus one fourth. We are going to set up this problem using sticks. On the left side of the minus sign, we will have three sticks in the numerator and four sticks in the denominator. On the right side of the minus sign, we will have one stick in the numerator and four sticks in the denominator. At the end of the problem we are going to put an equal sign. We also need to identify that the first fraction is positive, so let's place a plus sign in front of it. Do we have common denominators? Yes. Now we can subtract, so let's move the signs up to the numerators. Remember, when we subtract fractions using the stick method, we begin by placing the common denominator (4) on the right side of the equal sign. Then, we move all the sticks in the numerator of the original fraction to the numerator of the new fraction on the right side of the equal sign. Then we can subtract one stick. What is our new fraction? $\frac{2}{4}$. This can be reduced by grouping by twos, making one group over two groups. $\frac{1}{2}$.

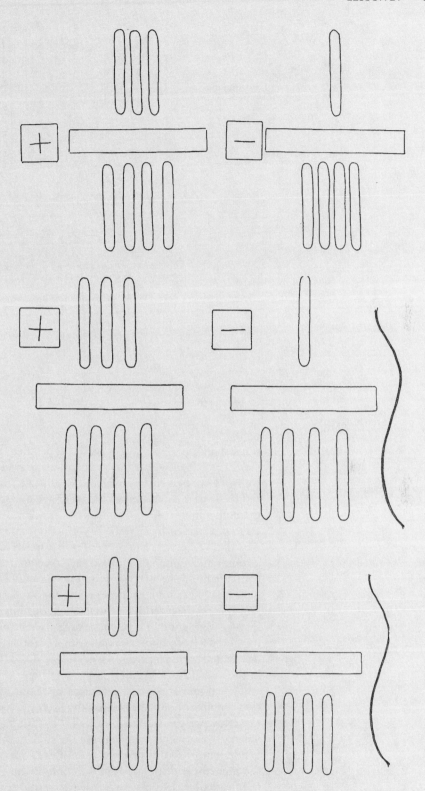

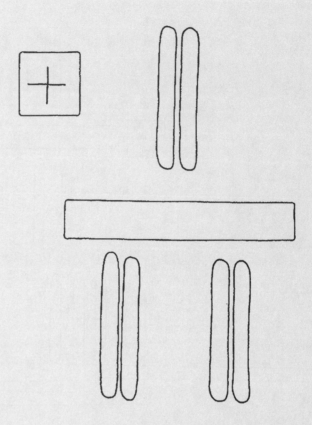

(Problem D: $\frac{2}{3} - \frac{1}{6} =$) Let's read this problem together. Two thirds minus one sixth. We are going to set up this problem using sticks. On the left side of the minus sign, we will have two sticks in the numerator and three sticks in the denominator. On the right side of the minus sign, we will have one stick in the numerator and six sticks in the denominator. At the end of the problem we are going to put an equal sign. We also need to identify that the first fraction is positive, so let's place a plus sign in front of it. Do we have common denominators? No. So before subtracting, we must find a common denominator. To do this, we will use our basic multiplication facts to find common multiples of the original denominator(s). Let's look at the denominators we have now. Let's look at the smallest denominator (3). Is there a way that we can use multiplication to get from three to six, our other denominator? Yes, we can multiply by two. Very good. Three sticks times two groups will be six sticks in the denominator of the first fraction. It is very important to remember that whatever we do to the denominator of a fraction we must also do to the numerator. So, what should we do in the numerator? Multiply by two groups. Good. So, two sticks times two groups will equal four sticks in the numerator of our first fraction. What is our new subtraction problem? Four sixths minus one sixth. Do we have common denominators now? Yes. Now we can subtract, so let's move the signs up to the numerators. Remember, when we subtract fractions using the stick method, we begin by placing the common denominator (6) on the right side of the equal sign. Then, we move all the sticks in the numerator of the original fraction to the numerator of the new fraction on the right side of the equal sign. Now we can subtract one stick from four sticks. What is our new fraction? $\frac{3}{6}$. This can be reduced by grouping by threes to create one group over two groups. $\frac{1}{2}$.

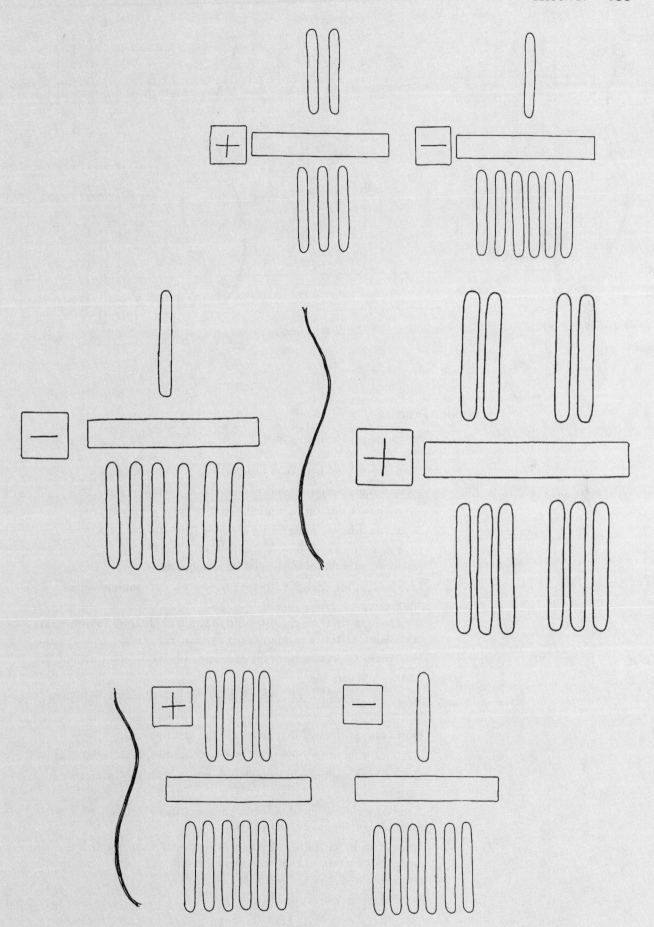

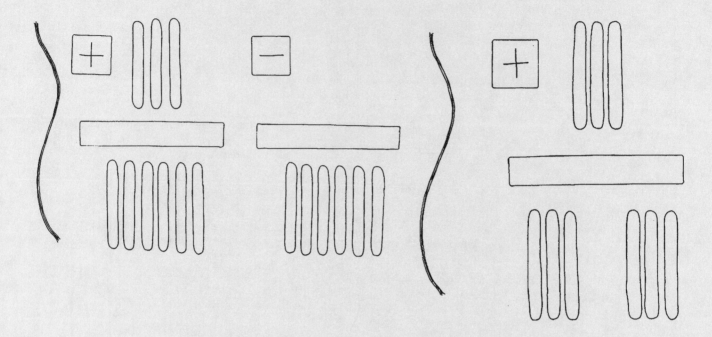

Guided Practice

Let's try some problems together.

(Problem E: $\frac{1}{4} + \frac{1}{8} =$) **Let's read this problem.** One fourth plus one eighth.

Set up this problem using sticks. + one stick/four sticks + one stick/eight sticks =

Do we have common denominators? No.

Before we add, we must find a common denominator.

How do we find the common denominator? Use basic multiplication facts to find common multiples of the original denominator(s).

Let's look at the denominators we have now. Let's look at the smallest denominator (4).

Is there a way that we can use multiplication to get from four to eight, our other denominator? Yes, we can multiply by two. **Very good.**

How many sticks will be in the denominator of this first fraction? 8.

Can we add yet? No.

What else do we need to do? Multiply by two groups in the numerator of the first fraction.

How many sticks will that give us in the first numerator? 2.

What is our new addition problem? Two eighths plus one eighth.

Do we have common denominators now? Yes. **Now we can add. Move the signs up.**

What do we know about the denominator in our new fraction? It will be the same as our common denominator (8).

Now what do we do to add when using the sticks method? Move all the sticks in the numerators of the two original fractions to the numerator of our new fraction.

What is our new fraction? $\frac{3}{8}$.

(Problem F: $\frac{5}{6} - \frac{2}{3} =$) **Let's read this problem.** Five sixths minus two thirds.

Set up this problem using sticks. + five sticks/six sticks − two sticks/three sticks =

Do we have common denominators? No.

Before we subtract, we must find a common denominator.

How do we find the common denominator? Use basic multiplication facts to find common multiples of the original denominator(s).

Let's look at the denominators we have now. Let's look at the smallest denominator (3).

Is there a way that we can use multiplication to get from three to six, our other denominator? Yes, we can multiply by two. Very good.

How many sticks will be in the denominator of this second fraction? 6.

Can we subtract yet? No.

What else do we need to do? Multiply by two groups in the numerator of the second fraction.

How many sticks will that give us in the second numerator? 4.

What is our new subtraction problem? Five sixths minus four sixths.

Do we have common denominators now? Yes. **Now we can subtract. Move the signs up.**

What do we know about the denominator in our new fraction? It will be the same as our common denominator (6).

Now what do we do to subtract when using the sticks method? Move all the sticks in the numerator of the original fraction to the numerator in the new fraction (5).

In this case, how many sticks do we need to subtract? 4.

What is our new fraction? $\frac{1}{6}$.

Word Problem

(Problem G) **Let's look at this scenario.** You borrow $\frac{1}{2}$ cup of milk from your neighbor to add to the $\frac{2}{8}$ cup you already have. If you combine the milk, how much will you have? **We will use concrete materials (sticks) to show our answers.**

To set this up as an addition problem, we will have $\frac{1}{2} + \frac{2}{8}$ **because we are combining the milk.**

Let's read this problem. One half plus two eighths.

Set up this problem using sticks. + one stick/two sticks + two sticks/eight sticks =

Do we have common denominators? No.

Before we add, we must find a common denominator.

How do we find the common denominator? Use basic multiplication facts to find common multiples of the original denominator(s).

Let's look at the denominators we have now. Let's look at the smallest denominator (2).

Is there a way that we can use multiplication to get from two to eight, our other denominator? Yes, we can multiply by four. Very good.

How many sticks will be in the denominator of this first fraction? 8.

Can we add yet? No.

What else do we need to do? Multiply by four groups in the numerator of the first fraction.

How many sticks will that give us in the first numerator? 4.

What is our new addition problem? Four eighths plus two eighths.

Do we have common denominators now? Yes. Now we can add. Move the signs up.

What do we know about the denominator in our new fraction? It will be the same as our common denominator (8).

Now what do we do to add when using the sticks method? Move all the sticks in the numerators of the two original fractions to the numerator of our new fraction.

What is our new fraction? $\frac{6}{8}$.

You will have $\frac{6}{8}$ cup of milk.

Independent Practice

Now you are going to add and subtract some fractions using sticks on your own. Remember to be sure you have common denominators before you add or subtract.

LESSON 28

Adding and Subtracting Fractions with Unlike Denominators 2.R *(representational only)*

Describe/Model

a) $\dfrac{1}{3} + \dfrac{2}{6} =$

b) $\dfrac{2}{3} + \dfrac{1}{2} =$

c) $\dfrac{1}{2} - \dfrac{1}{4} =$

d) $\dfrac{2}{3} - \dfrac{1}{4} =$

Guided Practice

e) $\dfrac{1}{2} + \dfrac{1}{8} =$

f) $\dfrac{4}{5} - \dfrac{1}{2} =$

Word Problem

g) You and your friend are putting up a group of posters in your room. You grab $\frac{1}{3}$ pack of tacks. Your friend already has $\frac{1}{2}$ pack. How much of a pack do you both have? Show your problem solving using pictorial representations.

Independent Practice

h) $\dfrac{1}{4} + \dfrac{1}{8} =$

i) $\dfrac{5}{6} - \dfrac{2}{3} =$

j) $\dfrac{3}{4} - \dfrac{1}{3} =$

k) $\dfrac{3}{2} + \dfrac{1}{3} =$

Teaching **LESSON 28**

Adding and Subtracting Fractions with Unlike Denominators *2.R* *(representational only)*

Describe/Model

Today we are going to continue adding and subtracting fractions. Like yesterday, we are going to have to pay close attention to be sure we have common denominators. Yesterday, we used sticks to work out these problems; today, we will replace the sticks with tally marks. I will work out some for you first and then you will work out some with me. At the end of the lesson, you will have the opportunity to work out some of these addition and subtraction problems on your own.

(Problem A: $\frac{1}{3} + \frac{2}{6} =$) Let's read this problem together. One third plus two sixths. We are going to set up this problem using tallies. On the left side of the plus sign, we will have one tally in the numerator and three tallies in the denominator. On the right side of the plus sign, we will have two tallies in the numerator and six tallies in the denominator. At the end of the problem, we are going to put an equal sign. Because there is no sign before the first fraction, we will write a plus sign. Do we have common denominators? No. So, before we add, we must find a common denominator. To do this, we will use our basic multiplication facts to find common multiples of the original denominator(s). Let's look at the denominators we have now. Let's look at the smallest denominator (3). Is there a way that we can use multiplication to get from three to six, our other denominator? Yes, we can multiply by two. Very good. Three tallies times two groups will be six tallies in the denominator of the first fraction. It is very important to remember that whatever we do to the denominator of a fraction we must also do to the numerator. So, what should we do here in the numerator? Multiply by two groups. Good. So, one tally times two groups will be two tallies in the numerator of our first fraction. What is our new addition problem? Three ninths plus two ninths. Do we have common denominators now? Yes. **Now we can add.** Remember, when we add fractions using the tallies method, we begin by placing the common denominator (6) on the right side of the equal sign. Then, we move all the tallies in both numerators of the original fractions to the numerator of the new fraction on the right side of the equal sign. Now we can count the tallies in the new numerator to find our answer. What is our new fraction? $\frac{4}{6}$.

(Problem B: $\frac{2}{3} + \frac{1}{2} =$) Let's read this problem together. Two thirds plus one half. We are going to set up this problem using tallies. On the left side of the plus sign, we will have two tallies in the numerator and three tallies in the denominator. On the right side of the plus sign, we will have one tally in the numerator and two tallies in the denominator. At the end of the problem, we are going to put an equal sign. Because there is no sign before the first fraction, we will write a plus sign. Do we have common denominators? No. So, before adding, we must find a common denominator. To do this, we will use our basic multiplication facts to find common multiples of the original denominator(s). Let's look at the denominators we have now. Let's look at the smallest denominator (2). Is there a way that we can use multiplication to get from two to three, our other denominator? No. So we must use another method to arrive at common denominators. Let's think of all the multiples of 2 (4, 6, 8, 10, 12 . . .) and all the multiples of 3 (6, 9, 12, 15 . . .). Do two and three have any common multiples? Yes, six. So, we will use six as our common denominator. First, we will change our original problem. How do we get from three to six using multiplication? Multiply by two. So, what must we do to the numerator? Multiply by two groups. What is our new first fraction? $\frac{4}{6}$. Now, let's change our second fraction. How do we use multiplication to get from two to six? Multiply by three groups. So, what must we do to the numerator? Multiply by three groups. What is our new second fraction? $\frac{3}{6}$. What is our new addition problem? Four sixths plus three sixths. Do we now have common denominators? Yes. Now we can add. Remember, when we add fractions using the tally method, we begin by placing the common denominator (6) on the right side of the equal sign. Then, we move all the tallies in both numerators of the original fractions to the numerator of the new fraction on the right side of the equal sign. Now we can count the tallies in the new numerator to find our answer. What is our new fraction? $\frac{7}{6}$.

(Problem C: $\frac{1}{2} - \frac{1}{4} =$) Let's read this problem together. One half minus one fourth. We are going to set up this problem using tallies. On the left side of the minus sign, we will have one tally in the numerator and two tallies in the denominator. On the right side of the minus sign, we will have one tally in the numerator and four tallies in the denominator. At the end of the problem, we are going to put an equal sign. Because there is no sign before the first fraction, we will write a plus sign. Do we have common denominators? No. So, before subtracting, we must find a common denominator. To do this, we will use our basic multiplication facts to find common multiples of the original denominator(s). Let's look at the denominators we have now. Let's look at the smallest denominator (2). Is there a way that we can use multiplication to get from two to four, our other denominator? Yes, we can multiply by two groups. Very good. Two tallies times two groups will be four tallies in the denominator of the first fraction. It is very important to remember that whatever we do to the denominator of a fraction, we must also do to the numerator. So, what should we do in the numerator? Multiply by two groups. Good. So, one tally times two groups will be two tallies in the numerator of our first fraction. What is our new subtraction problem? Two fourths minus one fourth. Do we have common denominators now? Yes. Now we can subtract. Remember, when we subtract fractions using the tallies method, we begin by placing the common denominator (4) on the right side of the equal sign. Then, we move all the tallies in the numerator of the original fraction to the numerator of the new fraction on the right side of the equal sign. Now we will subtract one tally. What is our new fraction? $\frac{1}{4}$.

(Problem D: $\frac{2}{3} - \frac{1}{4} =$) Let's read this problem together. Two thirds minus one fourth. We are going to set up this problem using tallies. On the left side of the minus sign, we will have two tallies in the numerator and three tallies in the denominator. On the right side of the minus sign, we will have one tally in the numerator and four tallies in the denominator. At the end of the problem, we are going to put an equal sign. Because there is no sign before the first fraction, we will write a plus sign. Do we have common denominators? No. So, before subtracting, we must find a common denominator. To do this, we will use our basic multiplication facts to find common multiples of the original denominator(s). Let's look at the denominators we have now. Let's look at the smallest denominator (3). Is there a way that we can use multiplication to get from three to four, our other denominator? No. So, we must use another method to arrive at common denominators. Let's think of all the multiples of four (8, 12, 16, 20 . . .) and all the multiples of 3 (6, 9, 12, 15 . . .). Do four and three have any common multiples? Yes, Twelve. So, we will use twelve as our common denominator. First we will change our original problem. How do we get from three to twelve using multiplication? Multiply by four. So what must we do to the numerator? Multiply by four groups. What is our new first fraction? $\frac{8}{12}$. Now, let's change our second fraction. How do we use multiplication to get from four to twelve? Multiply by three groups. So, what must we do to the numerator? Multiply by three groups. What is our new second fraction? $\frac{3}{12}$. What is our new subtraction problem? Eight twelfths minus three twelfths. Do we have common denominators now? Yes. Now we can subtract. Remember, when we subtract fractions using the tallies method, we begin by placing the common denominator (12) on the right side of the equal sign (12). Then, we move all the tallies in the numerator of the original fraction to the numerator of the new fraction on the right side of the equal sign. Now we will subtract three tallies. What is our new fraction? $\frac{5}{12}$.

a) $+\frac{|}{|||} + \frac{||}{||||} \bigg\} + \frac{|\ |}{||\ |||} + \frac{||}{|||||} \bigg\} + \frac{||}{||||||} \quad \frac{+||}{||||||} \bigg\} + \frac{\cup\cup}{\cup\cup\cup} \bigg\}$

b) $+\frac{||}{|||} + \frac{|}{||} \bigg\} + \frac{||}{|||} + \frac{|\ |}{||\ ||} \bigg\} + \frac{||\ ||}{|||\ |||} + \frac{|\ |\ |}{||\ ||\ ||} \bigg\} + \frac{|||||}{||||||} \quad \frac{+|||}{||||||} \bigg\} + \frac{\cup\cup\cup\cup|}{\cup\cup\cup\cup}$

c) $+\frac{|}{||} - \frac{|}{||||} \bigg\} + \frac{|\ |}{||\ ||} - \frac{|}{||||} \bigg\} + \frac{||}{||||} \quad \frac{-|}{||||} \bigg\} + \frac{|}{||||}$

d) $+\frac{||}{|||} - \frac{|}{||||} \bigg\} + \frac{||\ ||}{|||\ |||} - \frac{|\ |}{|||\ ||||} \bigg\} + \frac{||\ ||\ ||}{|||\ |||\ |||} - \frac{|\ |\ |}{|||\ |||\ |||} \bigg\} + \frac{|||||\text{卅}}{||||||||||} \quad - \frac{\text{卅}}{||||||||||} \bigg\}$

$$+ \frac{|||||}{||||||||||}$$

Guided Practice

Let's try some problems together.

(Problem E: $\frac{1}{2} + \frac{1}{8} =$) **Let's read this problem.** One half plus one eighth.

Set up this problem using tallies. + one tally/two tallies + one tally/eight tallies =

Do we have common denominators? No.

Before we add, we must find a common denominator.

How do we find the common denominator? Use basic multiplication facts to find common multiples of the original denominator(s).

Let's look at the denominators we have now. Let's look at the smallest denominator (2).

Is there a way that we can use multiplication to get from two to eight, our other denominator? Yes, we can multiply by four. **Very good.**

How many sticks will be in the denominator of this first fraction? 8.

Can we add yet? No.

What else do we need to do? Multiply by four groups in the numerator of the first fraction.

How many tallies will that give us in the first numerator? 4.

What is our new addition problem? Four eighths plus one eighth.

Do we have common denominators now? Yes. **Now we can add.**

What do we know about the denominator in our new fraction? It will be the same as our common denominator (8).

Now what do we do to add when using the tallies method? Move all the tallies in the numerators of the two original fractions to the numerator of our new fraction.

What is our new fraction? $\frac{5}{8}$.

(Problem F: $\frac{4}{5} - \frac{1}{2} =$) **Let's read this problem.** Four fifths minus one half.

Now set this problem up using tallies. + four tallies/five tallies − one tally/two tallies =

Do we have common denominators? No.

Before we subtract, we must find a common denominator.

How do we find the common denominator? Use basic multiplication facts to find common multiples of the original denominator(s).

Let's look at the denominators we have now. Let's look at the smallest denominator (2).

Is there a way that we can use multiplication to get from two to five, our other denominator? No.

What must we do from here? Compare the common multiples of five and two.

What are the first five multiples of five? 10, 15, 20, 25, 30.

What are the first five multiples of two? 4, 6, 8, 10, 12.

Are there any common multiples? Yes, 10.

So that will be our common denominator.

We will change the first fraction.

How do we get from five to ten? Multiply by two.

So, what must we do to the numerator? Multiply by two.

What will our numerator be? 8.

Now we will change the second fraction.

How do we get from two to ten? Multiply by five.

So, what must we do to the numerator? Multiply by five.

What is our new numerator? 5.

What is our new subtraction problem? Eight tenths minus five tenths.

Do we have common denominators now? Yes. Now we can subtract.

What do we know about the denominator in our new fraction? It will be the same as our common denominator (10).

Now what do we do to subtract when using the sticks method? Move all the tallies in the numerators of the two original fractions to the numerator in the new fraction.

In this case, how many tallies do we need to subtract? 5.

What is our new fraction? $\frac{3}{10}$.

Word Problem

(Problem G) **Let's look at this scenario.** You and your friend are putting up a group of posters in your room. You grab $\frac{1}{3}$ pack of tacks. Your friend already has $\frac{1}{2}$ pack. **How much of a pack do you both have?** We will use tallies to show our answer.

To set this up as an addition problem, we will have $\frac{1}{3} + \frac{1}{2}$ because we are combining the tacks.

Let's read this problem. One third plus one half.

Set up this problem using tallies. + one tally/three tallies + one tally/two tallies =

Do we have common denominators? No.

Before we add, we must find a common denominator.

How do we find the common denominator? Use basic multiplication facts to find common multiples of the original denominator(s).

Let's look at the denominators we have now. Let's look at the smallest denominator (2).

Is there a way that we can use multiplication to get from two to three, our other denominator? No.

What must we do from here? Compare the common multiples of three and two.

What are the first five multiples of three? 6, 9, 12, 15, 18.

What are the first five multiples of two? 4, 6, 8, 10, 12.

Are there any common multiples? Yes, 6.

That will be our common denominator.

We will change the first fraction.

How do we get from three to six? Multiply by two.

So, what must we do to the numerator? Multiply by two.

What will our numerator be? 2.

Now we will change the second fraction.

How do we get from two to six? Multiply by three.

So, what must we do to the numerator? Multiply by three.

What is our new numerator? 3.

What is our new addition problem? Two sixths plus three sixths.

Do we have common denominators now? Yes. Now we can add.

What do we know about the denominator in our new fraction? It will be the same as our common denominator (6).

Now what do we do to add when using the tallies method? Move all the tallies in the numerators of the two original fractions to the numerator of our new fraction.

What is our new fraction? $\frac{5}{6}$.

So, after combining the tacks there is $\frac{5}{6}$ of a pack.

Independent Practice

Now you are going to add and subtract some fractions using tallies on your own. Remember to be sure you have common denominators before you add or subtract.

LESSON 29

Adding and Subtracting Fractions with Unlike Denominators   *3.A   (abstract only)*

Describe/Model

a) $\dfrac{1}{3} + \dfrac{5}{6} =$

b) $\dfrac{1}{2} - \dfrac{1}{3} =$

Guided Practice

c) $\dfrac{1}{4} - \dfrac{1}{8} =$

d) $\dfrac{2}{5} + \dfrac{1}{3} =$

Word Problem

e) You and a cousin are cleaning. You scrub $\frac{3}{8}$ of the floor and your cousin scrubs $\frac{1}{3}$ of the floor. How much of the floor have you cleaned so far? Show your problem solving using abstract notation.

Independent Practice

f) $\dfrac{3}{8} - \dfrac{1}{3} =$

g) $\dfrac{4}{5} - \dfrac{1}{6} =$

h) $\dfrac{1}{4} + \dfrac{1}{6} =$

i) $\dfrac{2}{4} - \dfrac{3}{6} =$

j) $\dfrac{1}{5} - \dfrac{1}{8} =$

k) $\dfrac{5}{6} + \dfrac{1}{3} =$

Teaching **LESSON 29**

Adding and Subtracting Fractions with Unlike Denominators   3.A *(abstract only)*

Describe/ Model

Today we are going to wrap up adding and subtracting fractions with unlike denominators. For the past couple of days we have been adding and subtracting fractions with unlike denominators using sticks and tallies. Today we will not be using either. We will practice the abstract method. In other words, we will be using our basic facts to solve these problems. I will work out some of these first before you work out some with me. At the end of the lesson, you will add and subtract more fractions on your own using the abstract method.

(Problem A: $\frac{1}{3} + \frac{5}{6} =$) Let's read the problem. One third plus five sixths. Write a plus sign in front of the first fraction because no signs are listed. Remember, before adding or subtracting fractions, we must have a common denominator. Do we have a common denominator? No. So, we must find one before we add. Just as we did with the sticks and tallies methods we are going to look at the smallest denominator first (3). Is there any way that we can use multiplication to get from three to six, our other denominator? Yes, you can multiply by two. Good. So, we will use six as our common denominator. Let's go ahead and change the first fraction. $3 \times 2 = 6$. Always remember that anything we do to the denominator of a fraction we must also do to the numerator. So, what is one times two? 2. Our new first fraction is $\frac{2}{6}$. Let's read our new addition problem. Two sixths plus five sixths. Now that we have common denominators we can add. We know that the denominator in the new fraction will be six so we will write six there. Now we can add the numerators. Two plus five is . . .? Seven. What is our new fraction? $\frac{7}{6}$.

(Problem B: $\frac{1}{2} + \frac{1}{3} =$) Let's read the problem. One half minus one third. Write a plus sign in front of the first fraction because no signs are listed. Remember, before adding or subtracting fractions we must have a common denominator. Do we have a common denominator here? No. So, we must find one before we subtract. Just as we did with the sticks and tallies methods, we are going to look at the smallest denominator first (2). Is there any way that we can use multiplication to get from two to three, our other denominator? No. Good. So, now we have to compare the multiples of two (4, 6, 8, 10) with the multiples of three (6, 9, 12, 15). Are there any common multiples? Yes, 6. So we will use six as our common denominator. We will change the first fraction. How do we get from two to six? Multiply by three. So, what must we do to the numerator? Multiply by three. What is one times three? 3. What is our new first fraction? $\frac{3}{6}$. Now we can change the second fraction. How do we get from three to six? Multiply by two. So, what must we do to the numerator? Multiply by two. One times two is . . .? 2. What is our new second fraction? $\frac{2}{6}$. Let's read our new subtraction problem. Three sixths minus two sixths. Now that we have common denominators we can subtract. We know that the denominator in the new fraction will be six so we will write six there. Now we can subtract the numerators. Three minus two is . . .? One. What is our new fraction? $\frac{1}{6}$.

Guided Practice

Let's try some problems together.

(Problem C: $\frac{1}{4} - \frac{1}{8} =$) Let's read the problem. One fourth minus one eighth.

Do we have a common denominator here? No.

Can we subtract? No.

What should we do first when trying to find a common denominator? Look at the smallest denominator and see if there is any way to get from that number to the larger denominator using multiplication.

Good. Is there a way to get from four to eight using multiplication? Yes, multiply by two.

If we multiply by two in the denominator, what must we do in the numerator? Multiply by two.

What is the new first fraction? $\frac{2}{8}$.

Let's read our new subtraction problem. Two eighths minus one eighth.

Now can we subtract? Yes.

What do we know about the denominator in our answer? It will be eight.

Good. Now subtract the numerators.

What is our new fraction? $\frac{1}{8}$.

So, $\frac{1}{4} - \frac{1}{8}$ is . . .? $\frac{1}{8}$.

(Problem D: $\frac{2}{5} + \frac{1}{3} =$) **Let's read the problem.** Two fifths plus one third.

Do we have a common denominator here? No.

Can we add? No.

What should you do first when trying to find a common denominator? Look at the smallest denominator and see if there is any way to get from that number to the larger denominator using multiplication.

Good. Is there a way to get from three to five using multiplication? No.

What should we do from here? Compare the multiples of five and three.

What are the first four multiples of five? 10, 15, 20, 25.

What are the first four multiples of three? 6, 9, 12, 15.

Are there any common multiples? Yes, 15.

So, what is our common denominator? 15. Good.

Take a minute to change the first fraction. What did you get? $\frac{6}{15}$.

Take a minute to change the second fraction. What did you get? $\frac{5}{15}$.

What is our new addition problem? Six fifteenths plus five fifteenths.

Now can we add? Yes.

What do we know about the denominator in our answer? It will be fifteen.

Good. Now add the numerators.

What is our new fraction? $\frac{11}{15}$.

So, $\frac{2}{5} + \frac{1}{3}$ is . . .? $\frac{11}{15}$.

Word Problem

(Problem E) **Let's look at this scenario.** You and a cousin are cleaning. You scrub $\frac{3}{8}$ of the floor and your cousin scrubs $\frac{1}{3}$ of the floor. How much of the floor have you cleaned so far? We will show our work using the abstract method.
To set this up as an addition problem we would have $\frac{3}{8} + \frac{1}{3}$.
Let's read the problem. Three eighths plus one third.

Do we have a common denominator? No.

Can we add? No.

What should we do first when trying to find a common denominator? Look at the smallest denominator and see if there is any way to get from that number to the larger denominator using multiplication.

Good. Is there a way to get from three to eight using multiplication? No.

What should we do from here? Compare the multiples of eight and three.

What are the first seven multiples of eight? 16, 24, 32, 40, 48, 56, 64.

What are the first seven multiples of three? 6, 9, 12, 15, 18, 21, 24.

Are there any common multiples? Yes, 24.

So, what is our common denominator? 24. Good.

Take a minute to change the first fraction. What did you get? $\frac{9}{24}$.

Take a minute to change the second fraction. What did you get? $\frac{8}{24}$.

Let's read our new addition problem. Nine twenty fourths plus eight twenty fourths.

Now can we add? Yes.

What do we know about the denominator in our answer? It will be twenty four.

Good. Now add the numerators.

What is our new fraction? $\frac{17}{24}$.

So, $\frac{3}{8} + \frac{1}{3}$ is . . .? $\frac{17}{24}$.

$\frac{17}{24}$ of the floor has been cleaned so far.

Independent Practice

Now you are going to add and subtract some fractions using this method on your own. Remember to make sure that you have a common denominator before you add or subtract.

LESSON 30

Adding and Subtracting Fractions with Unlike Denominators   *4.A (generalized)*

Describe/Model

a) $2\dfrac{1}{3} + \dfrac{2}{6} =$

b) $\dfrac{1}{2} - \dfrac{1}{4} =$

Guided Practice

c) $3\dfrac{1}{5} + \dfrac{2}{10} =$

d) $\dfrac{2}{3} - 1\dfrac{1}{3} =$

Word Problem

e) A manager is determining how much of her motel is full. She had it $\dfrac{3}{4}$ filled last night but $\dfrac{1}{5}$ of that group left today. How much of the motel is now full?

Independent Practice

f) $\dfrac{1}{2} + \dfrac{1}{8} =$

g) $2\dfrac{1}{3} - \dfrac{1}{2} =$

h) $3\dfrac{1}{8} + \dfrac{1}{2} =$

i) $\dfrac{2}{3} - \dfrac{5}{6} =$

j) $\dfrac{5}{4} - 1\dfrac{1}{6} =$

k) $\dfrac{3}{2} + \dfrac{1}{3} =$

Note: To review adding and subtracting fractions with unlike denominations, see Cumulative Review G starting on page 157.

Cumulative Review
Problem Sets A-G

 ### CUMULATIVE REVIEW A: DIVISION WITH
FRACTIONAL ANSWERS/MIXED NUMBERS

After Lesson 7—solve each problem with your partner using abstract notation (numbers only). Make sure to explain each step to your partner and do not move to the next problem until both you and your partner can explain the answer.

Peer-Tutoring Directions and Prompts:

Tutor: *The purpose of this lesson is to practice division with fractional answers and mixed numbers. We have already learned about this. This lesson will help us not to forget.*
   If necessary, use these prompts to help your group solve the problems in Set A.

Prompt 1	*How do you read this problem?*
Prompt 2	*What's another way to read this problem?*
Prompt 3	*How many groups are we working with?*
Prompt 4	*What do we need to do first?*
Prompt 5	*How many times does the denominator go into the numerator evenly?*
Prompt 6	*How many are left over?*
Prompt 7	*Remember to write your answer.*

Note to teacher: You may provide more specific detail in the prompts above if necessary, depending on the level of your students.

 ### SET A: DIVISION WITH FRACTIONAL ANSWERS/MIXED NUMBERS

Solve each problem using appropriate terms.

a) $\dfrac{18}{4}$ b) $\dfrac{17}{4}$

c) $\dfrac{6 \text{ pens}}{4 \text{ persons}}$ d) $\dfrac{8 \text{ dollars}}{3 \text{ candies}}$

e) $\dfrac{9 \text{ sticks}}{3 \text{ groups}}$ f) $\dfrac{15 \text{ tallies}}{6 \text{ groups}}$

g) At lunch, 20 glasses of tea were given to 6 people. How many glasses per person were given? Use abstract notation to set up and answer the problem. Show all your work.

h) $\dfrac{9 \text{ sticks}}{4 \text{ sticks}}$ i) $\dfrac{3 \text{ sticks}}{9 \text{ sticks}}$

j) For helping build a wheelchair ramp, a family paid three high school students $25. If each student earned the same amount, how much would each person receive? Use abstract notation to set up and answer the problem. Show all your work.

 ### CUMULATIVE REVIEW B: MULTIPLICATION OF FRACTIONS

After Lesson 10—solve each problem with your partner using abstract notation (numbers only). Make sure to explain each step to your partner and do not move to the next problem until both you and your partner can explain the answer. Use the prompts provided if your partner gets stuck.

Peer-Tutoring Directions and Prompts:

Tutor: *The purpose of this lesson is to practice multiplication of fractions. We have already learned about this. This lesson will help us not to forget.*
  If necessary, use these prompts to help your group solve the problems in Set B, problems a–g.

Prompt 1 *How do you read this problem?*
Prompt 2 *What's another way to read this problem?*
Prompt 3 *How many groups are we working with?*
Prompt 4 *What do we need to do first?*
Prompt 5 *How many times does the denominator go into the numerator evenly?*
Prompt 6 *How many are left over?*
Prompt 7 *Remember to write your answer.*

Use these prompts for problems h–j.

Prompt 1 *How do you read this problem?*
Prompt 2 *Let's write this as a multiplication problem.*
Prompt 3 *What should we multiply first?*
Prompt 4 *What do we need to do first?*
Prompt 5 *Where do we write that number?*
Prompt 6 *What do we do next?*
Prompt 7 *Where do we write that number?*
Prompt 8 *Let's read our fraction.*

 ### SET B: MULTIPLICATION OF FRACTIONS

Solve each problem using appropriate terms.

a) $\dfrac{2 \text{ sticks}}{6 \text{ cups}}$ b) $\dfrac{16 \text{ dollars}}{9 \text{ sodas}}$

c) $\dfrac{14 \text{ rabbits}}{3 \text{ cabbages}}$ d) $\dfrac{7 \text{ rooms}}{3 \text{ people}}$

e) $\dfrac{15 \text{ pounds}}{4 \text{ inches}}$ f) $\dfrac{19 \text{ tallies}}{4 \text{ groups}}$

g) Five hamsters were sharing dinner. They had 18 pellets of food. If each hamster ate the same amount of food, how many pellets would each eat? Use abstract notation to set up and answer the problem. Show all your work.

h) A young woman has $\frac{3}{2}$ cup of mix to make biscuits. She only wants to use $\frac{1}{3}$ of the mix. How much mix will she use? Use abstract notation to set up and answer the problem. Show all your work.

i) $\left(\dfrac{1}{3}\right)$ cups of $\left(\dfrac{1}{4}\right)$ sticks   j) $\left(\dfrac{2}{3}\right)\left(\dfrac{3}{4}\right)$

CUMULATIVE REVIEW C: DIVISION OF FRACTIONS

After Lesson 14—solve each problem with your partner using abstract notation (numbers only). Make sure to explain each step to your partner and do not move to the next problem until both you and your partner can explain the answer. Use the prompts provided if your partner gets stuck.

Peer-Tutoring Directions and Prompts:

Tutor: *The purpose of this lesson is to practice division of fractions. We have already learned about this. This lesson will help us not to forget.*

Students should no longer need prompts for Set C, problems a–c. If they are still struggling, reteach Lessons 2 and 3.

Use these prompts for problem d.

Prompt 1	*How do you read this problem?*
Prompt 2	*Let's write this as a multiplication problem.*
Prompt 3	*What should we multiply first?*
Prompt 4	*What do we need to do first?*
Prompt 5	*Where do we write that number?*
Prompt 6	*What do we do next?*
Prompt 7	*Where do we write that number?*
Prompt 8	*Let's read our fraction.*

Use these prompts for problems e–i.

Prompt 1	*How do you read this problem?*
Prompt 2	*What kind of problem is this?*
Prompt 3	*What should we do first?*
Prompt 4	*What do we need to do second?*
Prompt 5	*What do we need to do third?*
Prompt 6	*What do we need to do fourth?*
Prompt 7	*Do we have a fraction that represents 1?*
Prompt 8	*Let's write and read our answer.*

SET C: DIVISION OF FRACTIONS

Solve each problem using appropriate terms.

a) A grandfather gave 10 cookies to his 3 grandchildren to split up evenly. How many cookies will each child receive? Use abstract notation to set up and answer the problem. Show all your work.

b) $\dfrac{12 \text{ quarters}}{4 \text{ teeth}}$ c) $\dfrac{30}{7}$

d) While making lemonade for friends, a young boy combines a mix with water. The recipe will make $\frac{5}{2}$ cups of lemonade, but he only wants to make $\frac{1}{3}$ of that amount. How much lemonade will he have? Use abstract notation to set up and answer the problem. Show all your work.

e) $\left(\dfrac{1}{4}\right)\left(\dfrac{3}{1}\right)\left(\dfrac{2}{5}\right)$ f) $\left(\dfrac{3}{4}\right)\left(\dfrac{6}{7}\right)$

g) $\left(\dfrac{2}{3}\right) \div \left(\dfrac{1}{5}\right)$ h) $\left(\dfrac{4}{1}\right) \text{ slices} \div \left(\dfrac{1}{2}\right)$

i) $\frac{3}{2}$ cups of water were divided into $\frac{1}{2}$-cup sets for watering plants. How many plants will be watered with the equal sets of water? Use abstract notation to set up and answer the problem. Show all your work.

 CUMULATIVE REVIEW D: FINDING EQUIVALENT FRACTIONS

After Lesson 18—solve each problem with your partner using abstract notation (numbers only). Make sure to explain each step to your partner and do not move to the next problem until both you and your partner can explain the answer. Use the prompts provided if your partner gets stuck.

Peer-Tutoring Directions and Prompts:

Tutor: *The purpose of this lesson is to practice finding equivalent fractions. We have already learned about this. This lesson will help us not to forget.*

Students should no longer need prompts for Set D, problems a–b. If they are still struggling, reteach Lessons 2 and 3.

Use these prompts for problems c–h.

Prompt 1   *How do you read this problem?*
Prompt 2   *Let's write this as a multiplication problem.*
Prompt 3   *What should we multiply first?*
Prompt 4   *What do we need to do first?*
Prompt 5   *Where do we write that number?*
Prompt 6   *What do we do next?*
Prompt 7   *Where do we write that number?*
Prompt 8   *Let's read our fraction.*

Use these prompts for problems i–l.

Prompt 1   *What is the fraction?*
Prompt 2   *How many groups of one do we need in the numerator?*
Prompt 3   *How many groups of one do we need in the denominator?*

Prompt 4   *What is the size of this group?*

Prompt 5   *What is our denominator?*

Prompt 6   *Can you read the new fraction?*

Prompt 7   *What is our new fraction also equal to?*

Note: Continue with prompts 2–6 as necessary to form other equivalent fractions.

SET D: FINDING EQUIVALENT FRACTIONS

Solve each problem using appropriate terms.

a) $\dfrac{23 \text{ computers}}{4 \text{ classroom}}$ b) $\dfrac{14 \text{ miles}}{5 \text{ hour}}$

c)   Five friends are sharing lunch. They can afford 12 chicken sandwiches to be split evenly between them. If each person eats the same amount, how many sandwiches will each person eat? Use abstract notation to set up and answer the problem. Show all your work.

d) $\left(\dfrac{3}{2}\right)$ bowls $\left(\dfrac{2}{3}\right)$ filled   e) $\left(\dfrac{2}{5}\right)\left(\dfrac{7}{3}\right)$

f)   Your mom tells you to share the ice cream with your three sisters. The four of you have to split the $\frac{5}{3}$ cups of ice cream equally. Use abstract notation to set up and answer the problem. Show all your work.

g) $\left(\dfrac{2}{3}\right)$ crate $\div \left(\dfrac{1}{4}\right)$ per customer   h) $\left(\dfrac{4}{1}\right) \div \left(\dfrac{1}{2}\right)$

i) $\dfrac{2}{7} = \underline{\quad} = \underline{\quad} = \underline{\quad} = \underline{\quad}$

j)   What was multiplied in the numerator and denominator to find the last equivalent fraction?

k) $\dfrac{3}{8} = \underline{\quad} = \underline{\quad} = \underline{\quad}$

l)   What was multiplied in the numerator and denominator to find the last equivalent fraction?

CUMULATIVE REVIEW E: REDUCING AND COMPARING FRACTIONS

After Lesson 22—solve each problem with your partner using abstract notation (numbers only). Make sure to explain each step to your partner and do not move to the next problem until both you and your partner can explain the answer. Use the prompts provided if your partner gets stuck.

Peer-Tutoring Directions and Prompts:

Tutor: *The purpose of this lesson is to practice finding equivalent fractions. We have already learned about this. This lesson will help us not to forget.*

Students should no longer need prompts for Set E, problems a–c. If they are still struggling, reteach Lessons 2 and 3.

Students should no longer need prompts for problems d–h. If they continue to need instructional support, consider reteaching, starting with Lesson 8.

Use these prompts for problems i–k.

Prompt 1   *What is the fraction we want to reduce?*

Prompt 2   *Which number is the numerator?*

Prompt 3   *Which number is the denominator?*

Prompt 4   *How many times can we group the numerator into the denominator evenly?*

Prompt 5   *If you can't, can you reduce the fraction?*

Prompt 6   *If you can, how many times can you group the numerator into the denominator?*

Prompt 7   *Can we divide any more groups into the denominator?*

Prompt 8   *Read your answer.*

SET E: REDUCING AND COMPARING FRACTIONS

Solve each problem using appropriate terms.

a) $\dfrac{18}{5}$

b) $\dfrac{38 \text{ feet}}{7 \text{ people}}$

c) Nine middle school students were tutoring 20 elementary school students. How many elementary school students per middle school student were being tutored?

Use abstract notation to set up and answer the problem. Show all your work.

d) $\left(\dfrac{5}{6}\right)$ apple trees $\left(\dfrac{1}{2}\right)$ filled

e) $\left(\dfrac{2}{4}\right)\left(\dfrac{1}{5}\right)$

f) $\left(\dfrac{2}{3}\right) \div \left(\dfrac{1}{3}\right)$

g) $\left(\dfrac{4}{5}\right)$ cup $\div$ (4) people

h) You want to climb $\frac{2}{3}$ of the way to the top of a large tower. After you start climbing, you realize that you have climbed $\frac{10}{15}$ flights of stairs. Did you climb $\frac{2}{3}$ of the way yet? Use equivalent fractions to find the answer. Show your problem solving using concrete materials.

Reduce these fractions to their simplest forms.

i) $\dfrac{4}{32} = $ ____

j) $\dfrac{9}{36} = $ ____

k) What did you divide by in the numerator and denominator of i and j?

CUMULATIVE REVIEW F: ADDING AND SUBTRACTING FRACTIONS WITH LIKE DENOMINATORS

After Lesson 26—solve each problem with your partner using abstract notation (numbers only). Make sure to explain each step to your partner and do not move to the next problem until both you and your partner can explain the answer. Use the prompts provided if your partner gets stuck.

Peer-Tutoring Directions and Prompts:

Tutor: *The purpose of this lesson is to practice adding and subtracting fractions with like denominators. We have already learned about this. This lesson will help us not to forget.*

Students should no longer need prompts for Set F, problems a–h.

Use these prompts for problems i–j.

Prompt 1   *What is the fraction we want to reduce?*

Prompt 2   *Which number is the numerator?*

Prompt 3   *Which number is the denominator?*

Prompt 4   *How many times can we group the numerator into the denominator evenly?*

Prompt 5   *If you can't, can you reduce the fraction?*

Prompt 6   *If you can, how many times can you group the numerator into the denominator?*

Prompt 7   *Can we divide any more groups into the denominator?*

Prompt 8   *Read your answer.*

Use these prompts for problem k.

Prompt 1   *Can you read the problem?*

Prompt 2   *Are we going to have to add or subtract?*

Prompt 3   *What does that tell us about our denominator?*

Prompt 4   *What numbers do we add or subtract?*

Prompt 5   *Do we have common denominators?*

Prompt 6   *Can you write the addition or subtraction problem?*

Prompt 7   *Now can we add or subtract?*

Prompt 8   *Read your answer.*

 ## SET F: ADDING AND SUBTRACTING FRACTIONS WITH LIKE DENOMINATORS

Solve each problem using appropriate terms.

a) $\dfrac{14 \text{ sticks}}{3 \text{ piles}}$ b) $\dfrac{30 \text{ books}}{8 \text{ children}}$

c) A student was asked to run $\frac{7}{2}$ times around the track. Instead, he only made it $\frac{1}{3}$ of that distance. How many times around did he make it? Use abstract notation to set up and answer the problem. Show all your work.

d) $\left(\dfrac{4}{3}\right) \div \left(\dfrac{1}{3}\right)$ e) $\left(\dfrac{2}{7}\right)$ candy bar $\div \left(\dfrac{2}{3}\right)$ pieces

f) Your friend says that a mix calls for $\frac{1}{2}$ cup of sugar. Using tablespoons, you have already poured $\frac{7}{16}$. Are these the same or different? Use equivalent fractions to find if $\frac{1}{2}$ is the same as $\frac{7}{16}$. If not, which one is larger? Use abstract notation to set up and answer the problem. Show all your work.

g) $\dfrac{2}{5} = $ ____ $ = $ ____ $ = $ ____

h) What was multiplied in the numerator and denominator to find the last equivalent fraction?

Reduce these fractions to their simplest forms.

i) $\dfrac{8}{6} = $ ____   j) $\dfrac{4}{10} = $ ____

k) What did you divide by in the numerator and denominator for i) and j)?

l) You bought $\frac{1}{6}$ dozen pies for a party. Your friend brings another $\frac{3}{6}$ dozen pies. How many dozen pies are there for the party? Show your problem solving using pictorial representations.

CUMULATIVE REVIEW G: ADDING AND SUBTRACTING FRACTIONS WITH UNLIKE DENOMINATORS

After Lesson 30—solve each problem with your partner using abstract notation (numbers only). Make sure to explain each step to your partner and do not move to the next problem until both you and your partner can explain the answer. Use the prompts provided if your partner gets stuck.

Peer-Tutoring Directions and Prompts:

Tutor: *The purpose of this lesson is to practice adding and subtracting fractions with unlike denominators. We have already learned about this. This lesson will help us not to forget.*
   Students should no longer need prompts for Set G, problems a–d.

Use these prompts for problems e–k.

Prompt 1   *Can you read the problem?*

Prompt 2   *Are we going to have to add or subtract?*

Prompt 3   *What does that tell us about our denominator?*

Prompt 4   *Do we have common denominators?*

Prompt 5   *If we don't have common denominators, what must we do?*

Prompt 6   *Let's write the addition or subtraction problem.*

Prompt 7   *What do we do first when trying to find a common denominator?*

Prompt 8   *What do we have to multiply the numerator by?*

Prompt 9   *What do we have to multiply the denominator by?*

Prompt 10   *What is the new fraction?*

Prompt 11   *Let's read our new addition or subtraction problem.*

Prompt 12   *Great! Now we can add or subtract because we have common denominators.*

Prompt 13   *What is our new fraction?*

SET G: ADDING AND SUBTRACTING FRACTIONS WITH UNLIKE DENOMINATORS

Solve each problem using appropriate terms.

a) Seven people were dividing cleaning duties. There were 18 duties altogether that were to be split between them. If each person were to complete the same amount, how many would each person complete? Use abstract computation to explain your answer.

b) (2)crates $\left(\frac{6}{7}\right)$packets $\left(\frac{1}{4}\right)$blocks   c) $\left(\frac{5}{3}\right) \div \left(\frac{8}{5}\right)$

d) Harold wants to buy $\frac{1}{3}$ set of playing cards. Instead, the store owner gives him carton. Which one is larger? How do you know? Use abstract computation to explain your answer.

e) $\dfrac{2}{3} - \dfrac{1}{3} =$

f) $\dfrac{5}{4}$ family $- \dfrac{3}{4}$ family $=$

g) $\dfrac{1}{4} - \dfrac{1}{8} =$

h) $\dfrac{2}{5}$ price $+ \dfrac{1}{3}$ price $=$

i) You borrow $\frac{2}{3}$ cup flour from your neighbor to add to the $\frac{6}{9}$ cup you already have. If you combine the flour, how much will you have? Show your problem solving using abstract notation.

j) $1\dfrac{2}{3} + \dfrac{1}{6} =$

k) $\dfrac{7}{3} - \dfrac{4}{5} =$

Posttest

Division with Fractional Answers

a) $\dfrac{9}{3}$

b) $\dfrac{7}{2}$

c) $\dfrac{23}{7}$

d) $\dfrac{12}{5}$

Multiplication of Fractions

e) $\left(\dfrac{2}{3}\right)\left(\dfrac{1}{5}\right)$

f) $\left(\dfrac{3}{2}\right)\left(\dfrac{5}{3}\right)$

Division of Fractions

g) $\left(\dfrac{1}{2}\right) \div \left(\dfrac{1}{4}\right)$

h) $\left(\dfrac{4}{5}\right) \div \left(\dfrac{1}{8}\right)$

Finding Equivalent Fractions

i) $\dfrac{2}{7} = $ _____ $= $ _____ $= $ _____

j) What was multiplied in the numerator and denominator to find the last equivalent fraction?

k) $\dfrac{1}{4} = $ _____ $= $ _____ $= $ _____ $= $ _____

l) What was multiplied in the numerator and denominator to find the last equivalent fraction?

Reducing and Comparing Fractions

m) $\dfrac{6}{24} = $ _____

n) What was divided equally in the numerator and denominator to find the fraction in its simplest form?

o) $\dfrac{4}{12} = $ _____

p) What was divided equally in the numerator and denominator to find the fraction in its simplest form?

Adding and Subtracting Fractions with Like Denominators

q) $\dfrac{1}{4} + \dfrac{2}{4} = $

r) $\dfrac{3}{5} + \dfrac{1}{5} = $

Adding and Subtracting Fractions with Unlike Denominators

s) $\dfrac{3}{4} + \dfrac{1}{12} = $

t) $\dfrac{1}{3} + \dfrac{2}{4} = $

Answer Key

PRETEST ASSESSMENT

Division with Fractional Answers

a) 2

b) $1\frac{2}{3}$

c) 7

d) $2\frac{1}{5}$

Multiplication of Fractions

e) $\frac{2}{3}$

f) $\frac{1}{4}$

Division of Fractions

g) $\frac{12}{1}$, or 12

h) $\frac{3}{2}$, or $1\frac{1}{2}$

Finding Equivalent Fractions

i) $\frac{3}{9} = \frac{4}{12}$

j) $\frac{4}{4}$

k) $\frac{9}{12} = \frac{12}{16}$

l) $\frac{4}{4}$

Reducing and Comparing Fractions

m) $\frac{2}{3}$

n) 4

o) $\frac{1}{3}$

p) 3

Adding and Subtracting Fractions with Like Denominators

q) $\frac{2}{3}$

r) $\frac{4}{4}$, or 1

Adding and Subtracting Fractions with Unlike Denominators

s) $\frac{5}{9}$

t) $\frac{7}{8}$

LESSON 1

a) 2 sticks per cup
Place 2 sticks each in 2 cups.

b) 1 stick/cup and 2 sticks/3 cups
Place 1 stick each per cup, with two sticks left over.

c) 3 sticks/4 cups
No sticks can be evenly divided into each cup.

d) 1 stick/cup and 2 sticks/4 cups
Place 1 stick each per cup, with 2 sticks left over.

e) 1 stick per cup
Place 1 stick per cup. There are no sticks left over.

f) 4 sticks per cup and 1 stick/2 cups
Place 4 sticks in each of the two cups, with one stick left over.

g) 10 dollars/4 children = 2 dollars per child and 2 dollars/4 children
Use 10 sticks for the dollars and 4 cups for the children.
Split 2 sticks evenly per 4 cups, with 2 dollars left over.

h) 1 stick per cup and 1 stick/3 cups
Place 1 stick per cup, with 1 stick left over.

i) 2 sticks per cup and 1 stick/3 cups
Place 2 sticks per cup, with 1 stick left over.

j) 2 sticks per cup
Place 2 sticks per cup, with no sticks left over.

k) 3 sticks per cup
Place 3 sticks in 1 cup.

 ## LESSON 2

a) 3 tallies per group
Split up the 12 tallies evenly between the 4 groups.

b) $2\frac{2}{3}$ tallies per group
Split up the 8 tallies evenly between the 3 groups so that 2 go into each group and 2 are left out.

c) $2\frac{3}{5}$ tallies per group
Each group should have 2 tallies, with 3 left out.

d) $7\frac{1}{2}$ tallies per group
Each group should have 7 tallies and 1 left out.

e) 1 tally per group
Each group should have 1 tally.

f) $4\frac{3}{4}$ tallies per group
Each group should have 4 tallies, with 3 left out.

g) $2\frac{2}{3}$ scoops per dog
Tallies could be used to represent scoops of food, and groups are used to represent the dogs. Each group should have 2 tallies, with 2 tallies left out.

h) 3 tallies per group
Each group should have 3 tallies.

i) 6 tallies per group
The 1 group should have all 6 tallies.

j) $3\frac{2}{3}$ tallies per group
Each group should have 3 tallies, with 2 tallies left out.

k) $3\frac{3}{5}$ tallies per group
Each group should have 3 tallies, with 3 tallies left out.

LESSON 3

a) $5\frac{3}{4}$

Twenty distributes evenly into four, with three left over that could not be evenly divided by four.

b) $2\frac{4}{5}$

Ten distributes evenly into five, with four left over that could not be evenly distributed into five.

c) $5\frac{2}{6}$, or $5\frac{1}{3}$

Thirty distributes evenly into six, with two left over that did not divide evenly into six.

d) $5\frac{2}{3}$

Fifteen distributes evenly into three, with two left over that did not divide evenly into three.

e) 4 or $\frac{4}{1}$

Sixteen distributes evenly into four.

f) $7\frac{4}{8}$ or $7\frac{1}{2}$

Fifty six distributes evenly into eight, with four left over that did not divide evenly into eight.

g) $3\frac{3}{5}$ slices per player; the fraction means that all the slices could not be divided evenly without cutting each left over slice into 5 slices.

Fifteen distributes evenly into five, with three slices that could not be distributed evenly between the five players.

h) $2\frac{5}{7}$

Fourteen distributes evenly into the seven, with five more that did not distribute into seven.

i) $6\frac{1}{9}$

Fifty four distributes evenly into nine, with one more left over that did not distribute evenly into nine.

j) $\frac{6}{1}$ or 6

Forty eight distributes evenly into eight.

k) $5\frac{1}{4}$

Twenty distributes evenly into four, with one left over that did not distribute evenly into four.

LESSON 4 (CALCULATORS WITHOUT FRACTION FUNCTIONS ARE ALLOWED)

a) 15 r.5, or $15\frac{5}{12}$

180 distributes evenly into 12, with 5 left over that did not distribute evenly into 12.

b) 7 r.2, or $7\frac{2}{9}$

63 distributes evenly into 9, with 2 left over that did not distribute evenly into 9.

c) 7 r.8, or $7\frac{8}{11}$

77 distributes evenly into 11, with 8 left over that did not distribute evenly into 11.

d) 4 r.22, or $4\frac{22}{25}$

100 distributes evenly into 25, with 22 left over that did not distribute evenly into 25.

e) 16 r.4, or $16\frac{4}{5}$, or 16 complete cars
80 cars distributes evenly across the 5 people, with 4 cars that did not distribute evenly across the 5.

f) 7 r.7, or $7\frac{7}{10}$
70 distributes evenly into 10, with 7 left over that did not distribute evenly into 10.

g) 7 r.4, or $7\frac{4}{7}$
49 distributes evenly into 7, with 4 left over that did not distribute evenly into 7.

h) 4 r.8, or $4\frac{8}{33}$
132 distributes evenly into 33, with 8 left over that did not distribute evenly into 33.

i) 4 r.14, or $4\frac{14}{21}$, or $4\frac{2}{3}$
84 distributes evenly into 21, with 14 left over that did not distribute evenly into 21.

 LESSON 5

a) 7 sticks/stick, or 7
7 sets of 2 sticks over 1 set of 2 sticks.

b) $2\frac{1}{5}$
2 sets of 5 over 1 set of 5, with 1 incomplete set of 1 stick over the 5 needed.

c) $2\frac{1}{6}$
2 sets of 6 over 1 set of 6, with 1 incomplete set of 1 stick over the 6 needed.

d) $\frac{1}{2}$
1 set of 4 over 2 sets of 4.

e) $2\frac{1}{4}$
2 sets of 4 over 1 set of 4, with 1 incomplete set of 1 stick over the 4 needed.

f) $\frac{1}{3}$
1 set of 3 over 3 sets of 3.

g) $1\frac{3}{4}$; the fraction means that 3 hamburgers need to be cut into fourths and three parts given to each friend.
1 set of 4 over 1 set of 4, with 1 incomplete set of 3 sticks over the 4 needed.

h) $2\frac{2}{3}$
2 sets of 3 over 1 set of 3, with 1 incomplete set of 2 sticks over the 3 needed.

i) $2\frac{1}{2}$
2 sets of 2 over 1 set of 2, with 1 incomplete set of 1 stick over the 2 needed.

j) $\frac{4}{1}$, or 4
4 sets of 3 over 1 set of 3.

k) $2\frac{3}{5}$
2 sets of 5 over 1 set of 5, with 1 incomplete set of 3 sticks over the 5 needed.

 LESSON 6

a) $3\frac{3}{4}$
3 sets of 4 over 1 set of 4, with 1 incomplete set of 3 sticks over the 4 needed.

b) $\frac{1}{2}$
1 set of 7 over 2 sets of 7.

c) $2\frac{5}{6}$
2 sets of 6 over 1 set of 6, with 1 incomplete set of 5 sticks over the 6 needed.

d) $\frac{2}{1}$, or 2
2 sets of 4 over 1 set of 4.

e) $\frac{3}{1}$, or 3
3 sets of 3 over 1 set of 3.

f) $2\frac{2}{6}$, or $2\frac{1}{3}$
2 sets of 6 over 1 set of 6, with 1 incomplete set of 2 sticks over the 6 needed.

g) $6\frac{2}{3}$ dollars per boy
6 sets of 3 over 1 set of 3, with 1 incomplete set of 2 sticks over the 3 needed.

h) Not a full dollar, about 67 cents.

i) $2\frac{4}{7}$
2 sets of 7 over 1 set of 7, with 1 incomplete set of 4 sticks over the 7 needed.

j) $1\frac{6}{9}$, or $1\frac{2}{3}$
1 set of 9 over 1 set of 9, with 1 incomplete set of 6 sticks over the 9 needed.

k) $\frac{2}{5}$
2 sets of 2 over 5 sets of 2.

l) $\frac{2}{1}$, or 2
2 sets of 5 over 1 set of 5.

 ## LESSON 7

a) $3\frac{1}{3}$
3 sets of 3 over 1 set of 3, with 1 incomplete set of 1 stick over the 3 needed.

b) $\frac{1}{3}$
1 set of 5 over 3 sets of 5.

c) $3\frac{1}{4}$
3 sets of 4 over 1 set of 4, with 1 incomplete set of 1 stick over the 4 needed.

d) $\frac{3}{1}$ or 3
3 sets of 4 over 1 set of 4.

e) $4\frac{1}{5}$
4 sets of 5 over 1 set of 5, with 1 incomplete set of 1 stick over the 5 needed.

f) $4\frac{1}{4}$
4 sets of 4 over 1 set of 4, with 1 incomplete set of 1 stick over the 4 needed.

g) $2\frac{2}{5}$ dollars per girl
2 sets of 5 over 1 set of 5, with 1 incomplete set of 2 sticks over the 5 needed.

h) Not a full dollar, 40 cents.

i) $4\frac{1}{6}$
4 sets of 6 over 1 set of 6, with 1 incomplete set of 1 stick over the 6 needed.

j) $3\frac{1}{7}$
3 sets of 7 over 1 set of 7, with 1 incomplete set of 1 stick over the 7 needed.

k) $3\frac{1}{10}$
3 sets of 10 over 1 set of 10, with 1 incomplete set of 1 stick over the 10 needed.

l) $3\frac{1}{5}$
3 sets of 5 over 1 set of 5, with 1 incomplete set of 1 stick over the 5 needed.

LESSON 8

a) $\frac{2}{3}$
2 cups of 1 stick over 1 cup of 3 sticks totals 2 sticks over 3 sticks.

b) $\frac{3}{12}$, or $\frac{1}{4}$
1 cup of 3 sticks over 3 cups of 4 sticks totals 3 sticks over 12 sticks. When grouped into sets of 3 sticks, the answer is simplified to 1 set of sticks over 4 sets of sticks.

c) $\frac{5}{4}$, or $1\frac{1}{4}$
1 cup of 5 sticks over 4 cups of 1 sticks totals 5 sticks over 4 sticks. When grouped into sets of the denominator of 4, the answer is simplified to 1 set of sticks over 1 set of sticks, with 1 incomplete set of 1 stick over the 4 needed.

d) $\frac{4}{3}$, or $1\frac{1}{3}$
2 cups of 2 sticks over 1 cup of 3 sticks totals 4 sticks over 3 sticks. When grouped into sets of the denominator of 3, the answer is simplified to 1 set of sticks over 1 set of sticks, with 1 incomplete set of 1 stick over the 3 needed.

e) $\frac{2}{6}$, or $\frac{1}{3}$
2 cups of 1 stick over 3 cups of 2 sticks totals 2 sticks over 6 sticks. When grouped into sets of 2 sticks, the answer is simplified to 1 set of sticks over 3 sets of sticks.

f) $\frac{6}{5}$, or $1\frac{1}{5}$
3 cups of 2 sticks over 1 cup of 5 sticks totals 6 sticks over 5 sticks. When grouped into sets of the denominator of 5, the answer is simplified to 1 set of sticks over 1 set of sticks, with 1 incomplete set of 1 stick over the 5 needed.

g) $\frac{2}{6}$, or $\frac{1}{3}$
1 cup of 2 sticks over 2 cups of 3 sticks totals 2 sticks over 6 sticks. When grouped into sets of 2 sticks, the answer is simplified to 1 set of sticks over 3 sets of sticks.
He needs to add less than the original amount.

h) $\frac{9}{1}$, or 9
3 cups of 3 sticks over 1 cup of 1 stick totals 9 sticks over 1 stick.

i) $\frac{2}{15}$
1 cup of 2 sticks over 5 cups of 3 sticks totals 2 sticks over 15 sticks.

j) $\frac{6}{20}$, or $\frac{3}{10}$
2 cups of 3 sticks over 4 cups of 5 sticks totals 6 sticks over 20 sticks. When grouped into sets of 2 sticks, the answer is simplified to 3 sets of sticks over 10 sets of sticks.

k) $\frac{1}{16}$
1 cup of 1 stick over 4 cups of 4 sticks totals 1 stick over 16 sticks.

LESSON 9

a) $\frac{6}{6}$, or $\frac{1}{1}$, or 1
3 cup of 2 sticks over 2 cups of 3 sticks totals 6 sticks over 6 sticks. When grouped into sets of 6 sticks, the answer is simplified to 1 set of sticks over 1 set of sticks, or 1.

b) $\frac{1}{16}$
1 cup of 1 stick over 4 cups of 4 sticks totals 1 stick over 16 sticks.

c) $\frac{3}{5}$

1 cup of 3 sticks over 1 cup of 5 sticks totals 3 sticks over 5 sticks.

d) $\frac{8}{5}$, or $1\frac{3}{5}$

4 cups of 2 sticks over 5 cups of 1 stick totals 8 sticks over 5 sticks. When grouped into sets of the denominator of 5, the answer is simplified to 1 set of sticks over 1 set of sticks, with 1 incomplete set of 3 sticks over the 5 needed.

e) $\frac{3}{12}$, or $\frac{1}{4}$

1 cup of 3 sticks over 3 cups of 4 sticks totals 3 sticks over 12 sticks. When grouped into sets of 3 sticks, the answer is simplified to 1 set of sticks over 4 sets of sticks.

f) $\frac{6}{6}$, or $\frac{1}{1}$, or 1

2 cups of 3 sticks over 1 cup of 6 sticks totals 6 sticks over 6 sticks. When grouped into sets of 6 sticks, the answer is simplified to 1 set of sticks over 1 set of sticks, or 1.

g) $\frac{2}{12}$, or $\frac{1}{6}$

1 cup of 2 sticks over 4 cups of 3 sticks totals 2 sticks over 12 sticks. When grouped into sets of 2 sticks, the answer is simplified to 1 set of sticks over 6 sets of sticks.

Less than one cup of formula is mixed.

h) $\frac{1}{12}$

1 cup of 1 stick over 2 cups of 6 sticks totals 1 stick over 12 sticks.

i) $\frac{2}{15}$

2 cups of 1 stick over 3 cups of 5 sticks totals 2 sticks over 15 sticks.

j) $\frac{4}{20}$, or $\frac{1}{5}$

1 cup of 4 sticks over 4 cups of 5 sticks totals 4 sticks over 20 sticks. When grouped into sets of 4 sticks, the answer is simplified to 1 set of sticks over 5 sets of sticks.

k) $\frac{2}{15}$

2 cups of 1 stick over 5 cups of 3 sticks totals 2 sticks over 15 sticks.

LESSON 10

a) $\frac{5}{12}$

5 times 1 over 6 times 2.

b) $\frac{6}{20}$, or $\frac{3}{10}$

2 times 3 over 4 times 5; when the numerator and denominator are divided by 2, the answer is 3 over 10.

c) $\frac{3}{4}$

1 times 3 over 4 times 1.

d) $\frac{3}{12}$, or $\frac{1}{4}$

3 times 1 over 2 times 6; when the numerator and denominator are divided by 3, the answer is 1 over 4.

e) $\frac{3}{8}$

3 times 1 over 4 times 2.

f) $\frac{4}{5}$

2 times 2 over 1 times 5.

g) $\left(\frac{1}{3}\right)\left(\frac{3}{2}\right) = \frac{3}{6}$ or $\frac{1}{2}$ tablespoon of cocoa
$\left(\frac{1}{3}\right)\left(\frac{1}{4}\right) = \frac{1}{12}$ teaspoon of vanilla
1 times 3 over 3 times 2;
1 times 1 over 3 times 4
Each person receives $\frac{1}{2}$ cup of milkshake.

h) $\frac{9}{5}$, or $1\frac{4}{5}$
3 times 3 over 1 times 5; when the numerator and denominator are divided by the denominator, 5, there is one set of 5 in the numerator and one set of 5 in the denominator, with 1 incomplete set of 4 that needs to be divided by 5.

i) $\frac{4}{6}$, or $\frac{2}{3}$
1 times 4 over 2 times 3; when the numerator and denominator are each divided by 2, the answer is 2 over 3.

j) $\frac{1}{18}$
1 times 1 over 6 times 3.

k) $\frac{4}{15}$
2 times 2 over 5 times 3.

 LESSON 11

a) $\frac{12}{28}$, or $\frac{3}{7}$
2 times 6 times 1 over 1 times 7 times 4; when the numerator and denominator are divided by 4, the answer is 3 over 7.

b) $\frac{24}{15}$, or $1\frac{9}{15}$, or $1\frac{3}{5}$
4 times 2 times 3 over 5 times 3 times 1; when the numerator and denominator are divided by the denominator, 15, there is 1 set over 1 set, with 1 incomplete set of 9 over 15. The 9 over 15 can be simplified by dividing the numerator and denominator by 3.

c) $\frac{2}{12}$, or $\frac{1}{6}$
1 times 2 times 1 over 2 times 3 times 2; when the numerator and denominator are each divided by 2 the answer is 1 over 6.

d) $\frac{18}{30}$, or $\frac{3}{5}$
2 times 9 over 3 times 10; when the numerator and denominator are divided by 6 the answer is 3 over 5.

e) $\frac{6}{20}$, or $\frac{3}{10}$
1 times 3 times 2 over 4 times 1 times 5; when the numerator and denominator are divided by 2, the answer is 3 over 10.

f) $\frac{28}{28}$, or $\frac{1}{1}$, or 1
1 times 4 times 7 over 2 times 7 times 2; when the numerator and denominator are divided by 28, the answer is 1.

g) $\frac{2}{6}$, or $\frac{1}{3}$
1 times 2 over 2 times 3; when the numerator and denominator are divided by 2, the answer is 1 over 3.
$\frac{1}{3}$ cup of water is needed.

h) $\frac{45}{10}$, or $4\frac{5}{10}$, or $4\frac{1}{2}$
5 times 3 times 3 over 1 times 2 times 5; when the numerator and denominator are divided by the denominator, 10, there are 4 sets over 1 set with 1 incomplete set of 5 over 10, or $\frac{1}{2}$.

i) $\frac{10}{36}$, or $\frac{5}{18}$

5 times 2 times 1 over 6 times 3 times 2; when the numerator and denominator are divided by 2, the answer is 5 over 18.

j) $\frac{1}{120}$

1 times 1 times 1 over 4 times 6 times 5.

k) $\frac{6}{48}$, or $\frac{1}{8}$

2 times 3 times 1 over 4 times 4 times 3; when the numerator and denominator are divided by 6, the answer is 1 over 8.

 LESSON 12

a) $\frac{12}{1}$, or 12

$\frac{3}{1}$ over $\frac{1}{4}$; to obtain a denominator of 1, multiply both fractions by the reciprocal of the denominator $\frac{1}{4}\left(\frac{4}{1}\right)$; the answer is $\frac{\frac{12}{1}}{1}$, or 12.

b) $\frac{3}{2}$, or $1\frac{1}{2}$

$\frac{1}{2}$ over $\frac{1}{3}$; to obtain a denominator of 1, multiply both fractions by $\frac{3}{1}$. The answer is $\frac{\frac{3}{2}}{1}$, or $\frac{3}{2}$. To simplify this fraction, divide both the numerator and denominator by 2; you are left with 1 set over 1 set with 1 incomplete set of 1 out of 2.

c) $\frac{6}{5}$, or $1\frac{1}{5}$

$\frac{3}{5}$ over $\frac{1}{2}$; to obtain a denominator of 1, multiply both fractions by $\frac{2}{1}$. The answer is $\frac{\frac{6}{5}}{1}$ or $\frac{6}{5}$. To simplify this fraction, divide both the numerator and denominator by 5; you are left with 1 set over 1 set, with 1 incomplete set of 1 out of 5.

d) $\frac{3}{3}$, or $\frac{1}{1}$, or 1

$\frac{1}{3}$ over $\frac{1}{3}$; to obtain a denominator of 1, multiply both fractions by the reciprocal of the denominator, or $\frac{3}{1}$. The answer is $\frac{\frac{3}{3}}{1}$, or 1.

e) $\frac{10}{3}$, or $3\frac{1}{3}$

$\frac{2}{3}$ over $\frac{1}{5}$; to obtain a denominator of 1, multiply both the numerator and denominator by $\frac{5}{1}$. The answer is $\frac{\frac{10}{3}}{1}$, or $\frac{10}{3}$; this can be simplified as $3\frac{1}{3}$.

f) $\frac{8}{1}$, or 8

$\frac{4}{1}$ over $\frac{1}{2}$; to obtain a denominator of 1, multiply both the numerator and denominator by $\frac{2}{1}$. The answer is $\frac{\frac{8}{1}}{1}$, or 8.

g) $\frac{6}{1}$, or 6

$\frac{3}{1}$ over $\frac{1}{2}$; to obtain a denominator of 1, multiply both the numerator and denominator by $\frac{2}{1}$. The answer is $\frac{\frac{6}{1}}{1}$, or 6.

He will make 6 one-half servings.

h) $\frac{6}{1}$, or 6

$\frac{2}{1}$ over $\frac{1}{3}$; to obtain a denominator of 1, multiply both the numerator and denominator by $\frac{3}{1}$. The answer is $\frac{\frac{6}{1}}{1}$, or 6.

i) $\frac{2}{4}$, or $\frac{1}{2}$

$\frac{1}{4}$ over $\frac{1}{2}$; to obtain a denominator of 1, multiply both the numerator and denominator by $\frac{2}{1}$. The answer is $\frac{\frac{2}{4}}{1}$, or $\frac{2}{4}$; this can be simplified as $\frac{1}{2}$.

j) $\frac{10}{3}$, or $3\frac{1}{3}$

$\frac{2}{3}$ over $\frac{1}{5}$; to obtain a denominator of 1, multiply both the numerator and denominator by $\frac{5}{1}$. The answer is $\frac{\frac{10}{3}}{1}$, or $\frac{10}{3}$; this can be simplified as $3\frac{1}{3}$.

k) $\frac{8}{5}$, or $1\frac{3}{5}$

$\frac{2}{5}$ over $\frac{1}{4}$; to obtain a denominator of 1, multiply both the numerator and denominator by $\frac{4}{1}$. The answer is $\frac{\frac{8}{5}}{1}$, or $\frac{8}{5}$; this can be simplified as $1\frac{3}{5}$.

LESSON 13

a) $\frac{6}{1}$, or 6

$\frac{2}{1}$ over $\frac{1}{3}$; to obtain a denominator of 1, multiply both the numerator and denominator by $\frac{3}{1}$. The answer is $\frac{\frac{6}{1}}{1}$, or 6.

b) $\frac{8}{10}$, or $\frac{4}{5}$

$\frac{2}{5}$ over $\frac{2}{4}$; to obtain a denominator of 1, multiply both the numerator and denominator by $\frac{4}{2}$. The answer is $\frac{\frac{8}{10}}{1}$, or $\frac{8}{10}$; this can be simplified as $\frac{4}{5}$.

c) $\frac{9}{2}$, or $4\frac{1}{2}$

$\frac{3}{1}$ over $\frac{2}{3}$; to obtain a denominator of 1, multiply both the numerator and denominator by $\frac{3}{2}$. The answer is $\frac{\frac{9}{2}}{1}$, or $\frac{9}{2}$; this can be simplified as $4\frac{1}{2}$.

d) $\frac{2}{9}$

$\frac{2}{3}$ over $\frac{3}{1}$; to obtain a denominator of 1, multiply both the numerator and denominator by $\frac{1}{3}$. The answer is $\frac{2}{9}$.

e) $\frac{4}{3}$, or $1\frac{1}{3}$

$\frac{2}{3}$ over $\frac{1}{2}$; to obtain a denominator of 1, multiply both the numerator and denominator by $\frac{2}{1}$. The answer is $\frac{\frac{4}{3}}{1}$, or $\frac{4}{3}$; this can be simplified as $1\frac{1}{3}$.

f) $\frac{16}{3}$, or $5\frac{1}{3}$

$\frac{4}{1}$ over $\frac{3}{4}$; to obtain a denominator of 1, multiply both the numerator and denominator by $\frac{4}{3}$. The answer is $\frac{\frac{16}{3}}{1}$, or $\frac{16}{3}$; this can be simplified as $5\frac{1}{3}$.

g) $\frac{12}{2}$, or $\frac{6}{1}$, or 6

$\frac{4}{1}$ over $\frac{2}{3}$; to obtain a denominator of 1, multiply both the numerator and denominator by $\frac{3}{2}$. The answer is $\frac{\frac{12}{2}}{1}$, or $\frac{6}{1}$, otherwise identified as 6.

6 stores bought crates.

h) $\frac{12}{1}$, or 12

$\frac{3}{1}$ over $\frac{1}{4}$; to obtain a denominator of 1, multiply both the numerator and denominator by $\frac{4}{1}$. The answer is $\frac{\frac{12}{1}}{1}$, or $\frac{12}{1}$, otherwise identified as 12.

i) $\frac{5}{12}$

$\frac{1}{4}$ over $\frac{3}{5}$; to obtain a denominator of 1, multiply both the numerator and denominator by $\frac{5}{3}$. The answer is $\frac{\frac{5}{12}}{1}$, or $\frac{5}{12}$.

j) $\frac{8}{6}$, or $1\frac{2}{6}$, or $1\frac{1}{3}$

$\frac{2}{3}$ over $\frac{2}{4}$; to obtain a denominator of 1, multiply both the numerator and denominator by $\frac{4}{2}$. The answer is $\frac{\frac{8}{6}}{1}$, or $\frac{8}{6}$; this can be simplified as $1\frac{1}{3}$.

k) $\frac{2}{20}$, or $\frac{1}{10}$

$\frac{2}{5}$ over $\frac{4}{1}$; to obtain a denominator of 1, multiply both the numerator and denominator by $\frac{1}{4}$. The answer is $\frac{\frac{2}{20}}{1}$, or $\frac{2}{20}$; this can be simplified as $\frac{1}{10}$.

LESSON 14

a) $\frac{25}{4}$, or $6\frac{1}{4}$

$\frac{5}{2}$ over $\frac{2}{5}$; to obtain a denominator of 1, multiply both the numerator and denominator by $\frac{5}{2}$. The answer is $\frac{\frac{25}{4}}{1}$, or $\frac{25}{4}$; this can be simplified as $6\frac{1}{4}$.

b) $\frac{15}{16}$

$\frac{3}{4}$ over $\frac{4}{5}$; to obtain a denominator of 1, multiply both the numerator and denominator by $\frac{5}{4}$. The answer is $\frac{\frac{15}{16}}{1}$, or $\frac{15}{16}$.

c) $\frac{3}{40}$

$\frac{1}{5}$ over $\frac{8}{3}$; to obtain a denominator of 1, multiply both the numerator and denominator by $\frac{3}{8}$. The answer is $\frac{\frac{3}{40}}{1}$, or $\frac{3}{40}$.

d) $\frac{36}{6}$, or $\frac{6}{1}$, or 6

$\frac{4}{3}$ over $\frac{2}{9}$; to obtain a denominator of 1, multiply both the numerator and denominator by $\frac{9}{2}$. The answer is $\frac{\frac{36}{6}}{1}$, or $\frac{36}{6}$; this can be simplified as $\frac{6}{1}$, otherwise identified as 6.

e) $\frac{2}{35}$

$\frac{1}{5}$ over $\frac{7}{2}$; to obtain a denominator of 1, multiply both the numerator and denominator by $\frac{2}{7}$. The answer is $\frac{\frac{2}{35}}{1}$, or $\frac{2}{35}$.

f) $\frac{5}{18}$

$\frac{5}{6}$ over $\frac{3}{1}$; to obtain a denominator of 1, multiply both the numerator and denominator by $\frac{1}{3}$. The answer is $\frac{\frac{15}{18}}{1}$, or $\frac{5}{18}$.

g) $\frac{24}{6}$, or $\frac{4}{1}$, or 4

$\frac{8}{3}$ over $\frac{2}{3}$; to obtain a denominator of 1, multiply both the numerator and denominator by $\frac{3}{2}$. The answer is $\frac{\frac{24}{6}}{1}$, or $\frac{24}{6}$; this can be simplified as $\frac{4}{1}$, otherwise identified as 4.
6 companies received bricks.

h) $\frac{12}{1}$, or 12

$\frac{6}{1}$ over $\frac{1}{2}$; to obtain a denominator of 1, multiply both the numerator and denominator by $\frac{2}{1}$. The answer is $\frac{\frac{12}{1}}{1}$, or $\frac{12}{1}$, otherwise identified as 12.

i) $\frac{15}{10}$, or $\frac{3}{2}$, or $1\frac{1}{2}$

$\frac{3}{5}$ over $\frac{2}{5}$; to obtain a denominator of 1, multiply both the numerator and denominator by $\frac{5}{2}$. The answer is $\frac{\frac{15}{10}}{1}$, or $\frac{15}{10}$; this can be simplified as $1\frac{1}{2}$.

j) $\frac{25}{24}$, or $1\frac{1}{24}$

$\frac{5}{3}$ over $\frac{8}{5}$; to obtain a denominator of 1, multiply both the numerator and denominator by $\frac{5}{8}$. The answer is $\frac{\frac{25}{24}}{1}$, or $\frac{25}{24}$; this can be simplified as $1\frac{1}{24}$.

k) $\frac{8}{14}$, or $\frac{4}{7}$

$\frac{2}{7}$ over $\frac{2}{4}$; to obtain a denominator of 1, multiply both the numerator and denominator by $\frac{4}{2}$. The answer is $\frac{\frac{8}{14}}{1}$, or $\frac{8}{14}$; this can be simplified as $\frac{4}{7}$.

LESSON 15

a) $\frac{3}{9} = \frac{4}{12}$
4 groups of 1 stick over 4 groups of 3 sticks.

b) $\frac{4}{4}$

c) $\frac{9}{12} = \frac{12}{6} = \frac{15}{20}$
5 groups of 3 sticks over 5 groups 4 sticks.

d) $\frac{5}{5}$

e) Circle the $\frac{4}{12}$ and $\frac{9}{12}$.
$\frac{9}{12}$ is the larger fraction.

f) 4 groups; numerator and denominator of $\frac{1}{2}$ is $\frac{4}{8}$.
4 groups of 1 stick over 4 groups of 2 sticks is the same as $\frac{4}{8}$.

g) $\frac{3}{6} = \frac{4}{8} = \frac{5}{10}$
5 groups of 1 stick over 5 groups 2 sticks.

h) $\frac{5}{5}$

i) $\frac{6}{9}$
3 groups of 2 sticks over 3 groups of 3 sticks.

j) $\frac{3}{3}$

k) Circle $\frac{3}{6}$ and $\frac{4}{6}$.
$\frac{4}{6}$ is the larger fraction.

LESSON 16

a) $\frac{4}{10} = \frac{6}{15} = \frac{8}{20}$
4 groups of 2 tallies over 4 groups of 5 tallies.

b) $\frac{4}{4}$

c) $\frac{2}{4} = \frac{3}{6} = \frac{4}{8} = \frac{5}{10}$
5 groups of 1 tally over 5 groups of 2 tallies.

d) $\frac{5}{5}$

e) Circle $\frac{4}{10}$ and $\frac{5}{10}$.
$\frac{5}{10}$ is the larger fraction.

f) Not the same.
When you multiply $\frac{1}{3}$ by $\frac{4}{4}$ you obtain the same denominator but a different fraction ($\frac{4}{12}$; not $\frac{5}{12}$).

g) $\frac{2}{6} = \frac{3}{9} = \frac{4}{12} = \frac{5}{15}$
   5 groups of 1 tally of 5 groups of 3 tallies.

h) $\frac{5}{5}$

i) $\frac{10}{12} = \frac{15}{18} = \frac{20}{24} = \frac{25}{30}$
   5 groups of 5 tallies over 5 groups of 6 tallies.

j) $\frac{5}{5}$

k) Circle $\frac{2}{6}$ and the $\frac{5}{6}$.
   $\frac{5}{6}$ is the larger fraction.

 LESSON 17

a) $\frac{10}{24} = \frac{15}{36}$
   3 × 5 over 3 × 12.

b) $\frac{3}{3}$

c) $\frac{2}{8} = \frac{3}{12} = \frac{4}{16} = \frac{5}{20}$
   5 × 1 over 5 × 4.

d) $\frac{5}{5}$

e) Circle $\frac{5}{12}$ and $\frac{3}{12}$.
   $\frac{5}{12}$ is the larger fraction.

f) Not the same; when the denominators are equal, the fractions are not equivalent
   ($\frac{9}{12}$ and $\frac{6}{12}$).
   Multiply the $\frac{1}{2}$ by $\frac{6}{6}$ to make the denominators the same.

g) $\frac{4}{18} = \frac{6}{27} = \frac{8}{36}$
   4 × 2 over 4 × 9.

h) $\frac{4}{4}$

i) $\frac{2}{12} = \frac{3}{18} = \frac{4}{24} = \frac{5}{30}$
   5 × 1 over 5 × 6.

j) $\frac{5}{5}$

k) Circle $\frac{4}{18}$ and $\frac{3}{18}$.
   $\frac{4}{18}$ is the larger fraction.

 LESSON 18

a) $\frac{3}{8} = \frac{6}{16} = \frac{9}{24} = \frac{12}{32}$
   4 × 3 over 4 × 8.

b) $\frac{4}{4}$

c) $\frac{2}{12} = \frac{3}{18} = \frac{4}{24}$
   4 × 1 over 4 × 6.

d) $\frac{4}{4}$

e) Circle $\frac{9}{24}$ and $\frac{4}{24}$.

f) They are different. To make the denominators the same, the $\frac{3}{10}$ becomes $\frac{6}{20}$ and
   the $\frac{1}{4}$ becomes $\frac{5}{20}$. $\frac{6}{20}$, or $\frac{3}{10}$, is greater than $\frac{1}{4}$, or $\frac{5}{20}$.
   Multiply $\frac{3}{10}$ by $\frac{2}{2}$ and $\frac{1}{4}$ by $\frac{5}{5}$.

g) $\frac{6}{20} = \frac{9}{30} = \frac{12}{40} = \frac{15}{50}$
   5 × 3 over 5 × 10.

h) $\frac{5}{5}$

i) $\frac{4}{14} = \frac{6}{21} = \frac{8}{28} = \frac{10}{35}$
   5 × 2 over 5 × 7.

j) $\frac{5}{5}$

k) None can be circled. You would have to continue multiplying by variations of $\frac{1}{1}$ to find equivalent denominators.

 LESSON 19

a) $\frac{2}{3}$
   2 groups of 4 sticks over 3 groups of 4 sticks.

b) $\frac{4}{4}$

c) $\frac{1}{3}$
   1 group of 3 sticks over 3 groups of 3 sticks.

d) $\frac{3}{3}$

e) a) is larger because when the denominators are the same, the numerator is greater.

f) $\frac{3}{5}$
   3 groups of 2 sticks over 5 groups of 2 sticks.

g) $\frac{2}{5}$
   2 groups of 3 sticks over 5 groups of 3 sticks.

h) $\frac{2}{2}$ for f) and $\frac{3}{3}$ for g); f) is larger.

i) $\frac{1}{4}$; $\frac{9}{12}$ reduced is $\frac{3}{4}$.
   $\frac{9}{12}$ is equivalent to 3 groups of 3 over 4 groups of 3, or $\frac{3}{4}$; $\frac{1}{4}$ is the right measuring cup because it has a matching denominator.

j) $\frac{3}{4}$
   3 groups of 4 sticks over 4 groups of 4 sticks.

k) $\frac{1}{4}$
   1 group of 2 sticks over 4 groups of 2 sticks.

l) $\frac{4}{4}$ for j) and $\frac{2}{2}$ for k).

m) $\frac{1}{2}$
   1 group of 3 sticks over 2 groups of 3 sticks.

n) $\frac{1}{2}$
   1 group of 7 sticks over 2 groups of 7 sticks.

o) $\frac{3}{3}$ for m) and $\frac{7}{7}$ for n).

 LESSON 20

a) $\frac{1}{4}$
   1 group of 5 tallies over 4 groups of 5 tallies.

b) $\frac{5}{5}$

c) $\frac{3}{4}$
   3 groups of 4 tallies over 4 groups of 4 tallies.

d) $\frac{4}{4}$

e) c) is larger because the numerator is larger when the denominators are the same.

f) $\frac{3}{5}$
   3 groups of 2 tallies over 5 groups of 2 tallies.

g) $\frac{4}{7}$
   4 groups of 2 tallies over 7 groups of 2 tallies.

h) $\frac{2}{2}$ for f) and $\frac{2}{2}$ for g).

i) Reducing $\frac{8}{10}$ equals $\frac{4}{5}$, so both toothpastes are the same.
   4 groups of 2 tallies over 5 groups of 2 tallies is equivalent to $\frac{8}{10}$.

j) $\frac{1}{2}$
   1 group of 3 tallies over 2 groups of 3 tallies.

k) $\frac{1}{2}$
   1 groups of 6 tallies over 2 groups of 6 tallies.

l) $\frac{3}{3}$ for j) and $\frac{6}{6}$ for k).
   Neither fraction is larger.

m) $\frac{2}{3}$
   2 groups of 3 tallies over 3 groups of 3 tallies.

n) $\frac{4}{5}$
   4 groups of 3 tallies over 5 groups of 3 tallies.

o) $\frac{3}{3}$ for m) and $\frac{3}{3}$ for n).

LESSON 21

a) $\frac{1}{3}$
   1×7 over 3×7.

b) $\frac{7}{7}$

c) $\frac{2}{3}$
   2×6 over 3×6.

d) $\frac{6}{6}$

e) c) is larger because the numerator is larger when the denominators are the same.

f) $\frac{2}{3}$
   2×5 over 3×5 or $10 \div 5$ over $15 \div 5$.

g) $\frac{1}{4}$
   1×5 over 4×5 or $5 \div 5$ over $20 \div 5$.

h) $\frac{5}{5}$ for f) and $\frac{5}{5}$ for g).

i) Finding equivalent fractions yields $\frac{2}{5}$ compared with $\frac{3}{5}$; you are not yet $\frac{3}{5}$ of the way there.

j) $\frac{1}{4}$
   1×8 over 4×8.

k) $\frac{3}{10}$
   3×4 over 10×4.

l) $\frac{8}{8}$ for j) and $\frac{4}{4}$ for k).

m) $\frac{3}{4}$
   3×9 over 4×9.

n) $\frac{1}{3}$

1×9 over 3×9.

o) $\frac{9}{9}$ for m) and $\frac{9}{9}$ for n).

 LESSON 22

a) $\frac{1}{3} < \frac{2}{3}$

b) $\frac{1}{4} < \frac{2}{4}$

c) $\frac{1}{5} < \frac{2}{5}$

d) $\frac{1}{4} = \frac{1}{4}$

e) $\frac{10}{15} > \frac{3}{15}$

f) $\frac{2}{3} > \frac{1}{3}$

g) $\frac{1}{2}\left(\frac{6}{6}\right) > \frac{5}{12}$, or $\frac{6}{12} > \frac{5}{12}$; The $\frac{1}{2}$ carton is bigger.

h) $\frac{6}{3} > \frac{1}{3}$

i) $\frac{4}{5} > \frac{3}{5}$

j) $\frac{2}{3} > \frac{1}{3}$

k) $\frac{8}{20} > \frac{5}{20}$

LESSON 23

a) $\frac{2}{3}$

A positive sign followed by 2 sticks over 3 sticks.

b) $\frac{4}{4}$, or $\frac{1}{1}$, or 1

A positive sign followed by 4 sticks over 4 sticks grouped by 4 is 1.

c) $\frac{2}{4}$, or $\frac{1}{2}$

A positive sign followed by 2 sticks over 4 sticks grouped by 2 is $\frac{1}{2}$.

d) $\frac{0}{5}$, or 0

A positive sign followed by no sticks over 5 sticks.

e) $\frac{3}{4}$

A positive sign followed by 3 sticks over 4 sticks.

f) $\frac{2}{5}$

A positive sign followed by 2 sticks over 5 sticks.

g) $\frac{2}{4}$, or $\frac{1}{2}$ carton

A positive sign followed by 2 sticks over 4 sticks grouped by 2 is $\frac{1}{2}$.

h) $\frac{4}{5}$

A positive sign followed by 4 sticks over 5 sticks.

i) $\frac{1}{4}$

A positive sign followed by 1 stick over 4 sticks.

j) $\frac{2}{3}$

A positive sign followed by 2 sticks over 3 sticks.

k) $\frac{3}{2}$, or $1\frac{1}{2}$

A positive sign followed by 3 sticks over 2 sticks grouped by the denominator is 1 complete set, with 1 incomplete set of 1 over 2.

LESSON 24

a) $\frac{3}{4}$
A positive sign followed by 3 tallies over 4 tallies.

b) $\frac{4}{5}$
A positive sign followed by 4 tallies over 5 tallies.

c) $\frac{1}{3}$
A positive sign followed by 1 tally over 3 tallies.

d) $\frac{2}{4}$, or $\frac{1}{2}$
A positive sign followed by 2 tallies over 4 tallies grouped by 2 is $\frac{1}{2}$.

e) $\frac{3}{3}$, or 1
A positive sign followed by 3 tallies over 3 tallies grouped by 3 is 1.

f) $\frac{1}{5}$
A positive sign followed by 1 tally over 5 tallies.

g) $\frac{2}{3} + \frac{2}{3} = \frac{4}{3}$, or $1\frac{1}{3}$ cases of soda
A positive sign followed by 4 tallies over 3 tallies grouped by the denominator is 1 complete set, with 1 incomplete set of 1 over $3\frac{1}{3}$.

h) $\frac{4}{4}$, or 1
A positive sign followed by 4 tallies over 4 tallies grouped by 4 is 1.

i) $\frac{2}{4}$, or $\frac{1}{2}$
A positive sign followed by 2 tallies over 4 tallies grouped by 2 is $\frac{1}{2}$.

j) $\frac{1}{3}$
A positive sign followed by 1 tally over 3 tallies.

k) $\frac{1}{2}$
A positive sign followed by 1 tally over 2 tallies.

 LESSON 25

a) $+\frac{3}{7}$

b) $+\frac{4}{4}$, or 1

c) $+\frac{3}{5}$

d) $+\frac{3}{6}$, or $+\frac{1}{2}$

e) $+\frac{3}{3}$, or 1

f) $+\frac{2}{5}$

g) $+\frac{2}{3} - \frac{1}{3} = \frac{1}{3}$ degree

h) $+\frac{5}{4}$, or $1\frac{1}{4}$

i) $+\frac{2}{6}$, or $\frac{1}{3}$

j) $+\frac{3}{5}$

k) $+\frac{6}{8}$, or $\frac{3}{4}$

LESSON 26

a) $+\frac{6}{3} + \frac{1}{3} + \frac{2}{3} = +\frac{9}{3} = 3$

b) $+\frac{3}{4} + \frac{4}{4} + \frac{1}{4} = +\frac{8}{4}$, or 2

c) $+3\frac{4}{5} - \frac{1}{5} = +3\frac{3}{5}$

d) $+\frac{6}{6} + \frac{1}{6} - \frac{5}{6} = +\frac{2}{6}$, or $\frac{1}{3}$

e) $+\frac{5}{7} + \frac{3}{7} = +\frac{8}{7}$, or $1\frac{1}{7}$; the bookshelf is overfilled

f) $+\frac{14}{7} + \frac{1}{7} + \frac{5}{7} = +\frac{20}{7}$, or $2\frac{6}{7}$

g) $+\frac{6}{6} + \frac{1}{6} - \frac{5}{6} = +\frac{2}{6}$, or $\frac{1}{3}$

h) $+\frac{5}{4}$, or $1\frac{1}{4}$

i) $+\frac{5}{6} + \frac{18}{6} + \frac{2}{6} = +\frac{25}{6}$, or $4\frac{1}{6}$

j) $+1\frac{4}{5} - \frac{3}{5} = +1\frac{1}{5}$

k) $+\frac{8}{8} + \frac{2}{8} - \frac{10}{8} = +\frac{0}{8}$, or 8

LESSON 27

a) $+\frac{3}{9} + \frac{2}{9} = +\frac{5}{9}$
A positive sign followed by 5 sticks over 9 sticks.

b) $+\frac{3}{8} + \frac{4}{8} = +\frac{7}{8}$
A positive sign followed by 7 sticks over 8 sticks.

c) $+\frac{2}{4}$, or $+\frac{1}{2}$
A positive sign followed by 2 sticks over 4 sticks grouped by 2 equals $\frac{1}{2}$.

d) $+\frac{4}{6} - \frac{1}{6} = +\frac{3}{6}$, or $+\frac{1}{2}$
A positive sign followed by 3 sticks over 6 sticks grouped by 2 equals $\frac{1}{2}$.

e) $+\frac{2}{8} + \frac{1}{8} = +\frac{3}{8}$
A positive sign followed by 3 sticks over 8 sticks.

f) $+\frac{5}{6} - \frac{4}{6} = +\frac{1}{6}$
A positive sign followed by 1 stick over 6 sticks.

g) $+\frac{4}{8} + \frac{2}{8} = +\frac{6}{8} = +\frac{3}{4}$ cup
A positive sign followed by 6 sticks over 8 sticks grouped by 2 equals $\frac{3}{4}$.

h) $+\frac{4}{8} + \frac{5}{8} = +\frac{9}{8}$, or $+1\frac{1}{8}$
A positive sign followed by 9 sticks over 8 sticks grouped by the denominator equals $1\frac{1}{8}$.

i) $+\frac{3}{9} - \frac{1}{9} = +\frac{2}{9}$
A positive sign followed by 2 sticks over 9 sticks.

j) $+\frac{3}{4} - \frac{2}{4} = +\frac{1}{4}$
A positive sign followed by 1 stick over 4 sticks.

k) $+\frac{5}{6} + \frac{2}{6} = +\frac{7}{6}$, or $+1\frac{1}{6}$
A positive sign followed by 7 sticks over 6 sticks grouped by the denominator equals $1\frac{1}{6}$.

LESSON 28

a) $\frac{2}{6} + \frac{2}{6} = \frac{4}{6}$, or $\frac{2}{3}$
A positive sign followed by 4 tallies over 6 tallies grouped by 2 equals $\frac{2}{3}$.

b) $\frac{4}{6} + \frac{3}{6} = \frac{7}{6}$, or $1\frac{1}{6}$
A positive sign followed by 7 tallies over 6 tallies grouped by the denominator equals $1\frac{1}{6}$.

c) $\frac{2}{4} - \frac{1}{4} = \frac{1}{4}$
A positive sign followed by 1 tally over 4 tallies.

d) $\frac{8}{12} - \frac{3}{12} = \frac{5}{12}$
A positive sign followed by 5 tallies over 12 tallies.

e) $\frac{4}{8} + \frac{1}{8} = \frac{5}{8}$
A positive sign followed by 5 tallies over 8 tallies.

f) $\frac{8}{10} - \frac{5}{10} = \frac{3}{10}$
A positive sign followed by 3 tallies over 10 tallies.

g) $\frac{2}{6} + \frac{3}{6} = \frac{5}{6}$ pack of tacks
A positive sign followed by 5 tallies over 6 tallies.

h) $\frac{2}{8} + \frac{1}{8} = \frac{3}{8}$
A positive sign followed by 3 tallies over 8 tallies.

i) $+\frac{5}{6} - \frac{4}{6} = +\frac{1}{6}$
A positive sign followed by 1 tally over 6 tallies.

j) $\frac{9}{12} - \frac{4}{12} = \frac{5}{12}$
A positive sign followed by 5 tallies over 12 tallies.

k) $\frac{9}{6} + \frac{2}{6} = \frac{11}{6}$, or $1\frac{5}{6}$
A positive sign followed by 11 tallies over 6 tallies grouped by the denominator equals $1\frac{5}{6}$.

 LESSON 29

a) $\frac{2}{6} + \frac{5}{6} = \frac{7}{6} = 1\frac{1}{6}$

b) $\frac{3}{6} - \frac{2}{6} = \frac{1}{6}$

c) $\frac{2}{8} - \frac{1}{8} = \frac{1}{8}$

d) $\frac{6}{15} + \frac{5}{15} = \frac{11}{15}$

e) $\frac{3}{8}\left(\frac{3}{3}\right) + \frac{1}{3}\left(\frac{8}{8}\right) = \frac{9}{24} + \frac{8}{24} = \frac{17}{24}$ of the floor

f) $\frac{9}{24} - \frac{8}{24} = \frac{1}{24}$

g) $\frac{24}{30} - \frac{5}{30} = \frac{19}{30}$

h) $\frac{3}{12} + \frac{2}{12} = \frac{5}{12}$

i) $\frac{6}{12} - \frac{6}{12} = \frac{0}{12}$, or $\frac{1}{2} - \frac{1}{2} = \frac{0}{2} = 0$

j) $\frac{8}{40} - \frac{5}{40} = \frac{3}{40}$

k) $\frac{5}{6} + \frac{2}{6} = \frac{7}{6}$, or $1\frac{1}{6}$

 LESSON 30

a) $\frac{12}{6} + \frac{2}{6} + \frac{2}{6} = \frac{16}{6} = \frac{8}{3}$, or $2\frac{2}{3}$, or $\frac{6}{3} + \frac{1}{3} + \frac{1}{3} = \frac{8}{3}$, or $2\frac{2}{3}$

b) $\frac{2}{4} - \frac{1}{4} = \frac{1}{4}$

c) $\frac{30}{10} + \frac{2}{10} + \frac{2}{10} = \frac{34}{10}$, or $3\frac{2}{5}$, or $\frac{15}{5} + \frac{1}{5} + \frac{1}{5} = \frac{17}{5}$, or $3\frac{2}{5}$

d) $\frac{2}{3} - \frac{3}{3} + \frac{1}{3} = \frac{0}{3}$, or 0

e) $\frac{3}{4} \times \frac{1}{5} = \frac{3}{20}$, $\frac{15}{20} - \frac{3}{20} = \frac{12}{20} = \frac{3}{5}$ full

f) $\frac{4}{8} + \frac{1}{8} = \frac{5}{8}$

g) $\frac{12}{6} + \frac{2}{6} - \frac{3}{6} = \frac{11}{6}$, or $1\frac{5}{6}$

h) $\frac{24}{8} + \frac{1}{8} + \frac{4}{8} = \frac{29}{8}$, or $3\frac{5}{8}$

i) $\frac{4}{6} - \frac{5}{6} = -\frac{1}{6}$

j) $\frac{15}{12} - \frac{12}{12} - \frac{2}{12} = \frac{1}{12}$

k) $\frac{9}{6} + \frac{2}{6} = \frac{11}{6}$, or $1\frac{5}{6}$

CUMULATIVE REVIEW A

a) $4\frac{1}{2}$

b) $4\frac{1}{4}$

c) $1\frac{1}{2}$ pens per person

d) $2\frac{2}{3}$ dollars per candy

e) 3 sticks per group

f) $2\frac{1}{2}$ tallies per group

g) $3\frac{1}{3}$ glasses per person

h) $2\frac{1}{4}$

i) $\frac{1}{3}$

j) $8\frac{1}{3}$ dollars per student

 CUMULATIVE REVIEW B

a) $\frac{1}{3}$ sticks per cup

b) $1\frac{7}{9}$ dollars per soda

c) $4\frac{2}{3}$ rabbits per cabbage

d) $2\frac{1}{3}$ rooms per person

e) $3\frac{3}{4}$ pounds per inch

f) $4\frac{3}{4}$ tallies per group

g) $\frac{18}{5} = 3\frac{3}{5}$ pellets per hamster

h) $\left(\frac{3}{2}\right)\left(\frac{1}{3}\right) = \frac{3}{6}$, or $\frac{1}{2}$ of the mix

i) $\frac{1}{12}$ sticks

j) $\frac{6}{12}$, or $\frac{1}{2}$

 CUMULATIVE REVIEW C

a) $\frac{10}{3} = 3\frac{1}{3}$ cookies per child

b) 3 quarters per tooth

c) $4\frac{2}{7}$

d) $\left(\frac{5}{2}\right)\left(\frac{1}{3}\right) = \frac{5}{6}$ cups

e) $\frac{6}{20}$, or $\frac{3}{10}$

f) $\frac{18}{28}$, or $\frac{9}{14}$

g) $\frac{10}{3}$, or $3\frac{1}{3}$

h) 8 slices

i) $\left(\frac{3}{2}\right) \div \left(\frac{1}{2}\right) = \frac{6}{2} = 3$ plants

 CUMULATIVE REVIEW D

a) $5\frac{3}{4}$ computers per classroom

b) $2\frac{4}{5}$ miles per hour

c) $\frac{12}{5} = 2\frac{2}{5}$ sandwiches per friend

d) $\frac{6}{6}$, or 1 filled

e) $\frac{14}{15}$

f) $\left(\frac{5}{3}\right) \div (4) = \frac{5}{12}$ cup of ice cream per person

g) $\frac{8}{3} = 2\frac{2}{3}$ crates per customer

h) 8

i) $\frac{4}{14} = \frac{6}{21} = \frac{8}{28} = \frac{10}{35}$

j) $\frac{5}{5}$

k) $\frac{6}{16} = \frac{9}{24} = \frac{12}{32}$

l) $\frac{4}{4}$

 CUMULATIVE REVIEW E

a) $3\frac{3}{5}$

b) $5\frac{3}{7}$ feet per person

c) $\frac{20}{9} = 2\frac{2}{9}$ students per tutor

d) $\frac{5}{12}$ filled trees

e) $\frac{2}{20} = \frac{1}{10}$

f) $\frac{6}{3}$, or 2

g) $\frac{4}{20} = \frac{1}{5}$

h) Yes, $\frac{2}{3}\left(\frac{5}{5}\right) = \frac{10}{15}$.

i) $\frac{1}{8}$

j) $\frac{1}{4}$

k) $\frac{4}{4}$ for i and $\frac{9}{9}$ for j

 ## CUMULATIVE REVIEW F

a) $4\frac{2}{3}$ sticks per pile

b) $3\frac{3}{4}$ books per child

c) $\left(\frac{7}{2}\right)\left(\frac{1}{3}\right) = \frac{7}{6}$, or $1\frac{1}{6}$ times around the track

d) $\frac{12}{3} = 4$

e) $\frac{6}{14} = \frac{3}{7}$ pieces of candy bar

f) $\frac{1}{2}\left(\frac{8}{8}\right)$, or $\frac{8}{16}$ is not the same as $\frac{7}{16}$. Because 8 is greater than 7, $\frac{1}{2}$ cup is larger.

g) $\frac{4}{10} = \frac{6}{15} = \frac{8}{20}$

h) $\frac{4}{4}$

i) $\frac{4}{3}$

j) $\frac{2}{5}$

k) $\frac{2}{2}$ for i and $\frac{2}{2}$ for j

 ## CUMULATIVE REVIEW G

a) $\frac{18}{7} = 2\frac{4}{7}$ of the duties

b) $\frac{12}{28} = \frac{3}{7}$ blocks

c) $\frac{25}{24}$, or $1\frac{1}{24}$

d) $\frac{1}{3}\left(\frac{4}{4}\right) = \frac{4}{12} < \frac{5}{12}$; $\frac{5}{12}$ carton is larger.

e) $\frac{1}{3}$

f) $\frac{2}{4}$, or $\frac{1}{2}$ family

g) $\frac{2}{8} - \frac{1}{8} = \frac{1}{8}$

h) $\frac{6}{15} + \frac{5}{15} = \frac{11}{15}$ price

i) $\frac{2}{3} + \frac{6}{9} = \frac{6}{9} + \frac{6}{9} = \frac{12}{9}$, or $1\frac{1}{3}$ cups of flour

j) $\frac{6}{6} + \frac{4}{6} + \frac{1}{6} = \frac{11}{6}$, or $1\frac{5}{6}$

k) $\frac{35}{15} - \frac{12}{15} = \frac{23}{15}$, or $1\frac{8}{15}$

POSTTEST

Division with Fractional Answers

a) 3

b) $3\frac{1}{2}$

c) $3\frac{2}{7}$

d) $2\frac{2}{5}$

Multiplication of Fractions

e) $\frac{2}{15}$

f) $\frac{15}{6}$, or $2\frac{1}{2}$

Division of Fractions

g) $\frac{4}{2}$, or 2

h) $\frac{32}{5}$, or $6\frac{2}{5}$

Finding Equivalent Fractions

i) $\frac{4}{14} = \frac{6}{21} = \frac{8}{28}$

j) $\frac{4}{4}$

k) $\frac{2}{8} = \frac{3}{12} = \frac{4}{16} = \frac{5}{20}$

l) $\frac{5}{5}$

Reducing and Comparing Fractions

m) $\frac{1}{4}$

n) $\frac{6}{6}$

o) $\frac{1}{3}$

p) $\frac{4}{4}$

Adding and Subtracting Fractions with Like Denominators

q) $\frac{3}{4}$

r) $\frac{4}{5}$

Adding and Subtracting Fractions with Unlike Denominators

s) $\frac{9}{12} + \frac{1}{12} = \frac{10}{12}$, or $\frac{5}{6}$

t) $\frac{4}{12} + \frac{6}{12} = \frac{10}{12}$, or $\frac{5}{6}$, or $\frac{2}{6} + \frac{3}{6} = \frac{5}{6}$

References

Butler, F. M., Miller, S. P., Crehan, K., Babbit, B., & Pierce, T. (2003). Fraction instruction for students with mathematics disabilities: Comparing two teaching sequences. *Learning Disabilities Research & Practice, 18*(2), 99–111.

Gagnon, J. G., & Maccini, P. (2007). Teacher-reported use of empirically validated standards-based instructional approaches in secondary mathematics. *Remedial and Special Education, 28*(1), 43–56.

Hutchinson, N. L. (1993). Second invited response: Students with disabilities and mathematics education reform—let the dialogue begin. *Remedial and Special Education, 14*(6), 20–23.

Jordan, L., Miller, M. D., & Mercer, C. D. (1999). The effects of concrete to semi-concrete to abstract instruction in the acquisition and retention of fraction concepts and skills. *Learning Disabilities: A Multidisciplinary Journal, 9*(3), 115–122.

Maccini, P., & Hughes, C. A. (2000). Effects of a problem-solving strategy on the introductory algebra performance of secondary students with learning disabilities. *Learning Disabilities Research & Practice, 15*(1), 10–21.

Maccini, P., Mulcahy, C. A., & Wilson, M. G. (2007). A follow-up of mathematics interventions for secondary students with learning disabilities. *Learning Disabilities Research & Practice, 22*(1), 58–74.

National Council of Teachers of Mathematics. (2000). *Principles and Standards for School Mathematics.* Reston, VA: Author.

Witzel, B. (2005). Using CRA to teach algebra to students with math difficulties in inclusive settings. *Learning Disabilities: A Contemporary Journal, 3*(2), 49–60.

Witzel, B. S., Mercer, C. D., & Miller, M. D. (2003). Teaching algebra to students with learning difficulties: An investigation of an explicit instruction model. *Learning Disabilities Research & Practice, 18*(2), 121–131.

Appendix

Summary Chart for Concrete to Representational to Abstract Sequence of Materials

Material samples	Overhead samples	Desktop samples	Pictorial representations	Abstract notation	
Digit			/	1-9	used for integers
Ten			|	10	used for ten
Group			◯ or ▢	0 or above may be an assumed 1	for groups of and per group
Divisor line			—	—	represents division
Equal sign			⌇	=	represents an equal sign
Positive, or Addition Symbol			+	+	represents addition
Negative, or Subtraction Symbol			–	–	represents subtraction

Multiplication Cards *(copy in blue)*

x	x	x	x

x	x	x	x

x	x	x	x

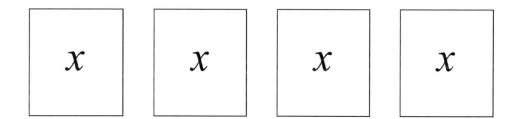

Plus, or Positive Cards *(copy in green)*

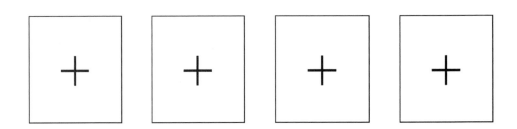

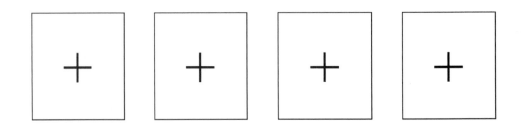

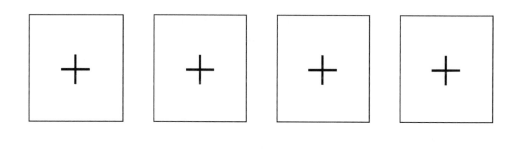

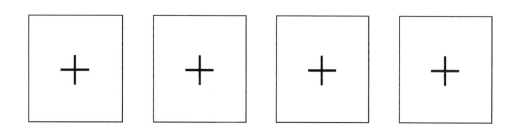

Negative, or Minus Cards *(copy in red)*

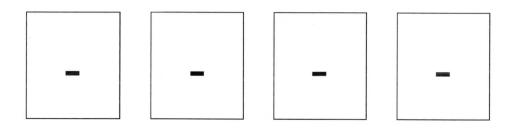

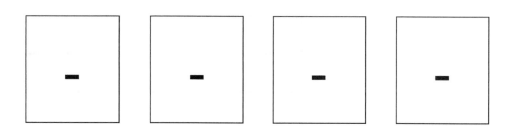

Divisor Lines *(copy in white)*

About the Authors

Dr. Bradley S. Witzel is an associate professor in the Department of Curriculum Instruction at Winthrop University in Rock Hill, South Carolina. He has experience in the classroom as an inclusive and self-contained teacher of students with high-incidence disabilities and as a classroom assistant and classroom teacher of students with low-incidence disabilities. He has written numerous research practitioner articles on mathematics and motivational instruction for students with and without disabilities. Additionally, he frequently provides professional presentations on mathematics-related topics. He also has patented an algebra technique. Dr. Witzel holds a B.S. in psychology and special education from James Madison University and an M.Ed. and Ph.D. in special education from the University of Florida.

Dr. Paul J. Riccomini is an associate professor in the Eugene T. Moore School of Education at Clemson University in Clemson, South Carolina. He has taught mathematics for several years to students in grades seven to twelve with high-incidence disabilities. He has also taught general education math classes to high school students. Dr. Riccomini conducts numerous professional development workshops focusing on improving the mathematics education of students with disabilities through the application of evidence-based instructional practices. Dr. Riccomini holds a B.A. in mathematics and an M.Ed. in special education from Edinboro University of Pennsylvania. He received his doctorate in special education from the Pennsylvania State University.

Much appreciation goes to Julie Jones with Peadiddles (www.peadiddle.com) for the artwork included in this manual.